Hemingway and Spain

A Pursuit

HEMINGWAY AND SPAIN

A Pursuit / *Edward F. Stanton*

Photographs by Gonzalo de la Serna

University of Washington Press / *Seattle & London*

This book was published with the assistance of a grant from the Program for
Cultural Cooperation Between Spain's Ministry of Culture and United
States' Universities.

Library of Congress Cataloging-in-Publication Data

Stanton, Edward F., 1942–

   Hemingway and Spain : a pursuit / Edward F. Stanton / photographs by
Gonzalo de la Serna.

    p. cm.

   Bibliography: p.

   Includes index.

   ISBN 0-295-96710-2

   1. Hemingway, Ernest, 1899–1961—Knowledge—Spain. 2. Hemingway,
Ernest, 1899–1961—Journeys—Spain. 3. Authors, American—20th
century—Biography. 4. Spain—Description and travel—1981– 5. Literary
landmarks—Spain. 6. Bullfights in literature. 7. Spain in literature. 8.
Bullfights—Spain. I. Title.

PS3515.E37Z877   1989

813'.52—dc19   88-22643

The paper used in this publication meets the minimum requirements
of American National Standard for Information Sciences — Permanence of
Paper for Printed Library Materials, ANSI Z39.48-1984. ∞

To the true María

Contents

Illustrations

Preface

Scholarship is a splendid thing. But I still believe you are stronger, on a wider base, if you have both Virgil and Mantova. Don Quixote de la Mancha and La Mancha. Santa Teresa and Avila including the wineplaces. Santa Teresa shook the dust of Avila off her shoes but it is good to have had the dust of Avila and Salamanca on your shoes. . . .
—EH to Fraser Drew, 30 September 1951

This book is a very personal one. It began when I read *Death in the Afternoon* in a public library at the age of fifteen, and it will not end with the writing. Because it is a personal book and because it will not end with the writing, I have called it a pursuit. To paraphrase Hemingway, everybody loves something and I love Spain and know it, in a small way, as he knew guns, rods, bulls, boats, drinks, maps, words. When he had the dust of Africa on his feet, Hemingway told us that happiness lies in the pursuit.

So this book is a pursuit of one of our few writers since Mark Twain who created an undeniable style. Hemingway whittled a style for our time in the 1920s, and as we enter the last years of the century, it may be the most intrinsic style our time will produce in America or elsewhere. Hemingway changed the language of English prose for good. Almost single-handed, he dealt a lasting blow to the rhetoric and affectations of all previous literature. At its best, Hemingway's style could make what he called a "mystery" with a simple declarative sentence. At its worst, it could degenerate into an imitation of itself. The rhythms of his prose are still in the ears of most young people who begin to write in English. It is a style that has reached even those who do not read: like Marx, Freud, and Einstein, Hemingway has achieved the status of a legend, an international password. No writer since Byron has reached so wide an audience. Like Byron, he has influenced attitudes and behavior as well as literature. If Ivy League undergraduates no longer affect the world-weary tones of the characters in *The Sun Also Rises,* and if doughboys no longer strike poses of tight-lipped stoicism like the protagonist of A *Farewell to Arms*, Hemingway remains one of the century's chief examples of courage in a broken, violent world. If his first books seemed to exaggerate violence and blood, since the Spanish Civil War we have watched with horror as the world has come to resemble its image in his work. Hemingway taught us how to live right with our eyes and our senses, as he put it, how to see things as if for the first time, and to tell about them that way. He showed us that to see clearly, and to tell what you see in a plain way, is one of the most difficult and most beautiful things a man or a woman can do.

In this book I will try to tell, as clearly as I know, how Hemingway discovered Spain and wrote about the country over a period of forty years. I will try to show how his prose style, his code of behavior, and his life cannot be seen clearly and wholly without an understanding of his Spanish experience. Indeed, it would be almost impossible to conceive of Hemingway without Spain: without *The Sun Also Rises*, *Death in the Afternoon*, "A Clean, Well-Lighted Place," *For Whom the Bell Tolls*, the Spanish-born Santiago of *The Old Man and the Sea*; without the bullfight and its tragic sense of life and death, its union of art and valor; without the Spanish word and feeling of *nada* or nothingness; without the writer's adoption of Catholicism and his turning away from the Church as a result of the Spanish Civil War; without his conversion to political and social consciousness as a result of the "Spanish thing"; without the extension of his Hispanic experience in Cuba between 1940 and 1960; without his return to Spain in the last years and his flawed effort to relive the old days of *ferias* and *fiestas*.

In telling the story of Hemingway and Spain, I will carry a razor blade in my pocket, like the one María carried in case of capture by the enemy in *For Whom the Bell Tolls*, to cut out what has already been said elsewhere. Whenever possible, I will let the author tell his own story by quoting or paraphrasing his own words; many of his unpublished letters and manuscripts have only been made available in the last few years. I will concentrate on the genesis of Hemingway's contacts with Spain when he was in his early and mid-twenties—the formative period in his and most careers. Everything is in the beginnings, his friend Picasso once said, because after the beginnings, there is only the end.

Before approaching Hemingway and Spain, we must remember that in some ways he was one of the most American of writers. He came straight out of the Midwest from Anglo-Saxon stock. He lived an almost classical American infancy and youth: his family life in Oak Park, Illinois, embodied the pattern of a dominant mother and a weak father, a conflict between a respectable, feminized culture on one hand, and a more masculine freedom in the outdoors on the other. When "everything went to hell in the family," Hemingway followed the path of many youths of the previous century—escape by going places and doing things. During the years of his willed exile in Italy, France, and Spain, he carried much of his country with him. "Americans are always in America," he wrote to Sherwood Anderson, "no matter whether they call it Paris or Paname. . . ." To the Europeans who met him, his love of action, exaltation of the body, intense energy, direct approach to life without ideological prejudices, and aversion to high culture all seemed to reek of the prairies. Even his wives came from the country's heartland—Missouri, Arkansas, Minnesota. Hemingway's devotion to work, his moral and esthetic pragmatism, were also in the Protestant-American grain. After he became a successful writer, his mobility, aggressiveness, and confidence reminded some people of the growing economic, political, and military power of the United States. His final years of paranoia and his suicide recall sadly William Carlos Williams's line: "the pure products of America go crazy."

The contrast between Hemingway's Midwestern rearing and his European experience gave a unique tension to his life and work. Some of the latest research on his early years has shown that he did not have a clear idea of his role as an artist, nor even a literary education to speak of, until well after he left his country to live in the Old World at the age of twenty-two. So much is this so that the novelist Mario Vargas Llosa has called Hemingway's American period his "prehistory." By leaving home and staking out new claims abroad, Ernest was following Nietzsche's advice: choose exile in order to be able to tell the truth. He believed every artist should either destroy or perpetuate in his work the place he is born in and knows best. He chose to destroy it: the urban, technological, industrial America whose business, Coolidge said when Hemingway was still a young writer, was business. Indirectly, but as surely as Picasso, he would paint a kind of American Guernica—nature and human life destroyed by technology. He understood, like Hawthorne in the previous century, that America, where there is "no shadow, no antiquity, no mystery, no picturesque and gloomy wrong," was the most difficult land for an artist to cultivate in fiction.

Hemingway's exile from the United States set him apart from the other members of his generation who did not leave home, or who returned and never changed substantially abroad, like his friend Scott Fitzgerald. Ernest wrote these cryptic and important words to William Faulkner:

> Difference with us guys is I always lived out of country (as mercenary or patriot) since kid. My own country gone. Trees cut down. Nothing left but gas stations, sub-divisions where we hunted snipe on the prairie, etc. Found good country outside, learned language as well as know English, and lost it the same way. Most people don't know this.

The good country Hemingway found abroad was not Italy or France— both marred by war and the process of mechanization that was destroying America. The last good country was Spain, and Ernest thought the Spaniards were the only good people left in Europe.

"Most people don't know about this," he said to Faulkner, and that has not changed more than a quarter-century after his death. Most American and British critics have ignored or misunderstood the Spanish elements in his works, due mainly to the radical differences between Anglo-Saxon and Hispanic cultures, and to Hemingway's unwillingness to state openly what he called "the secret things" about Spain. On the other hand, Spaniards have usually read him in poor or censored translations, ignored his profound American roots, and often attempted to annex him to their cultural patrimony for the greater glory of Spain. From here on I will rarely mention the vast fund of errors and misinterpretations already in print, preferring simply to tell the most important events of Hemingway's Spanish experience between 1919 and 1961.

In his forty years of contacts with Spain, there was a symbiosis unique in the history of literature. Other foreigners have known as much or more about the Iberian Peninsula, but none has made such an imaginative rendering of the country and its people in his work. Ernesto, as his Spanish friends called him—out of both affection and an inability to pronounce his surname—said that Spain was the country he loved more than any other except his own. Dozens of newspaper and magazine articles, some of his best short stories, four of his books, the one play, and the only movie in which he participated directly all deal with the peninsula. He spent a total of some three years on Spanish soil. He knew the people of all classes and regions, their artists and writers of the past and present. He knew the landscape the way he had known the plains of Illinois before they were built over, the hunting and fishing grounds of the West, the coast of south Florida. He knew Spain's language, smells, sounds, wines, foods, roads, birds, animals, trees, skies, and how the weather was. "I love Spain the way I love Idaho, Wyoming and Montana," he said, "and I feel just as much at home. In Madrid I feel more at home than in New York."

Almost everything about Hemingway bore a trace of Spain, from his art to the houses he chose to live in. His build and size, for example, were unmistakably American, but Spaniards who knew him have told me that his bearing, gestures, élan, and penchant for obscenity made him resemble their countrymen. Like the partly autobiographical Frederic Henry in A *Farewell to Arms*, Hemingway probably passed more than once for a "Latin." In his physical presence there was a kind of vital intensity, perhaps born from danger and exposure to death, that recalled the matador's. The dark or night side of his personality (what he called "black ass") found its closest parallel in the Spanish sense of nada—the anguish of nightmare, oblivion, and death—a realm of terror and the grotesque evoked by some of his favorite Spanish artists like Goya, Quevedo, and Picasso.

After his wounding and near death on the Italian front in World War I, Hemingway would find in the national spectacle of Spain, the bullfight, the only place in the modern world where a man could observe death at first hand, often surrounded by the most astonishing beauty, and thus come to terms with his own mortality. In this sense Spain was a healing country for him. He saw that the Spaniards' commonsensical acceptance of death as a natural function, and their constant awareness of it, paradoxically enabled them to live more intensely than other peoples. Hemingway immersed himself in their celebrations of life and death, especially in the ritual festivals of spring and summer. He felt himself attracted by this "fiesta concept of life," the release and sensual enjoyment that contrasted so sharply with his cheerless upbringing in the Midwest. He was drawn to the Spaniards' conviviality and code of generosity; to their elevation of the individual man of flesh and blood, rather than material products or abstract ideas, as the supreme human value; to the tribal nature of their society in which the bonds of blood and friendship take precedence over theoretical principles of justice, the law, or the State; to a religion based on what he called an "almost tribal faith" rather than on knowledge and reason.

Most of all, in Spain Hemingway found "the secret things" that had disappeared from most parts of the world, that nourished his inspiration and form the real substance of what he called the "fourth or fifth dimension" in his prose. Consistent with his famous iceberg theory of fiction, in which the author conceals the most profound level of his understanding, these secret things are hidden deep in the texture of Hemingway's books, manuscripts, and letters, as they are buried deep in the layers of Spanish life. They are things that well up from the subconscious mind out of the ancient past of Western man, and have survived, tenuously, in the Iberian Peninsula. They are related to the earth, sun, wine and food, woman, the sacrifice of the bull, blood, death, tragedy, a sense of the sacred, and the magical power of language. Hemingway believed that Spanish itself was a "secret language" because it had managed to preserve many ancient echoes, especially in cursing, blasphemy, and slang. The secret things of Spain are bound up with his style and will lead to what I believe is a new comprehension of his prose. They form a blank space on the map of his work, an "Undiscovered Country"—his original favorite among twenty-six possible titles for his novel, *For Whom the Bell Tolls*. The secret things are "way past what we know about," can only be intuited darkly, and must be elucidated in the context of Hemingway's Spanish experience.

"Spain is no peninsula but a continent," he said. It is many countries tied flimsily into one, like a bundle held together by a rope of sand. Anyone who attempts to write about Spain, and about Hemingway, learns that those two words can hardly contain the multiple phenomena to which they refer. Both have been overgrown through the years by a thicket of ideas, theories, half-truths, and errors. The writer who approaches them must hack away at the thicket alone; he undertakes a battle as uneven as Don Quixote's against the formidable windmills of La Mancha. The knight was destined to lose the battle: his victory was one of daring, not of succeeding. A writer cannot hope for more.

Robert Browning said that if you had opened his heart, you would have seen Italy graved inside of it. If you had opened the heart of that other old Veneto boy, Ernest Hemingway, you would have found Spain there, writ large—along with certain places in America and Africa, parts of Cuba, Paris and Venice. He told us that the heart or soul of a country assuredly does not exist; "it is only your own heart." The only country a novelist knows is the country of his heart. The Spain in Hemingway's heart did not always correspond to the country shaped like a bull's hide on the western edge of the Old World. In this book I will try to discover not only the figure in the carpet of his Spanish experience, but the figure under the carpet; not only the secret things, but his own secret myth, his dreams of himself and Spain—his hidden Spanish self.

The main chapters that follow describe Hemingway's life in Spain and his most important writings on the country. In the preludes to these chapters I will attempt to show what is left of his Spain and its people today, and what has disappeared. In this way, his story emerges not from secondary sources, but from my pursuit of his trail in the places and among the people he loved most, and from what he wrote about them. The entire book forms a contrast and comparison between past and present, a counterpoint between Hemingway's voice and my own—they may overlap—to create a new tone or melody. In some sections I have even parodied his style, with affection, in order to avoid the solemnity he despised. After all, he showed us that a serious writer does not have to be a solemn one.

Nobody has ever told Hemingway's story in this way, nor perhaps will anyone again, since much of his Spain and most of the people he knew are dead or dying. This book is a pursuit in which there is both Hemingway and Spain including the wineplaces, *The Sun Also Rises* and Pamplona, *Death in the Afternoon* and the bullfight, *For Whom the Bell Tolls* and the Sierra de Guadarrama, the 1920s and the 1980s. It is only a part of the story, but he taught us that if you make any part truly, it can represent the whole.

Madrid, Spain, and Lexington, Kentucky   *Edward F. Stanton*
1980–1988

Hemingway and Spain

A Pursuit

Prelude:
Madrid, 1984

I t is hot and bright. As lunch time approaches, the traffic has begun to thin out. The houses on the sunny side of the street look sharply white. You reach the old Calle de Cuchilleros, Street of the Knifesmiths, down the stairs from the Plaza Mayor, and see Botín on your right. Number 17. The burnished blond panelling of the facade looks smooth against the Mudéjar brick. You enter and it is noisy and cool. Behind the counter you see Antonio talking to some people. He smiles, making a graceful movement of hand and arm meaning he will be with you in a minute. You walk over in front of the entrance to the cone-shaped tile ovens that have not changed since the Antigua Casa Sobrino de Botín was founded in 1725. The man who cooks the meat says *"Buenos días"* to you and places an oak plank, held on a long pole, inside the oven; a suckling pig rests on the plank. Evergreen oak logs used for the fire are stacked on the worn tile floor.

Antonio comes over and shakes hands, smiling. His smile always brings you happiness; it is one of the finest you know, self-effacing and generous. He follows you up the creaking stairway the waiters also use to carry food from the kitchen. It is crowded in the dining room upstairs.

"I have a table in the corner where we can talk when it quiets down," Antonio says. "Go ahead and order your meal. I'll return."

You sit in a simple oak chair and tell the waiter to bring you suckling pig with red wine from Valdepeñas. Like most of the waiters, he is old and has been with the house for years. You look at the walls of white plaster with their rows of blue and white Talavera tiles, wrought-iron lanterns, and dark oil paintings, mostly still lifes. Oak beams support the ceiling. All the wood seems to be oak at Botín—beams, tables, chairs, counters. It is the Castilian tree, rough, durable, full of buckles and gnarls. Between walls and ceiling, the junctures are slightly askew.

Antonio González, owner and host of Botín, Madrid, June 1984.
(Photo Gonzalo de la Serna)

In his starched white coat, napkin folded gracefully over his arm, the waiter brings a liter pitcher of the house's wine and another of water with beads of sweat on the outside. The Valdepeñas is cold and slightly acid. Antonio sends up a plate of *jamón serrano* as an appetizer—the reddest, most tender cured ham in Spain, not too salty. With the jamón the wine smoothes out. You have a mushroom omelette for first course. Antonio arrives and sits down. He is wearing a light cream-colored suit.

"Are you going to have something to eat?" you ask him.

"No, my waiters eat before we open but I wait until we close. I will accompany you with a Scotch and some jamón."

The waiter brings him a glass with ice and a bottle of Johnnie Walker on a silver tray.

You raise your glasses and say *"Salud!"*

"In the beginning he would sit over there because the light was good." With a subtle motion of his brow and clear blue eyes, so that the customers will not notice, Antonio indicates a table across the room from us. It is next to one of the small, fortress-like windows facing Cuchilleros; now there is an air conditioner in the lower pane. An enormous, pink-faced man with rolls of fat under his chin sits alone there, picking baby clams out of their shells.

"Ernesto used to arrive before we opened, around noon," Antonio says. "He would ask for a bottle of wine and a glass, spread his books and papers on the table and work until his friends arrived for lunch. In those days, hardly anyone would eat before two o'clock."

"What years were these?"

"Mid-twenties. I was just a boy. Ernesto told my father he had a novel that was probably going to be published, in which the last scene would be set at Botín. This must have been *Fiesta*—what you call *The Sun Also Rises* in English—but my father never knew this. He did not read books."

The waiter brings your plate of suckling pig. It is a golden quarter of a three-week-old *cochinillo* and it covers the entire plate. The only garnish is a small, roasted new potato. The skin of the pork is so hot that it crackles. This is the only suckling pig you know that can be cut with a fork.

"*Buen provecho*," Antonio says. "I remember one time Ernesto asked my father what his normal day was. This must have been in the '30s before the Civil War, because I was already a student and a tireless reader. My father told Ernesto that he got up at seven in the morning to do the buying at the market, clean the fish and vegetables, fire up the oven, and wait for the people to come for lunch. After closing the restaurant at four or five, the kitchen would be used to make fried Castilian pastries like *pestiños* and *bartolillos* because we needed the extra money; the restaurant had only twenty-one tables. My mother and father would knead the dough with their hands and elbows. Until the restaurant opened again at night, we ran a pastry shop. Then the kitchen had to be prepared for supper and the last customers did not leave until two or three in the morning.

"When Ernest heard this, he told my father in Spanish: 'Emilio, you work like a man in the time of Dickens.' My father asked: '*Quién es ese señor?* Who is that gentleman?'"

You both laugh and drink. The suckling pig and Valdepeñas are beginning to make you feel good. One of the waiters comes to the table and tells Antonio, in low tones, that two old customers downstairs are vying with each other to pay the bill.

"He who makes the reservation for the table has the right to pay," Antonio tells him like an oracle. "That is holy—*Eso es sagrado.*"

Your waiter brings more Valdepeñas. The wine makes you remember the next-to-last scene of *The Sun Also Rises*, where Jake dines with Brett at Botín and puts away five bottles of *Rioja alta* almost by himself. Not to mention the three martinis each drank before lunch at the fine old bar of the Hotel Palace. You ask Antonio about the five bottles of Rioja.

"Probably an exaggeration, but not inconceivable. The wine in that novel is not there by accident. It is almost a sacrament; through wine Ernesto knew that the Dionysian man could emerge. That is what he was seeking in Spain from the very beginning."

"But why the Rioja? Nearly all your customers drink an ordinary Valdepeñas instead of finer, more expensive Riojas or French vintages."

"French wine would not be correct here, Eduardo. Our fare is essentially the food of the Castilian peasant."

"But prepared with the same skill and care as *haute cuisine* in Paris."

Antonio laughs and narrows his eyes. He rises to say goodbye to the wife of the German ambassador in Madrid. His father may not have read, but Antonio speaks English impeccably, and has learned French, German, Italian, and Russian by himself.

You are finishing the suckling pig when he comes back to the table. "I would recommend a light salad after the cochinillo," he says. "It has too much fat to digest well on a day like this."

You have forgotten about the heat of Madrid outside. Botín is like a cave or fortress that envelops you once you begin to eat and drink here: it seems a place unto itself, separate from the world outside. Yet it contains all the richness and bounty of the Spanish earth and seas: Castilian lambs, pigs, veal, beef; blood-sausages of Burgos, goat cheeses of La Mancha, snapbeans, asparagus, and strawberries of Aranjuez; cured hams from the mountains of Granada, trout from Navarre, Mediterranean squid and langostinos, Biscayan eels and hake, Galician mussels, clams, oysters. It is still one of the best restaurants in the world, and Spain is one of the last paradises of good food.

"What do you remember about the old man during the Civil War, Antonio?"

"That was the only time we have had to close the restaurant in more than sixty years. Not enough provisions. I remember a massive man, unshaved, with a leather jacket and a pistol strapped to his waist. He would stop by for a drink and talk with my father. 'Emilio,' he would say, 'don't worry about these bad times. A few years after the war, many Americans will come to Botín and make you prosper.' We had to wait fifteen years for that to happen, but his prophecy was true. He gave me the impression of a man who could see into things and change them with the power of his work. I was only a teenager at the time, but already Ernesto reminded me of a man who knew exactly what he wanted and how he was going to get it. Already he was acting and dressing and talking as he imagined was appropriate for a hero of those times. Would you like dessert?"

"Lord, no." You have finished the salad.

"A *copa* then," Antonio says. You smile your assent. He beckons a waiter and orders a brandy.

Antonio is still talking. "He would have been a great general or guerrilla leader. Even a politician, if he had not been a writer with the obligation to see many sides of a question. He had a way of inspiring loyalty that I have never seen in any other man. Perhaps because he gave you the feeling that he would give his own life—on the spot—for anyone or anything he considered to be right. I would have done anything for him."

A waiter comes for Antonio to solve a problem of another bill. They whisper; you cannot understand them. When the waiter leaves, Antonio explains.

"An old friend of the house who has been widowed. She has to make her living as a tour guide now. She is with an American couple who want to split the bill. I told the waiter to have her make a *garabato* or squiggle on the check to let them think she is charging her share."

"Who pays for her then?" you ask, feeling chagrined by your compatriots' ignorance of the Spanish code of generosity.

Antonio looks surprised: "The house, of course. She and her husband were regular customers for twenty-five years. One must preserve a sense of dignity."

The waiter brings the bulbous snifter that has been warmed to the temperature of the hand. He pours out the caramel-colored Spanish brandy, Duque de Alba. You hold it to the light, swirl it, breathe in the fumes rising from the heated glass, and taste it. Spanish brandy will never be cognac, but after suckling pig and a few pitchers of Valdepeñas at Botín, what does it matter?

The brandy is warming your mind. "You know, Antonio, Hemingway heard about Botín before he made his first trip to Spain. He came here that year—'23—and returned every time he was in Madrid. In some ways, his Spain was Botín—almost like a fighting bull's *querencia* for him. It was one of the few things that did not change, in Madrid or anywhere else. Why did he keep returning for nearly forty years?"

"Already you have said it: because it did not change." Antonio forms his smile that always has something sad and wise about it. "And with modesty speaking, as the Italians say, he kept returning because the food and wine were good. He knew they would not change. He felt comfortable here because he was in *su casa:* we lived on the top floor in those early days. Eduardo, you must understand that Botín was a home as well as a place of work—and it still is for me in some ways. My older son Antonio is already learning to be host, and his wife is pregnant with a third generation of González."

A large group of American tourists files out of the dining room led by their Spanish guide, a small, dark man who looks Arabic.

"Antonio, you know how much I love Botín. Only one thing bothers me—there are too many foreigners here, especially Americans. When people come to a restaurant in a group, they act collectively and they must be treated that way. The personal bond between client and waiter, between client and owner—what you hold sacred—it becomes vulgarized. The sense of responsibility, of personal involvement, of mutual respect and knowledge, the feeling of reciprocity—all that breaks down."

"*Al buen entendedor, pocas palabras.* Few words for the man who understands," he says with another smile. He is too much of a gentleman to make even the slightest derogatory comment about his customers or your countrymen.

You say, "This too is the heritage of Hemingway. He was one of our greatest writers and also our greatest tourist."

All of the customers have left now. You look around the room. The waiters are preparing the tables for supper, white napkins still draped ritually on their forearms. Except for the air conditioner in Hemingway's window, nothing significant has changed in this room for sixty years.

Only the people who have come or gone or stayed. You are happy: it is difficult not to be happy when you dine on suckling pig and Valdepeñas at Botín's. The happiness, you know, is somehow related to the wine and the sacrifice of all those lambs, pigs, calfs, steers. Outside the window is the heat of Madrid. The city will be waking and going back to work. You look Antonio in the eyes and you both smile. When you are at Botín's, you know what matters is not understanding what the world is all about, but learning how to live in it.

A Strange Country

Any one who knows a damned thing about it is aware that the artist, like the cabbage and the head lettuce, which he often resembles in intelligence, needs transplanting. It is not where they work, but what they have inside of them. . . . El Greco, you know, was not a native of Toledo. . . .
—Unpublished passage from manuscript,
  Death in the Afternoon

Nothing could repress Ernest's enthusiasm as he and his wife Hadley prepared to board the S.S. *Leopoldina* bound for Europe in late 1921. He sang, shouted, danced, and shadow-boxed. The ship's first port of call was in northwestern Spain on December 18. The Atlantic coast of the country looked long and brown and very old. Although it was almost the winter solstice, the sun shone bright and warm over the bay of Vigo; the water was blue as a chromo of Naples. The harbor reminded Hemingway of Little Traverse Bay in northern Michigan, where he spent summers as a child, but it was surrounded by mountains and crossed by lateen-sailed fishing boats. The waters were alive with schools of strange, rainbow-colored fish, packs of long Spanish mackerel, heavy sea bass with odd, soft-sounding names, and above all, the big silver and slate-blue tuna leaping out of the water.

Ernest and Hadley went ashore in a motor launch for a few hours; they walked up the cobblestone streets to the fish market where some of the tuna lay gutted on marble slabs. After the cold of Chicago and New York, Ernest was too hot wearing only a sweater. For two pesetas you could buy a quart of three-year-old wine, at a time when alcohol could not be bought legally at all in the U.S. "Gaw what a place," Hemingway wrote to one of his friends. "Vigo, Spain. That's the place for a male."

Although the *Leopoldina* stayed only four hours in Vigo, the town left a strong impression on the young couple. They fired off four letters home, and Ernest described it in an article for the *Toronto Star Weekly*, which had signed him on to do a series of European letters. The article projects a clear, vigorous impression of Vigo. Hemingway's enthusiasm led him to write in a style more exuberant than the one he had used at the *Kansas City Star* and in earlier pieces for the *Weekly*. The terse, short sentences of his American journalism now overflow in longer periods with rhythmic clauses and a richer vocabulary to describe action: "Sometimes five and six tuna will be in the air at once in Vigo Bay, shouldering out of the water like porpoises as they herd sardines, then leaping in a towering jump that is as clean and beautiful as the first leap of a well-hooked rainbow." He describes Vigo itself as an unattractive village with an ugly gray church and fort. This sullen, flat world of human institutions contrasts sharply with the deep, bright sea, teeming with life and in particular with the "king of all fish," the silver and blue tuna. The best men, the strong, "good fishermen," enter that natural world, where they are purified when they land a tuna after a "back-sickening, sinew-straining" fight. Only then are they worthy of entering the presence of the "cheerful, brown-faced gods that judge over the happy hunting grounds" and live up in the mountains above the bay. Perhaps only half seriously, Hemingway identified the Spanish fishermen with American Indians as men who lived a simple but strenuous life in contact with nature and its elemental forces. They foreshadow the world of *The Old Man and the Sea*, where the fisherman Santiago, born in the Canary Islands, leaves his Cuban village behind to enter the fecund waters of the Gulf Stream; he too undergoes a kind of purification after his struggle with that other great fish, the giant marlin.

"We're going back there," Hemingway wrote to a friend as the *Leopoldina* sailed away from Vigo, by Cape Finisterre and across the Bay of Biscay.

But the aspiring writer would have to wait more than a year before going back to Spain. First there was Paris. The Hemingways would live in the city on and off, mostly on, for the next eight years. In France and the other European countries where he was sent as a correspondent for the *Toronto Star*, Ernest witnessed and recorded the postwar devastation of the Old World. Spain was the only major country of Western "Yarrup" —as he disparagingly called it—that he did not cover as a journalist. After the luminous hours he had spent in Vigo, Ernest was eager to learn more about the peninsula: he avidly queried the Spanish friends he made in

Paris, such as the painters Picasso, Miró, and Luis Quintanilla. Gertrude Stein and the American artist Henry (Mike) Strater spoke to him of the bullfight, which Hemingway sensed might offer a different heroism after the wars. As Ezra Pound said of the young writer in Paris: "The son of a bitch's instincts are right!" Hemingway's instincts told him that he needed to find a new kind of courage in peacetime, among men who "by their actual physical conduct gave you a real feeling of admiration."

Breaking his own rule of writing only what he knew firsthand, he began a short prose sketch of the bullfight about a year after settling in Paris. It is important for revealing to us Hemingway's preconceptions of the bullfight before he traveled to Spain:

> The first matador got the horn through his sword hand and the crowd hooted him. The second matador slipped and the bull caught him through the belly and he hung on to the horn with one hand and held the other tight against the place, and the bull rammed him wham against the wall and the horn came out, and he lay in the sand, and then got up like crazy drunk and tried to slug the men carrying him away and yelled for his sword but he fainted. The kid came out and had to kill five bulls because you can't have more than three matadors, and the last bull he was so tired he couldn't get the sword in. He couldn't hardly lift his arm. He tried five times and the crowd was quiet because it was a good bull and it looked like him or the bull and then he finally made it. He sat down in the sand and puked and they held a cape over him while the crowd hollered and threw things down into the bull ring.

Hemingway intended his paragraph to be a kind of miniature in motion that would explode like a grenade in the reader's head. The problem is that the grenade seems to have exploded in the bullring instead, with two men wounded, one fainting, another vomiting, and five bulls dead. Later Hemingway would learn that good writing should give a "kick" to the reader, not to the characters or to the writer as happens here. Another problem is that the sketch is based on hearsay and secondary sources. Ernest had done some homework in conversations with Stein, Picasso, Quintanilla, and Strater; the detail of the wounded matador fighting off the members of his *cuadrilla* as he yells for his sword, for example, has been seen by most people who attend *corridas* and is certainly based on fact. The miniature partly reflects Strater's view of bullfighting—young, brave toreros and a cowardly, unsympathetic crowd. The painter described the public in this way: "The kind of a cheap crowd that one gets at some American race-tracks, sitting safely in their seats and criticizing the bull-fighters. . . ." In fact Hemingway's sketch even seems to be couched in the unliterate vernacular tone and vocabulary of a Ring Lardner, with echoes of the racetrack and the prizefight: "the kid . . . couldn't hardly lift his arm . . . it looked like him or the bull." The author might have read Vicente Blasco Ibáñez's bullfight novel by this time too; *Blood and Sand* was available in English, had already been referred to by Ernest in an early newspaper article for the *Toronto Star,* and ends with a famous scene portraying the crowd as a roaring, bloodthirsty beast.

Almost everything he had read about the bullfight insisted on its barbarity, sickening horror, and cruelty. As such he describes it in the sketch, yet the kid who kills five bulls alone, who is almost killed himself by the last one, and who must bear the abuse of the whole crowd after risking his life, is probably the first character in Hemingway's fiction whose actual physical conduct could give any feeling of admiration to the careful reader. In contrast, the American protagonists of his *Three Stories and Ten Poems,* published a few months later in Paris, are insensitive, dishonest, or indecisive.

At this early stage of his career, Hemingway was trying to learn how to live right with his eyes, to describe the sequence of motion and fact but not the emotion they made. That would come later. In the early prose sketch, there is an almost total absence of stated emotion in the flat, dry language. Edmund Wilson was correct in saying that this and the other vignettes of the same period had the "dry sharpness" of Goya's series of etchings, *La Tauromaquia.* Hemingway's first bullfight sketch was literally dry in a very peculiar sense: in spite of all the horn wounds, sword thrusts, and dead bulls, there is no blood on this sand. The absence of blood amid so much wounding, pain, and death gives the piece a colorless, aseptic quality. The flow of blood would have made this vignette less grating, more natural, perhaps even cathartic. Hemingway would learn the visual, esthetic, and emotional value of blood during his first trip to Spain in the spring of 1923.

From the first bullfight sketch, some of his early journalism, and the unpublished manuscripts, we can reconstruct Hemingway's attitude toward Spain before he actually traveled and lived there. Since the Latin peoples he knew best, the French and Italians, seemed venal to him, Ernest assumed the Spaniards would be the same. From an American painter in Paris he had apparently heard about an obsequious postman in Majorca whom it was necessary to tip for every letter; even then the Spaniard would cut pictures out of magazines before delivering them in order to brighten the walls of the local post office. "If you have been in Spain long enough," said Hemingway (implying that he had been), "you are able to hang on to your temper. It is the climate that does it, they say. The climate is so soft and gentle that it makes it seem not worth while to kill the postman. Life is mellow in Spain."

Hemingway did not know exactly what to expect in Spain, but he imagined that he "wanted something like Italy before the war and Senoritas instead of senorinas only with more castanets." Like thousands of northern travelers before him, perhaps with more skepticism and irony, he envisioned Spain as an exotic, romantic country with a soft, enervating climate; nubile, sensuous women; corruptible, fulsome men who contrasted with the honest Anglo-Saxon tourists; cruel, barbarous customs like bullfighting, redeemed only in part by occasional displays of solitary courage by simple men who lived in contact with the natural world, like toreros and the fisherman of Vigo. In short, almost the Spain of Mérimée's *Carmen* and of American writers like Irving, Longfellow, and Lowell, which could be summed up in a capital phrase by the nineteenth-century English Hispanophile, Richard Ford: "bull-fights, bandits, and black eyes."

At a Paris restaurant one day in the spring of 1923, Hemingway began to promote the idea of a trip to Spain with some friends. He felt perhaps that life there would be more exciting and less artificial than in Paris. Also, Spain and Portugal were the only Latin countries in Europe he could not boast of knowing from the inside. His friends were Robert McAlmon and William Bird, soon to be the publishers of his first books—*Three Stories and Ten Poems* and *in our time*. McAlmon, married to a British heiress, had money to burn and was willing to pay for the trip.

The painter Mike Strater drew a map on the back of the menu with crosses for Burgos and Madrid, Cordova, Seville, Granada, and Ronda.

He had been to Spain a few years before and annoyed Hemingway by pronouncing Madrid as Madreeth and Sevilla as Theveeya. Ernest thought his friend was talking through his hat and using a phony Spanish accent, but what really bothered him was that Strater had traveled in the peninsula and actually seen a bullfight, while he had only been there on port call. He could not stand for anyone he knew to be more of an insider about something that mattered to him. Spain mattered all right: after hearing so much about the corrida and trying his hand at the vignette earlier that spring, Hemingway wanted to know how it really was inside the bullrings of Spain. It was a matter of artistic integrity for him to see with his own eyes what he wrote about.

On the same menu, Strater jotted down the name of a bullfighters' pension on the "Via" San Jerónimo and of a picturesque old tavern where the specialty was roasted suckling pig. He also drew a plan showing where the Grecos were hung in the Prado. The sketch and words on the back of the menu were almost a microcosm of the romantic Spain that travelers from northern Europe and America had been seeking for more than a century: the country of the Cid, the national hero from Burgos; Madrid with its bullfighters, quaint locales, hearty food, and famous museum with the mystical paintings of El Greco; most of all, southern Spain, sunny Andalusia with its local color and exotic old Moorish towns like Cordova and Seville, Granada and Ronda.

The friends left on the southbound train from Paris to Madrid with "one objective—to see bull fights." Spain was nothing like what Hemingway had expected; it never is. At first it seemed a terrible place. Instead of finding a country like Italy before the war, he saw a bleak, bare land that reminded him curiously of the American West. Distances were enormous, the food was abundant but awful compared to France's, and the weather was not sunny—it seemed to rain all the time. "In the rain in the rain in the rain in the rain in Spain," he wrote in a poem after the manner of Gertrude Stein.

In 1923 Spain was still a substantially rural country, with nearly 60 percent of the population working in agriculture. Outside the major cities, the people lived a mainly agrarian, communal life that had not changed significantly since the Middle Ages. The industrialization that had blemished the American, Italian, French, and German landscapes was con-

fined to a few pockets in the north and northeast like Bilbao and Barcelona—not seen by Hemingway on his first trip. Spain looked "very big
and very bare" to him, but he got used to it quickly. Soon he thought it
was "unspoiled and unbelievably tough and wonderful," the only country
left in Europe that hadn't been "shot to pieces." As a bonus, it had the
best trout fishing on the continent.

While he admired the unspoiled Spanish landscape, Hemingway seems
to have been blissfully unaware of the political and economic conditions
of the country. Because he had never been given an assignment by the
Star in Madrid, he had not learned Spanish politics from the inside as
he had in France, Italy, Germany, and Greece. Spain was undergoing its
most serious national crisis since the Spanish-American War of 1898. The
situation had come to a head with the waning of the artificial prosperity of
the World War I years and the unpopular military campaign in Spanish
Morocco. Within four months of Hemingway's first trip to Spain, the
Army under Primo de Rivera, with the connivance of King Alfonso XIII,
would set up a military dictatorship openly sympathetic to fascism.

The shock that Ernest felt that spring of 1923 in Spain was almost as
great as the one he had known on his first trip to Europe in 1918. One
morning he had been in Paris with its safe, civilized feeling, and the
afternoon of the following day he was seated in the first-row *barrera* of the
Plaza de Toros in Madrid, observing a strange ritual of life and death more
ancient than any other in Europe, with the possible exception of Catholic
liturgy. When the first bull came shooting out into the arena and charged
one of the toreros, he suddenly knew what bullfighting was all about.
In spite of what the books and people said—that a fighting bull would
charge only if provoked—he saw with his eyes that this beautiful animal,
looking like some "terrible almost prehistoric" creature, charged from pure
instinct and was "absolutely deadly and absolutely vicious." With his own
unfailing instinct, he knew that the corrida meant the bull more than the
man. The animal was unearthly, wonderful, and horrifying; it gave him a
feeling of religious awe he had not known since his youthful days in the
primitive hemlock forests of Michigan, and a sense of exhilaration he had
not felt since the war in Italy. In fact, sitting in a barrera at a bullfight was
"just like having a ringside seat at the war with nothing going to happen
to you."

In the matadores' grace and courage, Hemingway recognized the kind of admirable physical conduct he had been seeking. "I have got ahold of it in bull fighting," he wrote to a friend. "Jesus Christ yes." He had also got ahold of a spectacle that embodied the kind of irrationality expressed by so many artists of the time. In the ancient ritual of life and death in the ring, a "survival of the days of the Roman Coliseum," Hemingway had discovered his own version of Picasso's African masks and the surrealists' exaltation of primitive life. Here was a territory that had not been claimed, incredibly, by any other major author. It would allow him, as Hadley said in a letter, to be "atavistic, to tear beauty out of chaos and dark things."

Hemingway was fortunate in seeing three of the best matadores in Spain that spring afternoon in Madrid—the short, clear-skinned Gitanillo, the chubby-faced gypsy Chicuelo, and the tall, wolflike Nicanor Villalta. It was almost as if destiny and poetic justice presided over his life in Spain: all three men would be important figures for him in the years to come. The toreros, especially the "dough-faced kid" Chicuelo, performed some slow, beautiful passes, elegantly, almost effortlessly, with great dignity. Hemingway had never suspected that such grace could be joined with valor to make a new kind of esthetic emotion. Even the goring and death of the horses did not bother him as much as he had anticipated; he watched with growing scorn as his friend McAlmon squirmed in his seat and gave a "sudden screeching intake of breath" at each encounter of bull and horse. Ernest already felt closer to the Spanish spectators than to his friend. A young American aficionado in a straw hat, seated at his left, explained to him the details of the corrida.

After the bullfight, Hemingway and McAlmon met the young American for dinner at Botín's, the little restaurant in downtown Madrid recommended by Strater. In the upstairs room of Botín's, the other American, whom they would come to "know and love as the Gin Bottle King," discoursed on the tragedy of the bullfight as they dined on mushroom omelettes and suckling pig, served on oak planks, washed down with red Valdepeñas wine.

The three Americans went on drinking that night, and the Gin Bottle King was apparently insulted by a despicable scion of the Madrid aristocracy, almost knifed, and framed for arrest. He extricated himself by wielding a bottle of Gordon's gin in what Hemingway described, in his tall-tale fashion, as "one of the four most dangerous situations I have ever seen" (he does not specify the other three). The evil aristocrat only confirmed his belief that Spaniards were crooks like the Italians, French, and other shifty Mediterranean peoples he had known. Back at the seedy pension on the Carrera de San Jerónimo, he thought one of the bullfighters had "eyes exactly like a rattlesnake."

In spite of the dangerous adventure with the Gin Bottle King, Madrid seemed slightly dull to Hemingway. It was modern rather than picturesque, without any costumes or local color. People stayed up later at night than in any other city he knew except Constantinople. But unlike "Old Constan" with its offal-strewn streets and debauchery, Madrid appeared to be a clean town where people merely stayed up and talked for hours, then got up late the next morning. This did not qualify as real night life: it was only "delaying the day."

Ernest was already acting like an initiate in the secret society of bullfighters at the boarding house on San Jerónimo, where he was laying plans for a trip to Andalusia in order to see more corridas. He talked of little but the bravery of bulls and the courage of the men who faced them. "Boxing looks paler and paler," he wrote on a postcard to Gertrude Stein. From Madrid, he dragged McAlmon and Bird to Seville; later he would boast that he had actually traveled with a crew of toreros.

By now it was late spring, the weather had warmed up, and Hemingway thought that "Spain is damn good in hot weather." The Americans saw a good bullfight on Corpus Christi day in Seville, but Ernest was beginning to be annoyed by the local color of Andalusia, which had been so noticeably absent in Madrid and the rest of Castile. When they saw some flamenco dancers one night, he kept saying "Oh, for Christ's sake, more flamingos!" Likewise, he thought that the gypsy caves of Granada—whitewashed walls, men dressed in "Valentino hats" strumming guitars, women dancers in flouncy dresses playing castanets—were a disgusting fake. Just as Old Constan's fabled "Magic of the East" was nothing but an illusion in the minds of foreigners, so the image of an exotic Spain was a stereotype forged by two centuries of northern European travelers in search of the romantic south, and favored by unscrupulous Andalusians in order to turn an easy profit.

The place Hemingway liked best in Andalusia was the little mountain town of Ronda, with the oldest bullring in Spain and a spectacular location on cliffs above a river. Ronda too had "romantic scenery," souvenir salesmen, and all the trappings for a honeymoon or an elopement. Like other tourists, Ernest shot photographs of a donkey in the dusty, quaint town, and of the picturesque gorge. In spite of all this, it was a fine place, because beneath the typical scenery and the local color Hemingway espied a deeper, more violent, and tragic quality in Ronda. He could not articulate his feelings yet, but he probably knew by intuition that he had found something very important. Ronda, with its old wooden *plaza de toros*, was the cradle of bullfighting in Spain. The ring stands on the edge of an enormous gash that splits the town in two parts. Jackdaws nested in the beetling cliffs, coming out to circle and dive in the gulch at dusk. When there was a bullfight, the dead horses were dragged over the edge of the cliffs, and the buzzards that had been wheeling high over the ring all day dropped down to feed on the rocks below the town.

As he rode the train back to Paris, Hemingway felt puzzled by Spain. He did not know the language well. "It took a while to learn even to speak it. You had to get rid of Italian, all of it." He had not found Spain as he expected. The exotic image of local color, costumes, and castanets was false, but at the same time, the country was radically different from all others where he had been, especially his own. Yet the landscape of Castile and Aragón was uncannily like the American West. He knew, when he found his own country there, "how the Spaniards must have felt finding their country in America and you share a common physical knowledge. . . ."

Northern Michigan had been the first peninsula loved by Hemingway, northern Italy the second; Spain would be the last. But Spain was more like a continent than a peninsula. The green Basque landscape through which the northbound train passed before crossing the French border was like a different country from the bare plains of Castile and Aragón, while Andalusia to the south was distinct from both. Driven by his need to understand from the inside, Hemingway decided not to wait another year and a half before returning to Spain. He would be back in less than three weeks, this time in Pamplona.

Pamplona, 1980: 1

It is the afternoon of the first full day of San Fermín, and you have had a lunch of langostinos the size of small lobsters; *alubias* or red beans; *marmitako*, a fisherman's dish of fresh bonito with red peppers in a tomato sauce, all washed down with rosé wine of the Navarrese Señorío de Sarriá; *cuajada* or sweet curded milk for dessert; coffee; *pacharán*, a Basque liqueur; and a cigar. Already you are learning that one of the secrets of the fiesta is to eat heartily in order to stay awake the whole day and night. You walk up the shady side of the Calle Jarauta; like the bullring, the street is divided by a line of sun and shadow. You stop at the makeshift bar that is the headquarters of the Peña Anaitasuna, one of the eating and drinking clubs that rule Pamplona during the festival. The members who are in the band, dressed like the others in white cotton shirt and pants, red kerchief and sash, are beating drums, tuning their instruments, unfurling the fifteen-foot banner they will carry in the procession to the bullring.

You see your friends Fernando Lizaúr and José Mari Torrabadella and give them an embrace. They are wearing outlandish hats that contrast with the traditional white costume: Fernando a gigantic Mexican sombrero, José Mari an old Robin Hood cap cocked to one side, a feather in the crown. The band starts playing and you all follow the swaying banner down the street to the plaza de toros.

Older people, women, and children watch from their balconies as you pass, waving and greeting the men they know in the *peña*. During San Fermín, everyone seems to know each other and for seven days all social barriers collapse. José Mari points out a member of ETA—the terrorist organization for Basque independence—who is dancing a *jota* with a member of the far more conservative National Basque Party. As you reach the square in front of the Town Hall, you hear the other peñas approaching with their pulsating music and songs.

A couple of drunken teenage boys with a *sifón* or flit gun squirt the crowd, and the cool soda water feels good in the bright, hot sunlight.

Another boy, with a string of garlic around his neck, comes up to you, holding the garlic toward you in one hand, a bottle of perfume in the other. You wonder if you have met him somewhere. He smiles: "*Cuál te gusta más?*" he asks, "Which do you like more?" Without hesitation you tell him the garlic, he says "*Sí,*" laughing, and hugs you. There is no place for perfume here, with the man-smell of clean sweat in the air. It is really true and nobody believes it who has not been in the streets during the feria with the men and boys of Pamplona.

You come out on the shady Paseo de Hemingway, full of cars, tourists and white-dressed Pamplonicans singing and dancing their way to the bullring in front of you, huge banners above them.

"It's still early" says Fernando, "we have forty minutes before the corrida —let's stop by Hartza's for a few minutes."

He grabs José Mari by one arm, you by the other, and takes you down the paseo, past the big statue of Hemingway with foreign boys and girls perched on it, down the hill and across the avenue to the only restaurant in Spain that can match Botín, for my money.

You walk up the stairs—there is no elevator—to the second floor where you see the unpretentious little sign saying "Hartza."

"They've already closed," says Fernando. He opens the door, gets down on his knees, motioning you to do the same like a platoon leader going into battle with his troops, and you all begin crawling toward the kitchen singing "La Cucaracha." You are right there with them and yet you cannot quite believe it: two middle-aged, successful businessmen, married, with kids, who have the freedom, the sense of the absurd, the fiesta sense of life to become like children for one week of the year. No wonder all the men in the peñas are called *mozos* during the feria, because in San Fermín they are all young. You try to think of a parallel in American life, you conjure up friends who might be similar to Fernando and José Mari, but you cannot picture them crawling on their knees in a public place singing "La Cucaracha" in front of the three sisters who own the restaurant, all of them laughing and calling the dishwashers in from the kitchen to see, a few remaining customers at their tables joining in the song. Then you are on your feet again, Give me a hug and taste this fresh *besugo*, try this *merluza* with small clams in a sauce of parsley and garlic, do you have a smoke for the corrida, take this hand-rolled Cuban cigar, and you are kissing the sisters goodbye until this evening, running down the stairs and

José Mari Torrabadella, Pamplona, July 1980.
(Photo Gonzalo de la Serna)

up the hill to the bullring, bumped by dancers from other peñas as you reach the entrance to the plaza.

All the members of the Anaitasuna are waiting for José Mari to pull his caper for the first bullfight of the fair. Each year he buys an *abono* or subscription for all nine corridas, but he refuses to show it, preferring the challenge to his ingenuity and the joy of crashing the gate. We are all watching him: he is short and almost entirely bald, but as he approaches the turnstile, arms spread-eagle and forefingers wagging No in rhythm to his slow, bouncy steps, an irresistible, beatific, all-the-teeth-in-his-mouth smile on his face as he sings "No, no no" to the ticketman—he seems to grow in stature before our eyes. We are all laughing so hard the tears are coming, the ticketman too, José Mari has crashed the gate once more. The fiesta sense of life. The festival is made up of thousands of just such acts. On the level of the individual man, these acts parallel the daring of those who run the *encierro* through the streets of the city, the more formal courage of the toreros in the ring, the bravery of the bulls. It only could happen in Pamplona for San Fermín.

2   A Wild Place
        Up in Navarre

Then this debonair giant turned up. He brought with him a combination of geniality, virility, and esthetic sensibility which for most Spaniards was a revelation. He was no longer the gaping tourist, the go-getter businessman, the Protestant ever ready to frown at Catholic superstition, the progressive commiserating on backward Spain. He was that rare thing, a human being; open-eyed, open-handed, open-hearted, open-minded, a man ready to learn, to understand, to appreciate, to see beneath the surface.
—Salvador de Madariaga

efore his first trip to Pamplona, Hemingway imagined the city as "a wild place up in Navarre in the edge of the mountains that run down into the Basque country." Like northern Italy, it fulfilled his preference for places with snow and mountains. Gertrude Stein had talked to him about the city and its bullfights, but neither Ernest nor Hadley had any idea of what was awaiting them when the annual fiesta of San Fermín exploded on July 6, 1923.

The Hemingways were some of the first English-speaking tourists to attend the ancient festival in Pamplona, celebrated for more than five hundred years. They entered a foreign, strange world when they arrived on the first night of the fair and carried their bags through the "carnival-mad streets," bumped by dancers snapping their fingers and whirling through the crowd. If Spain had puzzled Hemingway before, what must have been his reaction to a week of "mad, whirling carnival"—fireworks, throbbing music, papier-mâché giants, and dancing in the streets night and day, religious processions with the statue of San Fermín looking like a dark little Buddha, men drinking far into the night and eating, eating always to have more energy and stay awake, the rockets fired at dawn each morning

The poster
Hemingway saw
on the walls of
Pamplona,
July 1923.

when the fighting bulls and boys race through the streets to the ring where those same bulls would be killed in the afternoon by the best toreros in the world?

How strange and different from the prim, teetotaling world of the household in Oak Park, where Dr. Hemingway had turned out Ernest's Italian-American friends because they drank and sang too loudly for the neighbors, and how far from the serious, joyless religion of the Oak Park Congregational Church! Much more than the Italians, the Basque-Navarrese people knew how to "really feel things" and to "live all the way." Even more generous than the Italians Hemingway had met during the war, they would often refuse to let the young American couple pay for drinks and would "never count the denomination of the bill. Pull out the first one you touched." While Hemingway thought the Italians were "worse crooks than the French," the Basque-Navarrese were mostly straightforward, honest, uncorruptible. And brave, loving to fight with their fists and run the bulls. They seemed to combine the *joie de vivre* and festiveness of a Mediterranean race with the proud toughness of a mountain people. Ernest began to realize that these inhabitants of northern Spain resembled the kind of Americans he admired: they were simple and open without the complexity and diffidence of the Andalusians and other southern Europeans; wary of too many words and reasons; men who found pleasure not in a subtle, continuous play of the senses but in outbursts of drink and violence; lovers of independence who would resist any coercion. For Hemingway, the Basque-Navarrese would be from this time on the best people in Spain. What he did not realize was that with the exception of the yearly feria, the people of Pamplona lived a rigid, repressed existence that made San Fermín a necessary release and liberation each July.

It rained for the first few days that year, then the clouds rolled away across the valley, the sun came out bright and hot, and Hemingway went to the best corrida he had ever seen. Manuel García, called Maera, "one of the very greatest toreros of all time," the writer said with the exaggeration of a neophyte, was on the *cartel* that afternoon. He was "dark, spare and deadly looking," but also "generous, humorous, proud, bitter, foulmouthed, and a great drinker." With Villalta, he was the Hemingways' favorite matador and was to become Ernest's new hero. Next to such men, only a year or two his senior, he felt slightly embarrassed and incompetent. You could not compete with toreros on their own ground, if anywhere. He thought the only reason husbands could maintain the respect of their wives was that "first there are only a limited number of bull fighters, second there are only a limited number of wives who have seen bull fights." To win back some of Hadley's esteem, Ernest went into the "amateurs" in the morning, when fighting cows with padded horns are released in the ring; yet he did not dare to run the encierro with the men of Pamplona. Any admiration Hadley might reacquire for her husband would be a mere "antidote to the real admiration" for the toreros. At least Ernest could be consoled by his theory that the bullfights might have a "stalwart pre-natal influence" on the baby his wife was carrying, who would in fact receive one of his middle names from the great Nicanor Villalta.

So Hemingway began to intuit the erotic undercurrent of the corrida and the sexual aura of toreros, derived from proximity to the animals that have been worshiped for millennia as symbols of the male principle. The festival of San Fermín itself was a masculine rite: the bullfight, the encierro or running of the bulls, the peñas, the leaping *riau-riau* dance were all male prerogatives forbidden to women. With wonder, Hemingway saw Pamplona boys walking with their mothers and sisters, glassy-eyed, barely able to stand, the women holding them up, smiling and bowing to their friends. The rough male camaraderie of drinking and dancing reminded him of his fishing and shooting trips to upper Michigan, and of the good stench of comrades at his Red Cross ambulance section in northern Italy. But those places were all gone and "nowhere except in our minds now." Michigan and Italy were the past, Spain was now and the future.

Hadley returned to Paris with a bad cold, Ernest with his mind full of new images:

. . . the big feria at Pamplona – 5 days of bull fighting dancing all day and all night – wonderful music – drums, reed pipes, fifes – faces of Velasquez's drinkers (?), Goya and Greco faces, all the men in blue shirts and red handkerchiefs circling lifting floating dance. We the only foreigners at the damn fair. Every morning the bulls that are going to fight that afternoon released from the Corralls on the far side of town and all of the young bucks of Pamplona running ahead of them! A mile and a half run – all the side streets barred off with big wooden gates and all this gang going like hell with the bulls trying to get them.

They were the images that would become the core of his first great novel, *The Sun Also Rises*.

During two months in the spring and summer of 1923, Hemingway had been converted to Spain and bullfighting, almost with the fervor of a religious experience. His typical preconceptions of the country had been exploded. He now realized that there was not one Spain or one Spanish people, but many Spains and many different Spaniards. Those he liked best—the Basque-Navarrese and the Castilians—were not just another venal Mediterranean people. As in all the other European countries he had visited, the aristocracy, the official class, and the laws were bad, yet Spain was "really a swell country and the people were fine."

Although he had punctured the stereotype of Spain as a mellow, southern country full of picturesque costumes and local color, Hemingway still idealized the Spanish people as the most noble in Europe. He had lived and traveled sufficiently by this time to know that such ideals usually turned out badly enough. Later he would say: "If it should ever be discovered that the Spaniards were not a very fine people it would be perfectly all right with me because I have had such a fine time while I was believing it." For Hemingway in 1923 and the following years, Spain and the Spaniards were the "real old stuff." They had all other people in the world beat: they were all "good guys" like the best inhabitants of northern Michigan, as "wild" as his old drinking buddies in Italy.

We see the familiar triad of three peninsulas in Hemingway's life— Michigan-Italy-Spain. As he had idealized the Ojibway Indians and the local inhabitants of upper Michigan, and the brave Italians during the war, he now enthroned the Spanish people in his heart, compelled as he was to maintain a current gallery of heroes. Michigan was gone with his youth; Italy was "all post war fascisti, bad food and hysterics." Traveling through Spain as if it were a vast carnival, Hemingway did not seem to notice or care about the country's tilt toward fascism in 1923. Even more than the Italians, the Spaniards, particularly the Basque-Navarrese, had a fiesta sense of life which he wanted to emulate: the feria of San Fermín was "the godamest wild time and fun you ever saw. . . . Honest to Gawd . . . there never is anything like it anywhere in the world."

In 1521, the Basque soldier Ignatius Loyola had suffered in Pamplona what Hemingway called the "wound that made him think": it led to his spiritual crisis and conversion. Almost exactly four centuries later, in the spring and summer of 1923, a young American writer suffered a figurative wound in Spain, especially in Pamplona, that was as important in some ways as his real wound in Italy. Only later would Hemingway discover that Spain itself is an "open wound . . . that cannot heal. . . ." Since he had decided to destroy rather than to perpetuate his own country in his books, and since the Italian and French experience had failed too, he needed a new land and people—ones he could believe in—to nourish his work. He found them in his Spanish conversion of 1923. Unlike the romantic country of European writers like Mérimée, and of Americans like Irving, Longfellow, and Lowell, Hemingway's Spain from now on was rooted not in literature but in his own experience. He was beginning to forge his own vision of the country that replaced America, Italy, and France as his artistic homeland.

3   The Bullfight and
        the Prose of Ecstasy

---

ecstasy. 1. *State of being beside oneself; state of being beyond all reason and self-control, as when obsessed by a powerful emotion.* 2. *A state of overmastering feeling, esp. joy; rapture.* 3. *A mystic, prophetic, or poetic trance.*
—Webster's New Collegiate Dictionary

Watching the kill of the bull time after time, and the torero's exposure to death through a ritual art during that spring and summer of 1923, Hemingway gradually began to relive, accept, and heal the terrible memory of his almost fatal wound in the war. As the matador transformed blood and death into art, the young writer would learn to transform his own suffering and experience into fiction. The bullfight was an exact, unique vehicle for him to integrate his own past with the present, and to fuse his life with his writing. That is why the bullfight was so urgently important to him, why he felt a literally religious passion for it, and why his "whole inner life" would be bullfights for the next year.

Hemingway returned to Paris from Pamplona with a new ideal of heroism learned from matadores like Maera and Villalta. If only he could find a way of uniting courage and beauty in his own work as these bullfighters did with the cape, *banderillas*, and *muleta*. If he could "make" the emotion of the corrida instead of merely describing it, perhaps he the writer, and the reader, could get something like what a torero and the public felt during a great *faena*. If a writer had lived right with his eyes and would "fight it out" with the pencil and paper, he and the reader could feel a pleasure and "bite" that was almost like the physical sensation of a corrida. The bullfight gave Hemingway not only a model for heroic conduct, but for his own art as well. Just as he learned how to "write about country so it would be there like Cezanne had done it in painting," he learned from the art of *toreo* to make writing an actual physical activity that gave a kick to him and to the reader, and the same kind of tired, emptied-out feeling when it was over. For Hemingway, writing was connected to the body as well as to the mind; "you don't write just out of yr. head but with all the senses you have on tap." Writing was driven by the "same motor" as sexual activity. If watching a great faena was like a man's "first real sexual intercourse," after a bout of good writing he felt "empty and both sad and happy," as though he had made love.

Back in Paris in the late summer of 1923, Hemingway labored over a series of miniatures for *in our time* which would reveal his new conception of writing. No fewer than five of the eleven pieces were inspired by his recent trips to Spain; they are his first writings on the bullfight derived not from hearsay but from his own experience.

In spite of what he might tell friends, the violence of the corrida, in particular the wounding of the horses, still bothered Hemingway. For this reason perhaps, and to shock his readers, he stressed the cruelest and most grotesque aspects of toreo in some of these miniatures, almost in the same way he had done in "The first matador . . ." earlier that year. Blood pumps regularly from between the legs of a white horse that has been gored; its entrails hang down "in a blue bunch" and swing backward and forward as he begins to canter. One bull roars blood while dying.

Although this emphasis on the negative dimensions of the bullfight is similar, there are telling differences between the new sketches and the single miniature of the spring. There "the kid" was a faint adumbration of the heroic conduct we see embodied fully here by the proud, oddly graceful Nicanor Villalta. Unlike the kid, he performs a rhythmic faena and kills his bull with one mighty thrust of the sword; he is not humiliated but loudly acclaimed by the crowd. Villalta is the first unqualified Spanish hero to appear in Hemingway's fiction.

In contrast to his first book, *Three Stories and Ten Poems*, the world of *in our time* with its new Spanish miniatures contains a possibility for courage and dignity, even amidst its violence. The change can be explained largely by Hemingway's experience in Spain between the writing of the two works. There is death and suffering in each book, but *in our time* does not have the sterile, bloodless quality of the earlier collection. Now blood, a symbol of death but also a sign of vitality, seems partly to cleanse and purify the violence of the world.

The new miniatures also differ strikingly from "The first matador . . ." because they are based on the closest, clearest observation, almost photographic in its precision. Hemingway was learning to convey in words the exact sequence of motion and fact in the bullfight, which was nothing less than a model for all life and death. The corridas he had seen in the spring and summer of 1923 were a kind of practical school of writing for him; he had engraved precise images in his mind and memory and now he rendered them into the right words in the right order. A picador's horse "kneed himself up" from the sand after being gored and spilled by a bull, then "cantered jerkily along the barrera." When Villalta received his bull's charge during the faena, he "swung back firmly like an oak when the wind hits it, his legs tight together, the muleta trailing and the sword following the curve behind." For the reader who had never seen a corrida, Hemingway probably "made" the bullfight in these passages as forcefully as anyone had ever done before. For the reader who had seen many corridas, especially with Villalta, each phrase jarred a corresponding image from his own experience, almost as if he were watching a movie of his own memory play across the page.

The prose of the new miniatures is "tight and hard and every thing hangs on everything else. . . ." In this sense, and in their reduced dimensions, they resemble poetry more than prose. In fact, the most important source of Hemingway's early writing was the doctrine and example of Ezra Pound's Imagism: hard and clear images expressed with the greatest possible concentration in a musical rhythm. Ernest admitted that nobody had taught him as much about writing as Pound.

Hemingway also confessed that Gertrude Stein had taught him the "wonderful rhythms in prose." Like her, he turned Flaubert's rules of writing upside down, stressing rather than avoiding repetition of similar words and phrases, even within the same sentence. As an example of Hemingway's new rhythmic, repetitive prose, let us look at one of the five bullfight miniatures for *in our time*. All of the repeated elements are italicized.

If it happened right down close *in front* of you, you could see *Villalta* snarl at the *bull* and *curse* him, and when the *bull charged* he *swung back firmly* like an oak when the wind hits it, *his legs* tight together, the *muleta* trailing and the *sword* following the *curve* behind. Then he *cursed* the *bull*, flopped the *muleta* at him, and *swung back* from the *charge* his feet *firm*, the *muleta curving* and at each *swing* the *crowd roaring*.

When he started to kill it was all in the *same* rush. The *bull looking* at him *straight in front*, hating. He drew out the *sword* from the folds of the *muleta* and sighted with the *same* movement and called to the *bull*, *Toro! Toro!* and the *bull charged* and *Villalta charged* and just for a moment they *became one*. *Villalta became one* with the *bull* and then it was over. *Villalta* standing *straight* and the red hilt of the *sword* sticking out dully between the *bull's* shoulders. *Villalta*, his hand up at the *crowd* and the *bull roaring* blood, *looking straight* at *Villalta* and *his legs* caving.

The repeated words and phrases give a definite rhythm to the prose. This rhythm is that of action: the language does not describe so much as imitate or "make" the rhythm of the matador's and the bull's movements in the ring.

It was not by chance that Hemingway's first consistent use of this rhythmic prose occured in conjunction with toreo. Rhythm is almost everything in the bullfight. A matador must not only work as closely as possible to the bull's horns; he must know how to *templar* or to "move the cape or muleta slowly, suavely, and calmly, thus prolonging the moment of the pass and the danger and giving a rhythm to the action of the man and bull and cape, or man, bull and muleta." Each pass should have this kind of *temple*, but the individual passes also should be linked in larger groups or series, thus giving a rhythmic, musical pattern to the entire faena.

In the Villalta miniature and others of *in our time*, we could say that Hemingway was "templando" or slowing, tempering, attuning his language to the particular action he wished to render. He was striving for something like the "absolute rhythm" espoused by Pound and the Imagists, one that "corresponds exactly to the emotion or shade of emotion to be expressed." Here is how Hemingway did it in an article written in the fall of 1923, describing the capework of Algabeño in Pamplona:

The bull turned like a cat and charged Algabeno and Algabeno met him with the cape. Once, twice, three times he made the perfect, floating, slow swing with the cape, perfectly, graceful, debonair, back on his heels, baffling the bull.

Hemingway still needed to purify his vocabulary of words like "debonair" and "baffling," but the language here goes a long way toward reenacting the actual physical motions of the bullfighter and the bull, and the emotion they create in the spectator, now the reader.

The first sentence of the passage describing Algabeño ("The bull charges . . ."), with its succession of clauses strung together by *and's*, is typical of Ernest's early journalism and fiction, and of what has come to be known loosely as the "Hemingway style." Philip Young has analyzed this well-known style; it is usually a regular and monotonous sequence of short sentences or clauses unrelieved by a break in the rhythm or by comment from the author. The short, terse sentences and the staccato rhythms, often employed to describe violence and death in the newspaper pieces, in *Three Stories and Ten Poems*, and *in our time*, reflect a dislocated and fragmented world. Young has deciphered this style as an expression of Hemingway's need to check and control the memories of his traumatic wounding in World War I. As the young veteran had to sleep with a light on in order to prevent his imagination from reevoking the nightmarish experience near Fossalta in 1918, a few years later the aspiring writer had to harness his unbearable memories and reorder the world through the tight, controlled medium of his style.

Young's theory of the genesis of the "Hemingway style" explains more facts than any other hypothesis. What his discussion underestimates, and others ignore, is the equally important reverse of the coin: the longer sentences and "loose" prose rhythms Hemingway used in the main part of the passage on Algabeño in 1923 and in all of his subsequent works on bullfighting. Two years after that first trip to Pamplona, Hemingway "makes" a faena and a kill by Pedro Romero in *The Sun Also Rises*:

All the passes he linked up, all completed, all slow, templed and smooth. . . . Romero's left hand dropped the muleta over the bull's muzzle to blind him, his left shoulder went forward between the horns as the sword went in, and for just an instant he and the bull were one, Romero way out over the bull, the right arm extended high up to where the hilt of the sword had gone in between the bull's shoulders.

In *Death in the Afternoon*, one of the most significant passages in all of Hemingway's work recreates the sense of "beauty and great emotion" in a complete faena:

> . . . the faena that takes a man out of himself and makes him feel immortal while it is proceeding, that gives him an ecstasy, that is, while momentary, as profound as any religious ecstasy; moving all the people in the ring together and increasing in emotional intensity as it proceeds, carrying the bullfighter with it, he playing on the crowd through the bull and being moved as it responds in a growing ecstasy of ordered, formal, passionate, increasing disregard for death that leaves you, when it is over, and the death administered to the animal that has made it possible, as empty, as changed and as sad as any major emotion will leave you.

In the physical action and emotion of bullfighting, when the matador and the spectators are momentarily united in an almost religious ecstasy, Hemingway found a model for this new prose I have called ecstatic. The ecstasy of the corrida is only momentary, but it may be as deep as any religious ecstasy because the bullfighter and his public forget themselves, they are "beside themselves" and "stand out" of their normal lives, united by a common, collective emotion. In the same way, the slow, loose rhythms of these passages in Hemingway's prose stand out from the normal succession of short, terse, monotonous sentences. The ecstatic passages are a liberation from the rigid control of the "Hemingway style": the pressure of memory and fear have disappeared. These passages are not "dry" and static, but dynamic and "wet" with all the fecundity of life. They do not represent conscious, rational control by the writer, but a tapping of the unconscious mind and an unleashing of irrational forces. As the bullfighter and the public are united by a common emotion, the creator who writes ecstatic prose and the public who reads it are united in a feeling of release, purification, and catharsis. For this reason Hemingway felt empty and hollow inside after a few hours of good writing, and we may feel something similar after reading his best work.

The ecstatic prose always recreates a physical, rhythmic action in the present: it is a release from the past and memory, an exaltation of the moment. Through it Hemingway achieved not only a ritual exorcism of his war experience, but an abrogation of his childhood, the past, history, tradition. The ecstatic prose is an intense concentration on the present, a perpetual now, like the religious trance described by mystics. The difference between the mystics and the writer is that Hemingway's ecstasy is always born from the body and the senses; it never attempts to surpass them. The person who knows this ecstasy—bullfighter or spectator, writer or reader—feels "integrated" with the world, not above or beyond the world. Yet the ecstatic event transcends the traditional limitations of time and self. While it lasts, time does not exist and the individual is not aware of himself; he is joined with others in a collective experience and freed from the boundaries of his own consciousness.

This ecstatic prose is just as important a part of the writer's art as the popular conception of the "Hemingway style." Of course the two manners do not always exist in isolation: they may be interwoven and overlap in the texture of any given work or passage. Indeed, taken together they explain the breadth of Hemingway's achievement. He was both a writer of great control and discipline and one who could create what he called "a mystery" with language. Jung theorized that all artistic creation tended to one of these two extremes—what he called the *psychological* and the *visionary* modes. The psychological artist derives his material and his method from "the sphere of conscious human experience—from the psychic foreground of life." He is the artist of consciousness, whose values are clarity and order and whose material comes from human experience as understood by the rational mind. On the other hand, the visionary artist draws his material from "the hinterland of man's mind, as if it had emerged from the abyss of prehuman ages. . . ." He is the artist of the unconscious, the irrational, the obscure. His subject matter is not the everyday world of human life but the "primordial experience which surpasses man's understanding." Hemingway fused the qualities of both the psychological and the visionary artist: the conscious world of clarity, discipline, and order in his terse manner, and the unconscious realm of numinous emotion and mystery in his ecstatic prose. To have limited his work to either of the two poles would have been artistic suicide—the result shallowness and sterility on one hand, chaos and confusion on the other. Hemingway's real stylistic innovation was the fusion of these two modes in a unique, flexible, powerful synthesis.

The bullfight was a perfect vehicle from which to create the new style.

It was the only art in the world which traded in death—a preoccupation of Hemingway's at least since 1918. It was not a static art enshrined in a museum, but a vital, organic ritual in the open air. The ecstasy of the bullfight, in the plaza and on the pages of Hemingway's work, was an ephemeral but "timeless" liberation from the strictures of everyday life, routine, memory, and the weight of tradition. Yet this ecstasy was not as dangerous as the terrible archetypes of the unconscious mind described by Jung and expressed by many visionary artists, because it was always revealed within the supremely orthodox form of the bullfight. The corrida was "an old tragedy" played in the "absolutely custom bound, law-laid-down way." The Spanish philosopher Miguel de Unamuno called toreo the most orthodox of the fine arts. If Hemingway's terse manner of short sentences and monotonous rhythm reflected a dislocated, fragmented world, his ecstatic prose expressed a new freedom and beauty within the ordered, formal world of the bullfight.

Although Jung's theory helps us to approach the writer's style, we do not know if Hemingway read the psychologist's work. We do know that Hemingway was familiar with Nietzsche, whose distinction between Apollonian versus Dionysian creativity paralleled roughly Jung's contrast between the psychological and visionary modes. The records of Sylvia Beach's lending library at Shakespeare and Company in Paris show that Hemingway checked out at least one of the philosopher's books; he undoubtedly knew others directly or from conversation with writers and artists. Nietzsche discovered two basic impulses in art: the Apollonian, related to the eye, observation, and discrimination, the visual arts, beauty, knowledge, individuation; and the Dionysian, related to the ear, rhythm, music, dissonance and even ugliness, intuition, the unconscious, primordial unity. For the author of *Thus Spake Zarathustra*, the Apollonian and Dionysian impulses were fused in the greatest works of art, such as Greek drama; there, beneath an Apollonian surface, the music expressed the secret, Dionysian sense of pain and tragedy. Like Greek drama, Hemingway's style and best works embodied a union of the two impulses—a clear surface with a dark current below. The underlying rhythms of the prose expressed as much as the words themselves. Not by coincidence, Hemingway realized from the very beginning that the bullfight was a tragedy, not a sport. It harmonized with his own tragic sense, born from an unhappy childhood and exposure to pain and death in World War I.

Like the Dionysian spirit, Hemingway's prose is fundamentally tragic or elegiac. From the earliest works, there is a sense of loss in the themes and images, but more importantly in the prose rhythms. For this very reason his books often fall flat in translation, where the words can be rendered literally, but not the cadences. Similarly, the film versions of his works are destined to failure in literary terms: the change from one medium to another destroys the fragile music of language in which lies the real substance of his vision.

Hemingway was very aware of the rhythmic or poetic quality of his prose, but he felt reluctant to discuss it in public; it would have been a profanation of an artistic secret to reveal it openly. "It is only with alchemy that you combine poetry and prose," he once said. It was not so much the words as the rhythm that "makes the emotion."

A letter from Hemingway to one of his editors throws a light on his rhythmic prose and its tragic or elegiac nature. In the fall of 1938, he sent "Night Before Battle," a story about the Spanish Civil War, to Arnold Gingrich at *Esquire*. It tells of a "good tank man," Al Wagner, who is doomed to die in a battle on impossible terrain the following day. Hemingway's original version of the story's last paragraph reads this way:

> If you *hadn't have* known him pretty well and if you *hadn't have* seen the terrain where he was going to attack tomorrow, you would have thought he was very angry about something.

The writer knew that the two uses of *hadn't have* (emphasis mine) were ungrammatical and that his editor would want to delete them. The sentence was "not grammar," but it sounded right. "Maybe the have's should come out," he told Gingrich, "but let's leave them in unless you have some objection. In some way they seem to be involved in the rhythm that makes the emotion." The editor won out however, and the passage was printed without the superfluous, offending *have's*:

> If you hadn't known him pretty well and if you hadn't seen the terrain. . .

If we scan the rhythm of the two versions, we see that the original was irregular in the alternation of stressed and unstressed syllables:

If yŏu hádn't hăve knówn hĭm prétty wéll aňd ĭf yŏu hádn't hăve
séen hĭm. . .

In contrast, the rhythm of the printed version is more regular and peri-
odic, consisting mostly of a pattern of one accented syllable followed by
an unaccented, and so on:

Ĭf yŏu hádn't knówn hĭm prétty wéll aňd ĭf yŏu hádn't séen
hĭm. . .

The extra, ungrammatical *have's* of Hemingway's original gave the passage
an irregular, flexible rhythm, basically a dactylic meter of one accented
syllable followed by two unaccented: ′ ˘ ˘ . For centuries this was the
primary rhythm of various artistic and religious expressions in the ancient
world—elegiac poetry, oracles like the one at Delphi, the utterances of
gods. In the modern world, this is often the rhythm of language in religious frenzy, as in glossolalia or "speaking in tongues." Such activities of
the "god-run man" have their seat in the right or nonrational hemisphere
of the brain. Of course Hemingway did not know much if anything about
dactylic rhythm, ancient oracles, or the structure of the brain. But he
had learned from Pound and the Imagists to compose in the rhythm of
the musical phrase rather than in the meter of a metronome. With his
nearly perfect ear and his unerring instinct, he knew that "in some way"
the irregular, nonperiodic cadences of his prose were what "makes the
emotion." And the emotion is normally tragic and elegiac, related to loss,
pain, and death. Even when he celebrates joy, the melody of his prose is
sad. In a sense, all of his books are farewells—to his country, to youth,
innocence, love, life.

Although Hemingway's ecstatic prose was born from the bullfight, he
soon began to extend it to other physical activities that were also charged
with numinous emotion. As in the theoretical writings of William James,
emotion is always equated with bodily sensation in Hemingway's work.
After creating his ecstatic prose as an imitation or reenactment of the bullfight, he used it for his first love—fishing. Like his second love, shooting,
and like the bullfight, fishing involved a link with nature and the animal
past. When a bullfighter makes a good kill, when a hunter drops something cleanly that is trying to get away, when a fisherman catches what

is fighting to tear loose, "you get that old, primitive sensation." All three activities require the "Godlike attribute" of administering death.

Hemingway's newspaper article on Vigo, with its exuberant description of tuna in the sea, already foreshadowed the use of ecstatic prose to make the emotion of fishing. In "Big Two-Hearted River" (written in 1924), Nick Adams, still healing his war wounds, goes camping and fishing in the Michigan wilderness. The prose is characteristically monotonous and staccato until a big strike from a trout intervenes; suddenly, as Philip Young has said, "the pressure is off the man, he is nowhere but right there playing the fish, and then the sentences lengthen greatly and become appropriately graceful":

> Nick unhooked him; heavy sides, good to hold, big undershot jaw, and slipped him, heaving and big sliding, into the long sack that hung from his shoulders in the water.

Something similar would happen in the fishing scenes of *The Sun Also Rises, The Old Man and the Sea,* and the posthumous *Islands in the Stream.*

In the Austrian Alps during the winter of 1924–25, Hemingway noticed that "dropping straight down a mountain slope on skis through powder snow" was a physical sensation comparable to the experience of witnessing a great faena in the bullring. His short story, "Cross-Country Snow," shows Nick Adams skiing down a steep slope:

> The rush and the sudden swoop as he dropped down a steep undula-tion in the mountain side plucked Nick's mind out and left him only the wonderful flying, dropping sensation in the body. He rose to a slight up-run and then the snow seemed to drop out from under him as he went down, down, faster and faster in a rush down the last, long steep slope.

It would take several years for Hemingway to use his ecstatic prose to reenact hunting. In "The Short Happy Life of Francis Macomber" (1936):

> Macomber did not know how the lion had felt before he started his rush, nor during it when the unbelievable smash of the .505 with a

muzzle velocity of two tons had hit him in the mouth, nor what kept him coming after that, when the second ripping crash had smashed his hind quarters and he had come crawling on toward the crashing blasting thing that had destroyed him.

Since Hemingway compared the emotion of a great faena to the sexual act as well as to skiing, it was not surprising that he would use his ecstatic prose to evoke Nick Adam's first intercourse —in the woods of northern Michigan with an Ojibway Indian girl:

> Could you say she did first what no one has ever done better and mention plump brown legs, flat belly, hard little breasts, well holding arms, quick searching tongue, the flat eyes, the good taste of mouth, then uncomfortably, tightly, sweetly, moistly, lovely, tightly, achingly, fully, finally, unendingly, never-endingly, never-to-endingly, suddenly ended, the great bird flown like an owl in the twilight, only it daylight in the woods and hemlock needles stuck against your belly. ("Fathers and Sons," 1933)

None of these experiences is "properly describable"—a great faena in a bullfight, fishing, hunting, skiing, lovemaking. Yet Hemingway's ecstatic prose came as close as any other writer's language to remaking these pure "pleasurable physical" sensations. Each ecstatic action involves some connection with the body, the senses, instinct; all are links to an atavistic past, to the "primordial experience" described by Jung. Malcolm Cowley was the first critic to notice that Hemingway's characters live in a hostile world which can be survived and exorcised only through "the almost continual performance of rites and ceremonies." Besides the bullfight and other physical actions like fishing and hunting, skiing and love, boxing and horseracing, Hemingway would convert drinking, friendship, and death into rituals; they too would be rendered with his ecstatic prose. As in the rituals of primitive peoples, in the language of his prose there seems to be a magical connection between words and the things or actions they describe. His prose is a kind of incantation used to create certain fundamental experiences that are "religious" in the root sense of the word: they tie or integrate man and nature, man and animal together in a primordial unity which cannot be fully expressed by words. Like the mystic trance, these experiences are irrational and ineffable, but they can be evoked or suggested through music and rhythm. Hearing is a "primitive" sense, highly developed in ancient man and animals; it reaches deeper conscious and unconscious levels than sight—the scientific or rational sense par excellence. Thus St. Paul referred to hearing as the sense of faith, of religion. In Nietzsche's terms, sight and observation are Apollonian, hearing and music Dionysian.

In his feeling for ritual and forgotten sacraments, Hemingway could be called a religious writer. His conversion to Catholicism can be explained in part by his preference for the ritual, sacramental aspects of religion. Yet his cast of mind was more properly sub-Christian, or as Cowley said, pre-Christian and prelogical. An important letter written in 1950 reveals the nature of Hemingway's God:

> My God painted many wonderful pictures and wrote some very good books and fought Napoleon's rear-guard actions in the retreat from Moskova and fought on both sides at Gettysburg and did away with yellow fever and taught Picasso how to draw and sired Citation. He is the best god-damned God you ever knew. But I have never met him. I've seen a lot of his pictures though in the Prado and I read his books and his short stories every year. And I know the exact details of how he killed George Armstrong Custer, which nobody else knows, and my God when he played football was Jim Thorpe and when he pitched he was Walter Johnson and the ball looked as big as a small marble and it would kill you if it hit you. So my God never dusted anybody off ever.

Although it would be an error to take this jocular letter too seriously, it is consistent with much of what we have seen already in Hemingway's life and work; he is describing the sources of his own inspiration. To begin with, his God is exclusively masculine; none of the names or actions enumerated in the letter is related to women. Second, this God reveals himself in physical actions similar to those recreated in Hemingway's ecstatic prose—sports such as horseracing, football, baseball, and war. Third, his God is esthetic, not ethical: he inspires good writing and painting but does not reward or punish. Hemingway's God is much closer to the artistic deities of Greece, like Apollo and Dionysus, than to the Hebrew Jehovah or the Christian Jesus.

The experiences recreated in ecstatic prose—the bullfight, fishing, hunting, skiing, love, drinking, friendship, death—are nothing less than the "mystery," the fourth or fifth dimension to which Hemingway alluded several times but never explained. Indeed, to have defined these irrational, mythic experiences would have been a contradiction: they can only be lived in an actual present, here and now, and would be profaned or killed by rational analysis. Like the Dionysian rituals and spirit described by Nietzsche, these experiences are intimately related to music and tragedy. The death of the ancient Greek god was reenacted through an ecstatic ritual of music and dance; the bull is sacrificed in a highly ordered, rhythmic rite, which conveys an ecstatic emotion to the celebrant or matador and to the public who watches him. In the ancient, atavistic ritual of the bullfight, Hemingway found an art which could serve as a model for his own art of writing, an experience of ecstasy that had managed to survive in the modern world of science, reason, and technology, and which found its roots in the Iberian Peninsula. The bullfight and his ecstatic prose were the first "secret things" he would discover in Spain.

Pamplona: 2

You enter the long, narrow hotel room with afternoon light coming through a window facing the gardens below. There are two single beds, unmade, strewn with clothes, books, newspapers. A modern chandelier is suspended from the ceiling. The matador Luis Francisco Esplá moves quickly around the room, naked except for a white towel around his waist. He has the straight bearing and pigeon-toed step of an athlete. He looks about twenty-five, with light skin, brown hair, a square face and jaw. The tobacco- and gold-colored jacket of his *traje de luces*, short and stiff, hangs over a desk chair. From the bathroom come steamy smells of soap, cologne, hair oil. Rock music plays in English on a Sony clock radio between the beds. Esplá's uncle, also his *apoderado* or manager, is preparing the underclothes and the suit of lights. A withered little man who must be the swordhandler waits for orders. Esplá does not let the others serve him; whatever he needs he fetches himself, impatient.

"Pepe, where's the change from the bottle of whisky?" he asks the little man. His shrill voice does not seem to fit his torso—muscular like a welterweight's or a soccer player's.

Pepe points to a tray on one of the nightstands. Esplá walks around the bed, takes the 100-peseta bills from a plate, wads them, and places them in a drawer.

"Let it not be that someone picks them up after the corrida," he says, smiling at us. "You've got to be as tight-fisted as the Catalans around here."

You feel embarrassed, as if this kind of frugality did not befit a matador de toros. Until now you have not noticed two men against the wall in a corner. One is a mature Japanese with a camera around his neck, the other a young man who looks Andalusian or Latin American.

Everyone becomes silent as Esplá modestly turns away from us, unwraps the towel and takes the long white underwear from his uncle. There are some reddish-blue welts, scars from horn wounds, on his legs. As you see him dressed all in white underclothes except for the pink silk hose, you remember the day your sister was married and the dressing of the bride. That was a feminine ritual from which you were excluded except as a last-minute messenger boy. This is a masculine ritual. Like the bride, the matador acknowledges and does not acknowledge your presence; both seem to draw away from you as their minds anticipate the moment when they will be alone with their opposite—the otherness of it—bridegroom or bull.

Esplá appears to come out of his abstraction and wipes sweat from his armpits with the towel. "*La guinda*," he says joking. "Frigging fear—we drew the worst bull."

Since he has given a sign to change the tone in the room, everyone follows, joking about women and money, the ears El Cordobés cut yesterday in a second-class ring. The photographer asks if he can take a picture of the matador with his *capote de paseo* or embroidered dress cape in front of the hotel. Esplá says yes; the Japanese leaves.

They make fun of the "Chinaman" and how much he charges for his portraits. "Most toreros are ignorant enough to pay what he asks," says Esplá.

"Who are your best friends among the matadores?" asks the young hanger-on, who turns out to be Peruvian.

"I don't have friends among toreros," he answers.

There is a knock on the door.

Esplá says, "If it's the girls, wait until I put on the *taleguilla*."

Pepe goes to the door, then returns to help the uncle prepare the tobacco-colored breeches. Esplá climbs into them, pushing against the legs held by the two helpers, hitching, twisting, forcing all of his weight into the tight garment. The two girls come in, unbeautiful, shaking hands with him. Esplá shows them the jacket for today and the suit for tomorrow, hung in the closet—silver and black. They fondle it and say it is precious, make a call on the phone, then tell him how he will be triumphant today as he puts on his black slippers, slings the suspenders over his shoulders. The two helpers wrap and knot the sash around his waist, help him assume the heavy, encrusted jacket. He puts on his *coleta* or pigtail after his uncle has affixed a clasp to the back of his head.

As the matador adjusts his *montera*, or black cap, and examines himself in the mirror, you notice a pair of Adidas shoes placed neatly beneath the desk, about a yard to his left. You will never forget his feet—black pumps and pink stockings—next to that pair of white jogging shoes.

The uncle stands straight up, raising his voice: "The matador would like to be alone." This is the signal for everyone to leave: Esplá will probably pray now. You notice that there is no portable altar visible, with the usual Virgins, crucifixes, saints' medals and tapers. You have been in the room about twenty minutes; the corrida begins in half an hour.

You thank him, shaking his hand once more and wishing him "*Suerte.*" By now his eyes are looking beyond your head.

You walk down the stairs to the lobby. Your friend Alfonso Saiz Valdi-vielso, bullfight critic of the Bilbao newspaper *Deia*, walks up to you.

"What do you think *pues*?" he asks.

"He is a very nice boy. You can't help feeling like an underling next to him; you must respect him. The tremendous responsibility and the aloneness of it. But all this luxury bothers me."

"That is the question, whether bullfighting can survive prosperity, modernity, and democracy." We come out the entrance of the hotel; it rises like a concrete skyscraper compared to the buildings of the old city.

"Take this hotel for example," Alfonso goes on. "It could be found in Bilbao, Madrid, Berlin, or New York. It is spacious with all the modern conveniences, but it does not have any of the worn charm of the Hotel Quintana, gone now—where Hemingway watched a bullfighter get dressed for the first time—or the old Perla and the Yoldi where some of the more traditional toreros still stay in Pamplona."

You look up at the facade of the Hotel Tres Reyes: a large golden crown and five stars indicate its deluxe category. A liveried doorman tips his hat at the entrance.

"Esplá's room was full of books," you tell Alfonso. "There was a volume of poems by Alberti, one by Neruda, another by Juan Ramón Jiménez, even a novel by Baroja. He has wide taste." In the parking lot there are autos with license plates from all over Spain and Europe—Seats, Mercedes, Triumphs, Renaults, BMWs.

Alfonso says, "I wonder if a man who makes his living with dangerous animals, who kills and exposes himself to wounds, I wonder if that kind of man should be an intellectual. Esplá is a university student; he studies fine arts and likes to paint. Perhaps the greatest athletes and performers are those who act instinctively and do not think too much."

In the taxi to the bullring Alfonso says, "It would be hard to deny that a man like Esplá represents a step forward for Spain in culture. When I was young, my father introduced me to the old toreros who really were men that smelled of sweat and tobacco, as the saying goes. What has been gained in progress has been lost in the mystery of those men who did not read, spoke little, and lived near animals."

"Esplá is a fine boy," you say, "but he is almost like any other young man who works in a bank or a store, except that he happens to work with bulls."

"Wait till you see him place the banderillas this afternoon."

4   *The Messiah of Bullfighting*

*He was in Spain, inside Spain, living her life. And his two great
works, "For Whom the Bell Tolls" and "The Sun Also Rises,"
blossomed out of this implantation of the roots of that powerful
American tree into Iberian soil. . . .*
—*Salvador de Madariaga*

At the festival of San Fermín in 1925, Ernest and Hadley
saw the spectacular Pamplona debut of the new "phenomenon" of bullfighting, nineteen-year-old Cayetano Ordóñez,
"Niño de la Palma." The matador came from Ronda, the
cradle of toreo and the city which had intrigued Hemingway
during his first trip to Spain. Ronda was famous for a style of bullfighting
—"sober, limited in repertoire, simple, classic and tragic." These were
some of the qualities Hemingway perceived in Cayetano's art; they were
very close to the qualities he was striving to achieve in his prose. Both
Ernest and Hadley became immediate devotees of this "messiah who had
come to save bullfighting."

On the afternoon before one of the bullfights of San Fermín, Juanito
Quintana, owner of the hotel where both Cayetano and the Hemingways
were lodged, probably invited the young writer and one of his male American friends to meet Niño de la Palma during the ritual dressing before
the corrida. Ernest would soon capture the scene in words, renaming the
matador as Pedro Romero, and the two Americans as Jake Barnes and Bill
Gorton: half-past three in the afternoon, a gloomy bedroom, silence of apprehension, the young torero standing straight and unsmiling, seemingly
alone in spite of the company of hangers-on, the awkward embarrassment
of the Americans. The bullfighter had an aloof seriousness, an almost
priestly dignity, like a young god in some ancient, sacrificial rite. This
scene was the original beginning of *The Sun Also Rises*.

The fictional bullfighter Pedro Romero, based on the real matador

Cayetano Ordóñez, Niño de la Palma, was the focus of the novel in its early version. Before settling on the character's final name, Hemingway called him Antonio Guerra, "Guerrita" ("little war[rrior]"), echoing the name of the famous nineteenth-century torero, Rafael Guerra, "Guerrita." But he would eventually cut this name, probably to eliminate the suggestion of war—precisely what Jake Barnes was attempting to forget and transcend in the novel—in favor of Pedro Romero, a name almost synonymous with bullfighter and torco, as we will see. The bullfight itself was Hemingway's immediate, concrete inspiration for *Sun*: in toreo he had discovered a model for his own art, one that would somehow unite the body and the mind, action and beauty, his public and his private lives. He wrote to Sylvia Beach just three weeks after San Fermín, while he and Hadley were still in Spain following the bulls and Niño de la Palma: "I've written six chapters on a novel and am going great about 15,000 words. . . . It's going to be good but will be harder when there aren't any bullfights."

Hemingway's working papers show that the scene of the matador dressing in his hotel room was almost certainly the original start of *The Sun Also Rises*. The first version has to do with the moral dangers for a nineteen-year-old bullfighter who gets involved with a "gang" of people like Jake Barnes's drunken friends. Hemingway even recalls his own mother's injunctions during his youth in Oak Park, when she declared that she would rather see her son in his grave than have him become an alcoholic. (Grace Hall Hemingway did not have her way; Ernest would become an alcoholic before he reached the grave.)

In the *Sun* notebooks, Jake Barnes goes to bed late the night after he and his friend have visited the bullfighter (still called Niño) in room number eight of the Hotel Quintana. Several hours later, at six a.m., Jake is awakened by three men coming into his room, carrying a fourth with legs dangling. They realize it is the wrong room and leave. "I couldn't quite see the face of the man they were carrying. But he looked like Niño. Anyway they put him in number Eight."

In the final version of *Sun*, any suggestion of Pedro Romero's drunkenness or moral weakness is scrupulously avoided, although the character is still lodged in the same room of the hotel (now called the Montoya). It is curious that this early draft was prophetic of the eventual professional and moral decline of the real bullfighter, Cayetano Ordóñez. After his first serious goring at the end of the 1925 season, Niño de la Palma lost his valor and "never got it back." A failure as a torero, he began to drink heavily, took the humiliating step of becoming a banderillero for another matador, and ended his life in squalor and delusion.

The reasons for Hemingway's idealization of the bullfighter Pedro Romero in the final draft of *Sun* are central to the meaning of the novel and to the writer's vision of Spain. For now, it is enough to know that after the initial episode of San Fermín in the original draft, Hemingway shifted the narration from Spain to France: "To understand the situation in Pamplona you have to understand Paris." Indeed, the novel would become a study in geographical and cultural contrasts between France and Spain, Paris and Pamplona, and of how those contrasts influence the characters, in particular the narrator, Jake Barnes.

With this background, we can approach *The Sun Also Rises* as it stands in its final version. As the author said, you have to understand Paris before you can understand the situation in Pamplona. If London was T. S. Eliot's waste land in the post-World War I years, Paris was Hemingway's. Because of his nostalgic recollection of the city in his later writings (as in *A Moveable Feast*), and because of the irrepressible lyricism that often seizes critics when they evoke the "lost generation," it is easy to forget the withering view of Paris in Hemingway's early journalism and in *Sun*. In the novel, everyone in the city has been blasted by "that dirty war." As Hemingway would ask his friend Scott Fitzgerald, "Who has vitality in Paris?" In their materialism and reduction of everything to the cash-value principle, the French resemble the Americans whom Hemingway had already left behind in his life and his fiction.

No wonder then that Jake Barnes flees France for Spain every summer, making a kind of pilgrimage to the festival of San Fermín in Pamplona. This time, after their trip by car through the luminous Spanish country-side and several marvelous days of fishing in the Pyrenees, Jake and his friend Bill reach Pamplona for San Fermín, where they meet Pedro Romero in his hotel room before the first bullfight of the feria. The hushed, sacramental atmosphere of this scene is like nothing else in Hemingway's work before—one of the secret things he had discovered in Spain and was only beginning to capture in prose.

Hemingway named his fictional torero after the legendary founder of modern toreo, Pedro Romero (1754–1839). Like this historical figure, Cayetano Ordóñez (Niño de la Palma) was from Ronda and fought in the classic *rondeño* style. The fictional Romero also has "the old thing" in his art. After the scene in the hotel room, he shows a style with cape and muleta in the bullring that is consistent with the qualities Jake Barnes discovers and admires in Spain and the Spanish people—purity, naturalness, authenticity.

The central theme of the Pamplona sections in *The Sun Also Rises* is the relationship between the bullfighter Pedro Romero and the foreigners in Pamplona—the original theme of the book. When Montoya goes to Barnes's room to tell him that the torero has been invited to meet the American ambassador at the Grand Hotel, Jake tells his friend, "Don't give Romero the message." The matador and the ambassador represent incompatible, antithetical cultures: one ancient, rural, and rooted in tradition, the other modern, urban, and industrial. People like the ambassador don't understand the worth of a young man like Romero nor the centuries of tradition that have made his art and character possible. A year of "this Grand Hotel business" can ruin a bullfighter by contaminating him with the values of the "other" world. When Jake advises Montoya not to convey the invitation from the American ambassador, in effect he renounces a set of values represented by his own country in favor of others, as Hemingway had done by leaving the United States in 1921.

That same evening in the dining room of the Hotel Montoya, there is another meeting of the two cultures: Barnes presents Romero to the gang. The bullfighter and Brett Ashley feel an immediate attraction to each other. As we have seen earlier, Hemingway had already recognized the sexual aura of the corrida and of the matador—the man who slays the bull, symbol of masculine power at least since the ancient myth of Europa's rape by the bull-god. With his entire bearing and prestige, Pedro Romero represents what D. H. Lawrence called the "ithyphallic authority" over women, which had been lost by Anglo-Saxon man. In *Sun*, the torero establishes his sexual dominance precisely over the character who is portrayed, half-seriously it is true, as a kind of sexual goddess of San Fermín—Brett. But the attraction between Romero and the Englishwoman is not merely erotic; more than any of the other foreigners except

Jake, she has felt the deep, almost religious quality of the corrida. She regards the beauty and strength of the fighting bull with awe, learns the technical details of toreo quickly from Jake, and feels the same sense of physical exhaustion as her teacher after a corrida: "These bull-fights are hell on one," she says. "I'm limp as a rag." She also feels at home in the matador's world of superstition; she has her fortune told at a gypsy camp outside Pamplona and reads Romero's palm herself. Brett is far more than an alcoholic nymphomaniac, as she has been classified by many readers and critics. She is more intelligent than most of the men who pursue her: "Chaps never know anything, do they?" Jake, and perhaps Romero, recognize that she has "different depths" in her eyes and a capacity to see, experience, and enjoy more than the others.

Pedro Romero contrasts sharply with the members of Barnes's crew. Because of his constant exposure to danger and his ability to overcome death through his art, he lives more intensely than ordinary men: "Nobody lives their life all the way up except bull-fighters." Unlike most members of the "lost generation" in the novel, Romero is a professional; he has métier, or to use the Spanish word admired by Hemingway, *oficio*. He is a living example of the kind of practical wisdom Jake is seeking: "Maybe if you found out how to live in it [the world] you learned from that what it was all about," Barnes thinks. Pedro Romero is a man who knows how to live and how to enjoy it, giving priority to the senses; bulls, food, drink, cigars, and women are the ingredients of his primal masculine domain. When Bill Gorton is with the matador, he feels "ashamed of being a writer," as Hemingway did when he met Niño de la Palma and other bullfighters in Spain: an author is a more passive creator who does not combine action and beauty in a vital synthesis as the torero can. Most of all, Romero contrasts with Robert Cohn, the character who embodies many of the ills of the modern world. When Cohn finds Brett in the torero's hotel room, he beats up Romero with his fists but is "ruined" by the Spaniard's superior honor and courage. The matador's dignity in defeat rounds off with human frailness an otherwise immaculate, aloof character.

Jake Barnes's acquaintance with the bullfighter forms a necessary stage in the narrator's growth. From Pedro Romero he learns to have courage in facing the "bulls" of his own life. He learns to have oficio too: after Spain he will return to Paris and become a novelist by writing the book we are reading. He also learns to give priority to his body and his senses, like Romero, as the surest way to experience and live in the world. Like Hemingway's, Jake's senses come alive in Spain, where he absorbs everything around him "as a starfish with its five stomachs and five eyes absorbs an oyster."

By introducing Brett to the matador, Barnes in effect admits the impossibility of his own love for her. Thus he learns to accept himself without illusions and partly to overcome the suffering over his impotence. There is no doubt that his complex decision to serve as an intermediary between Brett and Romero is the key moral action of the book. (By conventional lights it would of course be considered an immoral action; Hemingway was not a conventional moralist.) By introducing Brett to Romero, Jake may feel a vicarious satisfaction in exposing the woman to the kind of man she needs for her own development—not the miserable, ineffectual Robert Cohn, not her drunken fiancé Mike Campbell, but Pedro Romero, who reflects some of Jake's best qualities, Jake's own best self. We might even say that bringing Brett to Romero is as close as Barnes will ever come to possessing her. Jake's decision is one of complete independence because he realizes it will alienate him both from his Spanish comrades, like Montoya, and from the Anglo-Saxon friends with a proprietary interest in Lady Brett—Cohn and Campbell. So Barnes's decision establishes his own moral independence and in certain ways brings a temporary fusion of the best elements of two worlds and two cultures portrayed in the novel: Brett and Romero, the female and the male principles, Anglo-American and Spanish. Jake probably intuits that the couple and the cultures they represent are too diverse to achieve a complete, permanent union, yet their liaison is necessary for their development and for his own. Barnes's decision moves his own character and the novel forward in a way that could not have been accomplished through any other action.

By this time we are ready to examine the reasons for Hemingway's whitewashing of the Pedro Romero character between the first and the final versions of *Sun*. In the earliest fragment of the novel, he showed Niño de la Palma being carried in a drunken stupor to his hotel room. The removal of this scene, the change in the character's name to prevent association with the historical Guerrita or the living Niño de la Palma, and the portrayal of the matador as a virtually unflawed person represent more than superficial changes, more than mere reductions consistent with the iceberg theory of fiction. Nowhere in the final version is there any suggestion that the bullfighter might lose his control and dignity. The omission of the original scene implies a substantial change in the ethical quality of the book. Although Jake believes that "everybody behaves badly" if given the proper chance, there is no evidence in the printed novel that these words might apply to Romero. Driven by his urge to idealize the Spanish males in his writings—Villalta and Maera were earlier examples—Hemingway needed to create in Pedro Romero an antidote to the flawed members of the gang, a heroic model and a touchstone of masculine conduct. Perhaps one of the weaknesses of the novel lies in the excessive idealization of a nineteen-year-old, semiliterate young man who is too vaguely sketched, too impeccable and anachronistic a figure to embody a real alternative mode of behavior. His importance in the novel lies not so much in himself as in his art and in his influence on Jake and Brett, and in their growth beyond a need to depend on others for their own well-being. Much earlier than his creator, Jake Barnes learns that there are no messiahs in the bullring.

Burguete and Roncesvalles, 1985

ou put on your Spanish hiking boots, sling a leather wine-skin over your shoulder and walk to the bus station. Several winos are celebrating their own San Fermín in the seedy waiting room. There are no buses to Burguete until afternoon and none returns to Pamplona, so you will have to hitchhike. You walk by the bullring, along the shady Paseo Hemingway, and across the Arga River.

It is a good day to be on the road—bright sky with clouds, a cool breeze. It does not seem very warm for July. The heat in Pamplona comes from the wine and the people as well as from the sun.

A man in an old Citroen Deux-chevaux picks you up. He is about fifty-five, unshaven, with large-knuckled hands. He has driven all the way from a furniture store in San Sebastián to deliver a mattress to an old client in a Navarrese town. Inside the Citroen it is stifling because the windows do not roll down. It smells of dust and man and engine. The road begins to climb, passing square fields ripe with wheat or hay on the hillsides and valleys. One man is cutting an entire field with a scythe. Here in Navarre you do not have the sensation of horizontal space as in Castile; everything is gathered in, on a human scale. You pass villages with white stone houses, churches, *pelota* courts, and the smell of manure. The driver says he is a *gallego*; he had to bring his family to the Basque country nine years ago because there were no jobs in Galicia.

He asks what you are doing in Navarre.

"The Sanfermines."

"Are you going to run the encierro?"

"Yes, tomorrow."

"*Ten cuidado*, be careful" he tells you like a father.

After going over the Erro Pass, you descend through green countryside to the town of Espinal where he must deliver the mattress. You say good-bye to the gallego and continue walking north by the side of the road, your feet hot against the pavement. Outside the town you see a stocky man pruning the thick trees and bushes back from the shoulder of the road. He stops as you approach, takes off his *boina*, wipes his forehead with his coatsleeve, puts the boina back on his head. He is not more than five feet four inches tall and he has the stubble of a white beard on his dry, brown face.

"*Buenos días*" you say to him.

"*Buenos.*" He wears the dark corduroy used by peasants in most of Spain.

"Is Burguete very far from here?"

"Not very far. It is the next town."

You take the *bota* off your shoulder and offer it to him, unscrewing the tit on the cap.

"Many thanks." He leans the pruning hook against his leg and takes the wineskin. Holding the neck of the bladder-shaped leather with his left hand and the fat part with the other, he raises it above his chin as he tilts his head back and squeezes with the right palm and fingers. Red wine begins to trickle into his mouth, becomes a fine stream and hisses in his throat as he extends his right arm as far as it will go and squeezes harder, his Adam's apple working up and down as he swallows. Then he draws the bota closer to his mouth, stopping the flow so cleanly that not a drop of the wine spills.

"It is very good, this little wine."

You drink, liking the coolness of the wine with its faint taste of pitch from the lining of the bota.

"You have much work to do," you tell him, pointing at the thicket along the roadside.

"Much" he answers. He is probably more than sixty years old. A man of his age would not be performing this kind of job in the United States, you think, then remember that nobody would do it by hand—a sickle mower would be used.

"You are coming from Pamplona," he says or asks.

"Yes. I wanted to see the country around Burguete. They tell me it is beautiful land."

"It is true. But still there is much poverty and ignorance. A few kilometers up in these hills there are villages where people do not know to speak Castilian. They must come down here to do their buying but they speak only Basque." His skin is burned dry as a nut. Hundreds of wrinkles groove his face and neck.

He still cannot figure you out. "You are a foreigner because of the accent," he says in the monotone that could be a statement or a question. By foreigner he might mean someone from abroad or simply outside of Navarre.

"Yes, from America." There are only two places you know in Europe where it is not an embarrassment to say you are American—the Basque-Navarrese country and southern Italy. For the people of these regions, with two of the most ancient cultures in Europe, the name of America still rings with a nostalgia of freedom and miracles.

"My father lived in America," he tells me, proud, smiling for the first time. Some of his teeth are missing, but the ones he has left are smooth, large and strong-looking like the teeth of an ancient mammal you might see in a museum.

"What part?" you ask.

"California. My father worked there five years, saved his money and returned here. He was a shepherd and a farmhand."

"I am from California also."

You offer him more wine. He wags his forefinger no.

"May you continue well" you say to him, slinging the bota onto your shoulder.

"Good trip" he answers, tipping his boina. The Navarrese are more courteous than Americans, like all Spaniards, you think.

You walk up the hill along the grassy shoulder of the road. At the crest you come to a wood of cork-oaks with cows grazing among the trees. A stone fountain flows in the shade. There is a sharp curve to the left and a plain opens out in front of you, split by the highway like an arrow— Burguete huddled along the road with its red roofs and white houses, a line of dark mountains behind it almost hidden by an immense bank of rolling gray fog, as if from a different world. Roncevaux, the Spanish Roncesvalles, must be up there but the fog is too dense to see it. On your right there is a campground along the stream that comes down from the Pyrenees.

You walk into the town. It is already cooler here. The houses and buildings, flush along the road with no sidestreets, are built mostly of stone, solid and clean. It seems you are in the Alps, in Germany or Switzerland rather than Spain. You pass immaculate open doorways giving onto large, airy rooms with shiny floors. In front of the church well-dressed people, probably from Pamplona, are gathering for a wedding.

You walk beyond the town into a pine and beech forest that extends on both sides of the road. It is sunny in Burguete as you look back, dark and foggy ahead. The sun vanishes and the fog thickens as you approach Roncesvalles. It is cold, really cold for July. Burguete is white buildings and red roofs, Roncesvalles is all gray—metal-sheathed roofs of the chapel and monastery. You watch the fog as it comes down fast from the Pyrenees and into the valley. There are no cars or people visible except an old hunchbacked monk pacing slowly back and forth in front of the monastery. You walk to the gray stone chapel and to the entrance of the cloister, both locked tight.

You approach the monk. A dog, old and shaggy as the man, lies on the grass watching his master shuffle to and fro. It barks at you and the monk scolds it with a handcarved wooden cane. He wears a grayish wool habit and a boina. With small, gray-green eyes, he squints at you suspiciously.

"*Buenas tardes,*" you say. It is probably afternoon by now.

"*Buenas,*" he answers.

"It is cold."

"Always it is cold here." He must be eighty. His hands tremble. He has bushy eyebrows that protrude from his forehead, long hairs growing from his ears and nostrils.

"Does one not get accustomed to the cold?" you ask him.

"It is more than twenty years that I have lived here, and still I am not accustomed. And I am Navarrese. It is never warm here, never. In the winter the snow drifts as high as a man's head."

You ask, "Do you not have heating?"

"Yes, but it gives shame to use it in July. It is a sin. *Es un pecado.*"

You would like to be with him longer—a man from another century. But his hands and lips are trembling and you realize he would rather be alone.

"Is there a way back to Burguete through the woods? I do not want to follow the road."

"Go down to your left below the chapel and follow a path by the stream."

"Many thanks."

"It is nothing."

When you reach the edge of the beech forest, you turn around to look at the monk once more. He paces still, so slowly that he seems almost to be standing. You look at the dark mountains, the fog and clouds, the gray buildings once more. The only sound is the wind loud in the trees. Madrid and Pamplona seem hundreds of miles and years away. Something new begins here in Europe, or something ends. Something different from all of Spain, Gibraltar to the Bay of Biscay.

You enter the beech forest and leave Roncesvalles behind. Never have you been in a wood like this. The sky is covered by the trees—spreading, gnarled, moss-barked. Fog rolls around the thick trunks, the wind blows through the twisted branches with their purplish-brown, waxy leaves. The trees are very old and they have covered the earth with a dense layer of leaves, soft under your feet. Hearing water, you come to the stream, stone-bedded and clear. Roots of some beeches bulk above the ground, growing from one shore to the other. Muffled by the fog, the sound of cowbells reaches you from the hills above. Except for the forest path you see no sign of human beings until you come out on the road near Burguete. This is country.

"This is country" (The Sun Also Rises).
Beech forest between Burguete and Roncesvalles, 1986.
(Photo Gonzalo de la Serna)

5   "*This Is Country*"

B efore San Fermín, Jake Barnes and Bill Gorton climb to the roof of a bus that will take them from Pamplona to Burguete, and the whole mood of the novel brightens. The two Americans sit in the sun with the Basque-Navarrese peasants. Following the ancient Iberian custom of generosity, the men have Jake and Bill cork up their bottles of wine and drink from a leather bota. The communal partaking of wine contrasts with the more sullen, solitary drinking in Paris that dominated the early part of the novel. These Basques are the only peasants to appear in the book, and this is the first scene where Jake has any significant contact with the Spanish or the French people. In Paris, relations between foreigners and the natives were formalized and based on the exchange of money.

"These Basques are swell people," Bill says. The peasants on the bus love good humor and hearty drinking among friends. They are a strong, simple people, dressed in black smocks, their skin tanned the color of saddle-leather. Even with their spontaneous friendliness, their actions are somehow ritualistic: the rules of generosity must be observed, wine must be drunk from the bota in the correct way—holding it at full arm's length and making the wine hiss into the mouth with a flat trajectory, then cutting off the stream sharply so that nothing will be lost. Although there are women on the bus, they do not join in the drinking or the banter. The male camaraderie, so characteristic of Basque-Navarrese and Hispanic culture in general, is part of Jake's recovery and healing from the sexual entanglements of life in Paris.

The bus stops at a *posada* in a town where vineyards come down to the houses. Jake and Bill get off and go inside:

> There was a low, dark room with saddles and harness, and hay-forks made of white wood, and clusters of canvas rope-soled shoes and hams and slabs of bacon and white garlics and long sausages hanging from the roof.

In contrast to Paris, where many things are artificial, objects are real here; they seem to stand out in relief because they are so basic, simple, and natural. There is nothing in this scene that could not have occurred in the nineteenth century, or in the Middle Ages for that matter. It is a kind of still life in prose which Hemingway would echo several years later in his great epilogue to *Death in the Afternoon*:

> If you could make . . . the feel of leather; rope soled shoes; the loops of twisted garlics; earthen pots; saddle bags carried across the shoulder; wine skins; the pitchforks made of natural wood . . .

The realness of things is reflected in the authenticity of the people. When Jake and Bill have a drink at the posada and leave ten centimes for a tip, the woman returns the copper coin, thinking the Americans have misunderstood the price. The Basques are a people with a strong traditional culture that has managed to keep its integrity in the modern world.

Back on the bus, an old stubble-bearded man tells Jake he spent fifteen years in the western United States. He is not significantly different from the other peasants, except that he speaks "American" and shows the union of two cultures, Old World and New, that Barnes himself is seeking.

As if to avoid any idealization of the Spanish people, in Burguete Hemingway has the woman innkeeper overcharge Jake and Bill for their room. But unlike the avaricious Parisians in the first part of the novel, the woman feels guilty about accepting too much money; therefore she includes wine in the price of the room. Since Jake and Bill are often tight on the wine of the country, she probably gets the short end of the deal.

The weather in Burguete, at the foot of the Pyrenees, is much cooler than in Pamplona. As in *A Farewell to Arms*, *For Whom the Bell Tolls*, and some of his best short stories, Hemingway associates the mountains— bracing air and unspoiled landscape—with a rarer moral climate than that of the cities on the plain, whether Paris or Pamplona, Milan or Madrid. Jake and Bill's hotel room in Burguete is almost monastic, in keeping with its location beneath the great shrine of Roncesvalles: "There were two beds, a washstand, a clothes-chest, and a big, framed steel-engraving of Nuestra Señora de Roncesvalles." Without the tugs of jealousy and rivalries among the members of the gang in Paris, the two men revel in their friendship and a youthful repartee. They eat abundantly—hot soup, fried trout, a stew, plenty of wine, wild strawberries. That evening Jake's profound sleep contrasts with his insomnia in Paris. In less than forty-eight hours on Spanish soil, he has taken in the countryside, eaten, drunk, and slept well, beginning the process of healing his physical and psychological wounds that was impossible in Paris.

Hemingway's manuscript of *Sun* has the following sentence with corrections:

> five
>
> ~~four~~
>
> We stayed ~~three~~ days at Burguete and had good fishing.

Actually, the number of days given to the fishing trip in the novel does not fit into the time available between Jake and Bill's departure from Paris and their return to Pamplona for the feria. Whether or not Hemingway was aware of this, the fact is that the mechanical, clock time of workaday Paris has been replaced by the fluid, mental time of the Pyrenees. "Wonderful how one loses track of the days up here in the mountains," says the Englishman Harris whom they meet at the inn. The three friends eat and drink together, dig worms from the moist, rich earth, fish trout in the streams of the Irati valley, picnic under the shade of the great trees in the ancient forests above the town. In the beech forests near Burguete, like his creator in the hemlock forests of northern Michigan, Jake feels strange, the way he should feel in church: "This is about the last good country there is left. . . ."

Like Nick Adams's fishing trip in "Big Two-Hearted River," written a year before *Sun*, the sojourn in the Pyrenees is curative and healing. In that short story, Nick is alone; in the novel, Jake has begun to outgrow the solitary stages of convalescence and to reenter the human community, first with the peasants on the bus, now with Bill Gorton and Harris. The actions of fishing, eating, and drinking together in the heady mountain scenery are a kind of therapy for Jake. He is beginning to give some peace and order to his life.

Like the drinking from the wineskin on the bus, the actions in the

Pyrenees are somewhat ritualistic, performed with care, in the proper way, or as the Spanish expression has it, *como Dios manda* (as God commands):

> I took the trout ashore, washed them in the cold, smoothly heavy water above the dam, and then picked some ferns and packed them all in the bag, three trout on a layer of ferns, then another layer of ferns, then three more trout, and then covered them with ferns.

The fishing bag is just one object which seems to integrate the human, the animal, and the vegetable worlds—Jake's hands packing the trout among the ferns. As in this passage, a series of prepositions usually establishes the narrator's connection with the natural world: in the stream, above the dam, in the bag, on the ferns, over the trout. Whatever Jake looks at, he looks into; he centers himself in the mountains, where there is a forest, where there is a stream, where there are trout in the water and ferns on the banks. He gravitates from the periphery to the center of things. He settles into the world, as if he were "pulling the blanket of his existence up close against him." But in contrast to other modern writers who have sought some kind of impossible return to nature, Hemingway does not have Jake and Bill retreat from the world; soothed by the water and the woods, they integrate their experience of nature into themselves in order to return to the human life of the city—Pamplona or Paris. The nature portrayed here is far from being a wilderness; it has been humanized by centuries of habitation. Jake and Bill follow roads and paths to reach the fishing spots, cross fields where sheep graze, hear cattle-bells in the woods, cross a stream on a foot-log, see a white house and a field of buckwheat, cool their wine in spring water flowing from an iron pipe.

The language Hemingway used to describe the landscape of the Pyrenees around Burguete is rhythmic prose at its best. These passages on the Spanish countryside reveal a tone that could be called religious in the root meaning of the word—a profound unity between man, animal, and nature. Hemingway admitted that he was deadly serious and "felt almost holy" about creating landscapes with words.

Having spent several marvelous days around Burguete in the summer of 1924—like being in heaven, he would tell Hadley—Ernest knew that the scenery there had a special power. He was aware of the historical, religious, literary, and mythic resonances of Roncesvalles: battles of French, Basques, and Arabs, Charlemagne, *The Song of Roland*, the famous monastery that offered shelter to medieval pilgrims on their way to the tomb of the apostle St. James in Santiago de Compostella. Following his iceberg theory, Hemingway awakened these resonances without referring explicitly to the past. Jake, Bill, and Harris go through the monastery of Roncesvalles that marks the historic spot, but they are "not much on those sort of places. . . . It isn't the same as fishing. . . ." They choose to enjoy one another's company in a nearby drinking place. Like their creator, the three friends prefer the present to the past, experience to books. "Eschew the monumental," Hemingway would write in a letter to his editor Max Perkins. "Shun the epic." The landscape of the Spanish Pyrenees, with its clean air, ancient beech and pine forests, and trout-filled streams, could bear the weight of its symbolic function in the novel by itself, without the excrescence of historical allusions. It was enough to assent to the wonder of an unspoiled, humanized nature, the Spanish earth, saying with Bill Gorton: "This is country."

Pamplona: 3

The bullring is pulsating with music and man-voices. You look for a seat with your friends of the Peña Anaitasuna in the sun. There is a great din of band music; each group has its own drums and fifes. Nobody pays attention to the numbers on the tickets: you sit wherever you can squeeze between two men. If you insisted on taking the seat shown on your stub, you would run the risk of being thrown out of the ring or, more likely, into the ring. You would not be thrown by the police but by the mozos themselves, the only authorities here.

When you sit on the sunny side at your first corrida in Pamplona, refrain from wearing clothes that will not be improved by immersion in wine, *sangría*, champagne, or beer, and by sprinklings of flour, bread, tomatoes, and soup. In prosperous post-Franco Pamplona, champagne prevails. As the bottles pop open, the champagne is sprayed on your neighbors. This is the only way to keep cool because there is no sun as bright, among the din and the closeness of the stone seats and the white-dressed men, as the sun in the bullring at Pamplona on an afternoon of San Fermín.

The figure of the bull underlies everything in Pamplona between July 7 and 14. San Fermín is the only festival of the bull in Spain—*Feria del Toro*. Pamplona is not the place to see the best bullfights in Spain; it is merely the place to see some of the best bulls, if you are lucky. Even in the torero, it is not esthetic grace that is most admired in Pamplona, but his animal bravery that is revealed in the presence of the bull and is an expression of the bull's power.

After the procession of the toreros, Esplá's cape work on his first animal is too hurried; he cannot slow the charge of the wide-horned bull of the Conde de la Corte. When he takes the banderillas, he runs longer and faster than anyone you have ever seen, even the Mexicans and the Girón brothers from Venezuela, zig-zagging in and out of the bull's terrain then finally driving the shafts straight down hard in the withers, his arms stiff, body straight as the horns pass. He places the second and third sets close to the first, high up on the shoulders where they should be. After each pair the mozos chant from the sun: *"Como Esplá no hay ninguno! Esplá es cojonudo!"* ("Like Esplá there's none! Esplá's well-hung!") The crowd is on its feet after this display of daring, speed, and timing. Risking a fine or suspension, Esplá takes advantage of the public's mood and walks to the sunny side of the ring to dedicate the bull's death to some political prisoners who belong to ETA. No matter what he does in the last third of the fight, he has won over the people. A cheap trick, some aficionados murmur, especially those on the shady side. Politics have invaded the bullring and San Fermín, and everything else in Spain.

With the muleta now, Esplá cannot control the bull's charge or dominate the animal; there is no slow running of the hand, no linking of the passes. It is almost as if his arms are not long enough to make it slow, smooth, and with the emotion. He goes in to kill with a strong thrust of the sword, the bull is dead and the plaza is full of white handkerchiefs demanding the award of an ear.

After the third bull the mozos begin to take out their *meriendas* or snacks of sausages, stuffed meat pies, omelettes, giant sandwiches, and the specialty of San Fermín, *ajoarriero*—codfish cooked with garlic, oil, tomatoes, and eggs. Many of the men in the sun are too drunk, unruly, or busy eating to pay much heed to the bullfight below. One boy of about seventeen in front of you is yelling *"Cabrón cabrón cabrón!"* at whatever matador happens to be facing the bull; he does not bother to look at the ring as he stuffs his mouth with an immense *bocadillo* of egg and sausage or sprays passersby with a plastic squirt gun. There are two spectacles competing against each other in the plaza—one in the ring, supposedly tragic; one in the stands, comical and even cruel, as when the seventeen-year-old splats a bocadillo in an usher's face right in front of us. The old communion between crowd, matador, and bull seems to have been lost. Perhaps the bullfight itself has deteriorated as much as the public. Never have the animals been so weak, the men so mediocre. Esplá, Ángel Teruel, and Paco Ojeda are no Pedro Romeros today, nor even Niños de la Palma.

The three bullfighters do not manage to recapture the public's attention after the merienda. The afternoon is over. Esplá has cut the only ear and won the day. His work with the banderillas has been brave, skilled, exciting, but it does not have the slowness, the depth, the mystery of the man and the bull together that you feel in a great faena. A performance that is mostly athletic, even if it shows courage, ultimately has something common about it.

The main gate to the ring opens and the boys and girls of Pamplona rush into the plaza. You go down to the first row with José Mari and the other members of the Peña Anaitasuna, jump into the *callejón* that runs around the ring, push your way through the crowd, following a track of smoothed-out sand and blood left by the dead bulls that have been dragged to the slaughterhouse by the mule team.

Only José Mari and his companion Fernando, with his gigantic sombrero, are allowed inside the open-door abattoir: you are admitted because of them. The last bull hangs upside down, headless, already flayed, swinging spread-legged from metal hooks. The slaughterhouse is about the size of a very high double-car garage. The organs of the bulls overflow a concrete trough. Another trough holds the fine, glass-eyed, black heads of the Conde de la Corte bulls that were running through the streets of Pamplona twelve hours ago. Still another contains their horns, widespread and point-lifted. The butchers are three big red-faced Navarrese with high rubber boots. One of the three puts the head of the last bull on the concrete floor, raises an ax and chops the horns from the skull, spraying the closely pressed crowd outside with blood, hair, and flesh. He places the head and horns in their troughs and hoses down the floor. It is cold inside the concrete walls and there is a damp, sweet smell of water, blood, and meat. One of the butchers gives José Mari the testicles of the bulls in a heavy sack. They will be used to prepare the delicacy of *cholas* for lunch tomorrow.

We go out into the heat again. There is a clean smell of sweat and a warm tiredness as we move slowly with the crowd, white banners fluttering over us, bands playing as we inch along like a slow river under the trees around the bullring, men singing hard-voiced, dancing where there is space to move hands and feet, down the hill in the early evening to the town where the bars have the lights on inside.

6   *The Fiesta Sense of Life*

A fter returning to Pamplona from the mountains, Jake Barnes and Bill Gorton accompany the other members of their crew to the unloading of the fighting bulls in the corrals by the Arga River. All are impressed by the supple beauty, speed, and fierceness of the animals, except Cohn of course. Brett comes closest to Jake in feeling an almost religious awe: "My God, isn't he beautiful?" she exclaims when the first bull shoots into the corral and charges a man with quick, searching thrusts of the horns. Like Barnes, she suffered terribly from the war—she lost her lover to dysentery —and thus she possesses the heightened awareness of death required to understand the tragedy of the bullfight. She is the only woman in the novel, and in all of Hemingway's fiction for that matter, who is worthy of the fellowship of aficionados to which Jake and the hotelkeeper Montoya belong. While Barnes believes in the validity of faith and prayer, Brett admits that official religion has never worked for her, yet she has not lost a sense of the sacred and she feels intuitively the "unearthly and unbeliev-able" quality of a brave fighting bull. Jake reminds us that San Fermín "is also a religious festival," but the most operative religion in Pamplona seems to be related to the bulls—the wonder they inspire in those who know how to see, their sacrifice in the collective ritual of the corrida every afternoon.

Then the fiesta explodes. "It kept up day and night for seven days." Hemingway gives his best description of the fiesta sense of life here: the constant drinking, dancing, and noise, the revelry, the breaking down of routine, the liberation of the senses, the feeling of unreality. Everybody, including the foreigners, is swept away by the impetus of the celebration.

It would be difficult to overestimate the impact of the feria on a man like Jake Barnes. His involvement in the eating, drinking, touching, and conviviality of the fiesta is a necessary phase in the healing of his wounds,

The fiesta of San Fermín "explodes" at noon, July 6, 1980.
(Photo Gonzalo de la Serna)

the cleansing of his memory, the restoration of his confidence, and his reintegration into the human community—a process begun in the fishing scenes. A sign of his participation in the spirit of the feria is the leather bota he buys himself. Yet it would be a mistake to believe that Jake achieves a total immersion in the festival. He remains alone at times, preferring the solitude of his hotel room to continual carousing with Brett, Mike Campbell, and the others. In a way, he stands between Montoya—a serious, dignified man and veteran of many Sanfermines—and the foreigners. For the two aficionados, Jake's companions are "simply a little something shameful between us, like the spilling open of the horses in bull-fighting." Unlike some members of his gang, Barnes never loses control of himself. He is almost halfway between the Spaniard and the Anglo-Saxons—between two cultures, two moralities, two kinds of life.

After watching Pedro Romero perform skilfully at the first bullfight of the festival, Jake has that "disturbed emotional feeling that always comes after a bull-fight, and the feeling of elation that comes after a good bull-fight." This and the other corridas in which Romero performs at San

Fermín will allow Barnes to forget for the time being his own terrible problems, the sense of devastation he has known since his wounding in the war, the anguish over his frustrated love for Brett Ashley. Jung has described the process by which a ritual celebration like the bullfight can free a spectator from the limitations of his own life. A powerful man or man-god, whom Jung called the universal hero, vanquishes evil in the form of a dangerous beast; the audience identifies with the hero and is gripped by numinous emotions:

> The ordinary man can be liberated from his personal impotence and misery and [be] endowed (at least temporarily) with an almost super-human quality. Often enough, such a conviction will sustain him for a long time and give a certain style to his life.

Jung's words are just as applicable to the young Hemingway in Spain as to his protagonist in *The Sun Also Rises*.

Like the novelist, Jake Barnes has *afición*—the quality of passionate understanding of the bullfight that is rare even among Spaniards. While the narrator has been unsure and ironic about himself in the French scenes of the novel, we see him with a new confidence in the world of toreo during the festival of San Fermín. Without false humility, Jake admits "I had aficion." His friend Montoya and the other aficionados at the hotel recognize and respect his knowledge. The brotherhood among Barnes and the Spaniards derives from an awareness of the fighting bull as a death-giving creature, and of the sacred nature of its ritual sacrifice in the corrida. Their camaraderie is expressed through a sparing use of words and by physical contact—the "actual touching" of a hand or shoulder, for example. The brotherhood among aficionados is another form of male conviviality in Hispanic life, manifested in the entire feria.

Again like his creator, Jake Barnes's experience in the war has allowed him to understand a spectacle based on death—the certain sacrifice of the bull, the potential sacrifice of horses and men. The narrator knows that "the only place where you could see life and death, *i.e.*, violent death now that the wars are over, was in the bull ring. . . ." Because of his experience in battle and in the bullfight, death is the "one thing" Barnes doesn't worry about. The remainder of the novel, and especially the corridas and the fiesta, will teach him to worry less about life also, by living it more spontaneously. His knowledge of death gives him the tragic sense possessed by Hemingway and so many Spaniards; paradoxically, it will permit him to live more joyfully. The tragic feeling is what makes the fiesta so intense. Probably more than any other time or place in the world, both exist side by side at San Fermín.

Pamplona: 4

Everything looks clear in the early light. It is Sunday and more men are in the streets than any other day of the week; from all the towns of Navarre they have arrived during the night. This will make the running more difficult for there is less space to keep away from the bulls. Also it is the thirteenth day of the month—nobody talks about that. San Fermín comes only once a year and one day of the fiesta must fall always on July 13.

The streets smell of the early morning. Like nearly everyone else, you have not gone to bed all night. You wonder if your body will do what you want it to do, but in the cool morning, with the knowledge of action to come, you feel alert and clear-headed. The people packed along the temporary wooden barricade offer wineskins and bottles to the runners. Above the course, balconies are solid with people. A drunk squeezes between the wood planks into the street, trips, and falls on his face. Two policemen rush over and carry him to the fence.

Around you restless men jog or exercise to warm up their muscles. In their faces you can see a kind of tense expectation. Thinking about the bulls may be worse than running from them. Some men sing the traditional song asking San Fermín for protection: "A *San Fermín pedimos* . . . ," making goose-pimples on your arms. Throughout the night people have moved and felt as groups, drinking, singing, and dancing the bobbing, floating dances of Navarre. Now there is a mounting sense of aloneness as each man thinks about the bulls that will come soon stampeding down the streets. Within a few minutes, every mother's son will have to run for himself. There are no women. The encierro, from the seven fighting bulls and six steers to the thousands of Spanish and foreign men along the course of 900 yards from the corrals to the bullring, is a masculine prerogative.

You hear a military band playing the last *diana* or reveille from a street beyond the runway. Also the traditional groups of three players, two flutes or *txistus*, and a drum, making plaintive music. When they finish, you know it is close to eight o'clock and it is almost time. The last minutes before the running of the bulls are the most strangely quiet in the whole week of the fiesta. You spit on the cobblestones of the street for good luck. Also to see if it is true that you cannot spit when you are really frightened.

Without warning the first rocket explodes to signal the opening of the corrals. Your heart races, everyone begins to move and shout. A few seconds later, another rocket means the bulls have passed through the gates and are galloping up the hill of Santo Domingo. Everything happens so fast and with such elation of gladness and fear that it is like a dream, except you feel more awake than any moment of your life. It is as if you were very awake and dreaming at the same time. You begin to jog across the large square of the Town Hall, decked with flowers and flags of Spain and Navarre, feeling the playful wonder and a dark knot in your belly and groin. You move slowly at first, ahead of the crowd, down the wide Mercaderes Street, around the sharp corner and up the long, narrow Estafeta. Behind you the noise of the crowd grows louder and more urgent, but you know from counting in your head that the bulls are still well behind, you cannot allow the panic of the mass to ruin your sense of time and distance. The crowd is running hard now and you must not be swept away by them, you are going a little faster, right up the middle of the street that leads to the bullring, every second looking over your shoulder. Then before seeing the animals you hear great clatter of hooves on the cobbles among the shouts and you feel the rumble of the ground, see them now coming fast and tight as a herd, the black bulls with ivory horns and the creamy brown steers scattering the white- and red-dressed men, someone falls huddled on the sidewalk but the animals pay no attention, they are gaining, nobody can run ahead of fighting bulls for long. The crowd is thinner in front of the herd, a little area opens out as if cleared by the horns, you fall into that magical space for a few seconds running full tilt and feeling the joy and fright, alert in the head but allowing your body to follow itself free, mouth dry, heart pounding you cannot stay ahead of them longer, you jump onto the sidewalk pressing against a doorway watch them pass galloping together, heavy, muddy-sided, tossing their heads. Smell of animal hangs in the air, a blond boy is lying flat on his back in the street, two white-suited Pamplonicans run over to pick him up and carry him to a doorway. Then the shouts behind and you know something has happened, one or more bulls have been separated from the pack, it will not be a clean run, cries of *"Toro rezagado!"* "Somebody gored!" *"Cogida!"* Minutes seem to elapse in terrible apprehension until you see it, alone, not galloping but charging jerkily, detached from the herd, head moving from side to side, turning to go back until it is lured forward by a man with a bullfighting cape. Pressing tightly against the doorway as it approaches, you see the horns with the bossed tips as it stops to charge a man, yes one horntip stained and shining red down to the fat part of its curve, blood all over the muzzle, dark little eyes with light circles around them, great hump of muscle on the neck, heavy power in him as he goes by, horns swinging. You run as fast as you can to reach the plaza before they close the gate behind him, the last bull, spectators along the barricade and in the balconies applauding the runners now, out on the open square and into the long chute that connects the course to the bullring. Just as you reach the end of the runway you see the big red gates go shut, you hear the shouts of 20,000 people inside and feel something bad is happening. You grab the top of the gate, wriggle up, and see the confusion in the ring, knowing there are too many people on the sand where a bull lopes around with a striped sweater caught on the left horn. There is a loud scream and you see a bearded man hanging on the right horn of a bull below you, he falls on his back as the bull moves off, he is holding his belly with both hands, another scream of horror as the crowd realizes he has been gored. Several men begin to pick up the fallen one, the bull turns and charges again, the crowd blocks your view then you can see the animal thrusting surely and quickly with its horns, lifting, shaking the same man like a rag then dropping him, you feel sick, the crowd groaning. The bull moves away and they pick up the man's body, intestines hanging to the ground, carry him toward the infirmary, slowed by the multitude. All the bulls have entered the gate from the ring to the corrals except two, then only the bloody-headed one remains, surrounded by steers with bells around their necks. The bull begins to move nervously toward the corral, a boy distracts him with a muleta in his hand, breaking the rule of the encierro never to spoil an animal for the professionals who must face it in the afternoon. Men attack the boy, hitting him with wadded newspapers or their fists until two policemen grab him and take him away. The bull reaches the gate, makes a final feint to turn before entering the darkness of the corrals amid the lumbering steers. Then a rocket goes up. The encierro is finished.

That afternoon in the papers we read that two men have been killed, more than thirty wounded. The encierro lasted ten minutes and fifty-five seconds, one of the longest ever, and it seemed twice as long; a clean run takes less than three minutes. The first victim was José Antonio Sánchez, twenty-six, son of a farmer from the Navarrese town of Cintruénigo. He was gored in front of the Town Hall and carried thirty meters on the horn of the bull that had been separated from the herd. They bore him on a stretcher to the Provincial Hospital, where he died after a blood transfusion of fifteen liters. Since the age of fourteen he had been running the bulls at San Fermín. This was to be his last encierro: he was scheduled to marry María J. Chivite on August 23, and young men who are engaged often promise their betrothed not to run the bulls after marriage. They often break the promise too.

The bull who killed José Antonio Sánchez was named Patirrota, Broken-Hoof, weight 522 kilos, was number 55 of the breeding establishment of Salvador Guardiola, Heirs. (Fifty-five years ago, also on July 13, a man was killed by a bull in *The Sun Also Rises*.) Out of respect for the dead man, they hosed the blood off Patirrota's horn and face before he entered the ring to be killed by Tomás Campuzano as the sixth bull of that same afternoon.

The second victim was Vicente Risco, twenty-nine. (The man who died in *Sun* was named Vicente Girones and he was twenty-eight years old.) A bachelor, native of Extremadura, he had lived in Navarre for twelve years and they say he had been training for a black belt in karate. He died three minutes after entering the infirmary.

The bull who killed Vicente Risco was named Antioquío, number 17, weight 543 kilos, also from the ranch of Salvador Guardiola. He was killed that afternoon by a matador in the same arena where he had gored the man to death eleven hours before. Some people believe this bull killed both men. The encierro happens with such speed and confusion that nobody will ever know for certain.

In the slaughterhouse after the corrida, the heads of Patirrota and Antioquío were auctioned to a collector. He says he will send them to a taxidermist for stuffing.

7   The Tragic Sense
      of Life

O n Sunday morning, the last day of the fiesta, Jake Barnes goes out into the streets to watch the running of the bulls. He watches the encierro from behind the fence that leads to the bullring: he is an observer, more a witness than a celebrant. In the runway leading to the plaza de toros, Jake sees a man gored to death. Afterward, he goes to a café where he tells a waiter about the man who has received the cogida or horn-wound. The waiter is an antitaurine proletarian straight out of a novel by Blasco Ibáñez: "What are bulls? Animals. Brute animals . . . Muerto. Dead . . . All for morning fun."

The goring and death of the man in the encierro was based on an event Hemingway witnessed at the Sanfermines of 1924: On Sunday, July 13 of that year, Esteban Domingo, twenty-eight, a bricklayer from the town of Sangüesa, had been gored fatally through the back and lung. Hemingway changed the victim's name to Vicente Girones, made him a farmer from the Navarrese town of Tafalla, and had the bull's horn go all the way through the man's back and out his chest. On the most basic level then, the sacrifice of Vicente Girones was a plausible, realistic event in the celebration of San Fermín. Beneath the surface of drinking and dancing of the fiesta, represented by the perpetual flow of wine, there is a deeper level of death and sacrifice symbolized by the blood of the bulls, horses, toreros, and the males who run the encierro every morning for seven days. "They took about twenty chaps to the infirmary," Mike Campbell says after the running of bulls on the day Girones dies. The toll for that morning: one dead and twenty wounded; that afternoon, the six bulls who have run through the streets will be slain at the corrida. In a very real way, the life of the festival is sustained by the blood of men and bulls. The farmer's sacrifice reveals the tragedy that flows beneath the fiesta.

The death of Vicente Girones is a key to the structure of *The Sun Also Rises*, which turns or "gyrates" (Spanish *girar*) around the event—the only human fatality in a book that treats the very matter of life in relation to death, as indicated by the passage from Ecclesiastes where Hemingway found his title: "One generation passeth away, and another generation cometh; but the earth abideth forever. . . ." After Girones' death in the morning, the narrator tells us that his wife and children came to Pamplona the next day to be with the body, and the day after there was a service in the chapel of San Fermín. The coffin was carried to the railway station by the members of the drinking and dancing society of Tafalla, followed by the male societies of the major towns in Navarre—Pamplona, Estella, Sangüesa. Then:

> The coffin was loaded into the baggage-car of the train, and the widow and the two children rode, sitting, all three together, in an open third-class railway-carriage. The train started with a jerk, and then ran smoothly, going down grade around the edge of the plateau and out into the fields of grain that blew in the wind on the plain on the way to Tafalla.

Here is Hemingway's best prose with its characteristic elegiac rhythm to express the emotion not of physical ecstasy as before—the bullfight, fishing, hunting, skiing, lovemaking—but of death, death in the midst of life:

> the fields of grain that blew in the wind on the plain on the way to Tafalla.

The past tense, in contrast to the earlier use of ecstatic prose in the present, increases the sense of loss.

Not only is this episode the one instance of death in the novel, but only here does the narration by Jake Barnes break out of present, chronological time to project itself into the future and into the freedom of the imagination. For when Jake describes the funeral and the train ride to us, he does so in the past tense but from present narrative time *before they have actually happened* and *without actually being there* in person, since he will leave Pamplona himself on the day the funeral takes place. Thus the episode represents an extraordinary break and "turning" point in the structure of the novel. The men who have observed the ritual of the bullfight become participants in a ritual of death. The body of Vicente Girones returns to its resting place in the Navarrese earth, the Spanish earth, which abides and brings forth new life: "fields of grain that blew in the wind . . ." These sad, beautiful words evoke the same kind of emotion as the last line in García Lorca's famous lament for the death of a bullfighter: "And I remember a sad breeze through the olive trees."

The episode of Vicente Girones in *Sun* has usually been ignored or undervalued by critics and readers. A writer as eminent as Edmund Wilson did not realize that the encierro is a collective ritual in which men choose to participate; he believed that Girones was "accidentally gored" on his leisurely way to the bullring. Wilson would have done well to see the relevance of this episode to his own accurate summary of Hemingway's world: "The condition of life is pain; and the joys of the most innocent surface are somehow tied to its stifled pangs." The entire fiesta of San Fermín, with its current of blood and death beneath a surface of wine and rejoicing, is a microcosm of Hemingway's vision. We can see why the death of Girones, which seems to be a brief and incidental scene, is a necessary sacrifice and an indispensable part of the novel. Without it, *Sun* would indeed resemble the "jazz superficial story" that some critics saw, and not the "damn tragedy with the earth abiding for ever as the hero" intended and achieved by Hemingway. Carlos Baker is probably accurate in describing *The Sun Also Rises* as a tragicomedy: its surface tone is somewhere within the range of the comic, but the tragic sense of life exists in the undertones of the novel. Wirt Williams has called it the "first major revelation of Hemingway's tragic vision."

Finally, the short but essential episode of Vicente Girones' death is the structural link between the most important events and characters in *Sun*. The bull who gored Girones to death will be killed that afternoon in the plaza de toros by Pedro Romero. One of the bull's ears will be awarded to the matador by popular acclamation. Romero "in turn," says the narrator, gives the ear to Brett, who will wrap it in a handkerchief belonging to Jake, and then leave it far back in the drawer of her nightstand in the Hotel Montoya. Girones and the bull that killed him thus connect the human and the animal worlds in the novel, high and low, Spaniards and foreigners, the humble people of Navarre and the tourists in Pamplona,

Romero with Brett and Jake. The death is not an isolated, absurd event but a necessary, meaningful sacrifice that joins the human community with nature and the rhythms of life. Girones's death is the sacrifice out of which will come a new kind of life for Jake, and perhaps also for Brett, some members of the gang, and other participants in the fiesta.

Pamplona Finale

They come from America, Canada, France, England, Germany, Holland, Belgium, Norway, Sweden, Australia. They come dressed in levis, shorts, corduroys, lederhosen, long dresses and short dresses, T-shirts, especially T-shirts, sweatshirts too, vests, sweaters, windbreakers, field jackets, leather jackets, red or black boinas, straw hats, cowboy hats, glasses, sunglasses, earrings, nose-rings, bracelets, rings, beads, pendants, necklaces, and the red kerchief of San Fermín around their necks. What are they searching for, with their short hair or long hair, their braids, their beards and mustaches and side-burns and seven days' stubble of sleeping on the ground in a sleeping bag or a blanket or newspapers rolled around them? They come here to the stone monument of the American writer under the shade of the trees by the bullring, the block of stone almost unfinished and rough like Michelangelo's slave, the bearded head of bronze rising out of the granite like an ancient tortoise sticking its head from a shell. Where will they go now that the fiesta is over and the wine drunk and the bulls of nine afternoons killed, flayed, drawn, quartered, and eaten, the two gored men from Navarre lie in their coffins, strips of gauze around their heads and jaws to keep the faces from collapsing, hands tied together in their laps with pieces of black silk, and two bronze candleholders at their heads? Where will they walk now in their hiking boots, tennis shoes, jogging shoes, canvas shoes of San Fermín, cork-soled sandals, thongs, bare feet? Where will they go laden with memories, their backpacks stuffed with bread, cheese, sausages, marijuana of Colombia, peyote of Mexico, pills of New York, Amsterdam, London, hashish of Morocco? Where will they travel with their tents, canteens, handbags, purses, plastic bags, Kodaks, Minoltas, Super-8's, Michelins, Fodors, *Europe on $5 a Day* and *Europe on $10 a Day* and the maps? What are they thinking or dreaming with the loops of twisted garlics and empty wineskins across their shoulders in the shade of the trees, always trees and shade under the trees with the cool morning smells, asleep against the stone monument or bleared eyes watching the people of Pamplona go back to work and the fiesta is over?

8   *Over the Wind-Blown Fields of Grain*

Vérité au deçà des Pyrénées, mensonge au delà.
—*Pascal*

In the morning, Monday July 14, the fiesta is finished. It is all over, and there is a sense of let-down and emptiness in the city and the people. The next day Jake leaves Pamplona with Bill and Mike. The good fellowship of the fiesta carries over among the three friends on their trip to the French border in a rented car, the last scene of male camaraderie in the novel. From now on, Jake will be almost entirely on his own, but the trip in the bus with the peasants, the idyll in the mountains with Gorton and Harris, the brotherhood between aficionados, and the conviviality of the fiesta in Pamplona have gone a long way toward healing his solitude and restoring his confidence.

In Bayonne, Barnes experiences a "safe, suburban feeling." Everything is very clear in France: if you have money, you can live well and buy people's respect. Human relations are based on an exchange of currency, which ultimately alienates men and women from one another. In Spain, food and wine flowed abundantly in the fiesta; now they are carefully apportioned with "that measured French feeling." France is the modern, industrial, capitalistic, urban nation par excellence. Spain represents just the opposite within European and Western culture: the old, preindustrial, precapitalistic, fundamentally rural way of life based on the individual human being with all his unpredictability. "In Spain you could not tell about anything." If life in France is simple and sound with its clear financial basis, life in Spain is complicated and "obscure." There love, friendship, success, power depend not only on money, but on the fragile, volatile relations between men and women. There is more risk, but also more possibility for discovery, growth, and change. In France, for example, Jake could buy the respect of a hotelkeeper with money; in

Pamplona, his friendship with Montoya derived from subtle moral and esthetic preferences. When Barnes violated those preferences in Montoya's eyes, their friendship had to terminate, at least for the time being.

All of Jake's perceptions seem to be fresh and clear after the fiesta. In Bayonne, he has a good meal at a restaurant, washed down with a bottle of Château Margaux. He has learned to savor and enjoy his food, his drink, and his solitude. "It was pleasant to be drinking slowly and to be tasting the wine and to be drinking alone. A bottle of wine was good company." When he crosses the border back into Spain for a stay in San Sebastián, his senses are still sharpened; he describes sights and sounds with great care. Time seems to slow down and collect itself.

In the manuscript of *Sun*, Hemingway says that San Sebastián was a good place to "get straightened around inside again." This portion of the novel is full of water images that give a sense of cooling, cleansing, and healing—similar to the water of the Irati River during the fishing trip to Burguete. Jake swims out into the bay of San Sebastián and dives cleanly and deeply, his eyes open, to the bottom, where it is green, dark, and cold. Like Nick Adams, he has a special, almost religious feeling about diving and being underwater: "there wasn't anybody but him that was that way underwater. . . . nobody knew about the water but him . . . ," Nick had said. Just as Jake penetrated deeper and deeper into the center of the forest near Burguete, here he literally dives into the center of nature, the sea. We have a sense that he has descended into the depths of his own memory, his unconscious, even death. He comes up to the surface, turns and floats, looking up at the sky, feeling the rise and fall of the swells like a newborn baby on his mother's breast. This is probably the most peaceful moment in the book. Jake has gotten "all straightened inside" and he is ready to return from his solitude into the human world again.

That will be taken care of by a telegram from Brett: she is in trouble and wants Jake to meet her at the Hotel Montana in Madrid. He does not sleep on the night train. In the morning he watches the rock and pine plateau between Ávila and Escorial through the window: the high, austere Castilian countryside adds to the therapeutic effect begun in the bay of San Sebastián. Yet Jake does not "give a damn" about the monastery of El Escorial itself, long and gray and cold in the sun. The sepulcher of Spanish kings since the sixteenth century, it represents the official Spanish religion and politics rejected by Barnes and his creator in favor of the profound, enduring Spain—the people and the land. This description of El Escorial by a Spanish contemporary of Hemingway's will make clear the reasons for Jake's apparently gratuitous rejection of the famous building: "El Escorial . . . is . . . the monumental manifestation of an intransigency, of a refusal to accept life as it is . . . paralytic inflexibility . . . a palace-monastery-tomb."

In Madrid, Jake and Brett are reunited. She has made Romero leave because she realized that a young matador should not live with anyone, much less with a foreign woman like herself. The bullfighter's ideas about women turn out to be antiquated, provincial, and *machistas:* he wanted Brett to grow her hair longer so that she would look more "womanly," and then to marry her so that she would never go away. Yet Romero has helped her to wipe out the affair with Cohn and enables her to make the ethical decision to leave him for his own good.

After reserving berths on the northbound train for Paris, Jake and Brett have martinis amidst the fine gentility of the Hotel Palace. They go for lunch to Botín's, the restaurant where Hemingway had his first complete meal in Spain that spring of 1923. Of course they order roast suckling pig and red wine. She eats little but he makes up for her by having a big meal and consuming most of the five bottles of Rioja alta.

"You like to eat, don't you?" Brett asks Jake. From his experience in France and especially in Spain over the past several months, he has learned to enjoy eating and many other things in his life. The fishing trip to Burguete, the feria in Pamplona, Pedro Romero, the day in San Sebastián have been so many steps in the education of Jake Barnes. By enjoying a large meal, he affirms his independence from Brett, the priority of his own senses, and the regenerative processes of life itself. He may not have discovered what life is all about, but he certainly has learned how to live better in the world, to know and accept himself. He will continue to be a friend of Brett, but we sense that he will never again be deluded into believing that they could love each other, nor will he depend on her and despair of her love as he did in Paris. Jake will live in the world of other men and women, but he knows that he must take care of himself and not depend on anyone else for his own well-being. The clarity with which he sees and describes things after the meal at Botín's is indicative of his disillusioned wisdom. "It was very hot and bright, and the houses looked sharply white." As in the bullfight scenes, light and truth are almost synonymous.

The Sun Also Rises is the story of how one man, Jake Barnes, heals his psychological wounds, restores his confidence, and achieves a kind of wholeness. It is not by chance that most of his convalescence takes place in Spain. In the rivers and forests of the Pyrenees, on the plain of Pamplona, in the bay of San Sebastián, on the high Castilian plateau, and in the sharp light of Madrid, he has perceived the obscure values and the secret things that will help him to live in the world with dignity and to create the novel we are reading.

Although Jake calls himself a rotten Catholic, the collective sense of religion and ritual in Spain is one of the first stages in his healing. "Some people have God," he tells Brett. *Sun* is a religious novel not because the protagonist goes to church and prays, but because it contains a sense of ritual, and a striving for unity between man and nature that is at the root of religion. In the unspoiled Spanish countryside, the ancient beech forests and rivers around Burguete, the bracing water of the sea at San Sebastián, Jake penetrates the natural world around him. He also feels a new sense of unity with the human world through the fiesta sense of life and its liberation from routine, its exaltation of the senses, its hearty eating and drinking, and its mostly male fellowship; through the camaraderie among aficionados, embodied by Montoya, high priest of their taboos, enigmatic values, and ritual touching; through the bullfight with its ceremony of life and death, action and beauty, its sacrifice of a noble animal, and the catharsis experienced by the public. At a deep level then, *Sun* can be seen as a religious novel in that there is a binding of men to nature and society through the ritual of the church, of the fiesta and the bullfight, and through the use of primordial symbols like earth, blood, and water.

Hemingway and Jake Barnes have turned around Pascal's famous, ironic words written from a French point of view: "the truth is on this side of the Pyrenees, falsehood on the other side." In *The Sun Also Rises*, France is the nation of the false values in the modern world—materialism, selfishness, a sterile rationalism, mechanization. Spain is the land of the ancient truths—nature, the body, fertility, religion, ritual. If *Sun* is Hemingway's *Waste Land*, and if Jake's existence in Paris was a kind of living death, he undergoes a rebirth in the mountains, rivers, and sea of Spain. In Eliot's poem the message of salvation comes down from the sky as life-giving rain; it comes up from the roots of the Spanish earth in this novel. Jake Barnes's trip from Paris to Pamplona is a modern pilgrimage along the ancient road to Santiago; he does not reach the end of the route because that would have been too easy. It would be utopian to believe that he or anyone else could be wholly transformed or saved by traveling to Spain or any other country. "You can't get away from yourself by moving from one place to another," Jake said early in the book. Life in France is unacceptable, but life in Spain is too demanding for a foreigner. Although more of an insider than the other members of his crew, Barnes remains as much an onlooker or witness as a participant in the festival of San Fermín. The standard for behavior represented by Montoya and his aficionado friends is too inflexible, provincial, and anachronistic for an inhabitant of the modern world like Jake Barnes. And of course the "code" character, Pedro Romero, is too unassailable and remote to be more than a heroic model. Yet with Romero and Montoya, with the Basque-Navarrese peasants, with his comrades on the fishing trip, and with the celebrants of the fiesta, Jake acquires a sense of integrity and a more natural, intuitive behavior that allow him to reinstate himself in the human community. He has acquired the faith in himself, in other people, and in nature that will enable him to return to Paris and create a novel out of his own suffering, memory, and imagination.

Writing the novel will be another (perhaps the final) step by Jake in putting his world together again, just as the writing of an elegiac poem is a way of restoring wholeness after the death of a cherished person. *The Sun Also Rises* is in many ways an elegiac work—in the rhythms of its prose, in its diffuse, melancholy sense of loss and of passing time. It is also a novel that embodies the tragic sense of life—the blood that flows beneath the wine of the fiesta, the necessity of suffering and death. The mounted policeman's raised baton in the last scene of the book, when Jake and Brett take a taxi after their meal at Botín's, is a reminder of the limitations of all human efforts. Hemingway would say later that death does not always come in the form of a skeleton with a scythe; "it can be two bicycle policemen as easily."

In a world bereft of tradition, there are no easy solutions for a wounded, sensitive man like Jake Barnes who has seen into the tragic nature of things. The novel ends as it begins, with Jake and Brett together in a hopeless relationship. Yet the scene is now Madrid instead of Paris, and the sharp light of the Spanish capital seems to reveal a new truth. Jake has accepted the truth about himself and other truths about life and death in the world. He does not have much more hope than before, but he does have more control of himself, more sense of his own integrity, and less despair. He will return to the center of civilization, Paris, to create a novel from his experience. He and Brett will not love each other, they and the other members of their generation will pass away as Vicente Girones passed away, but the race and the earth will abide. The sun will continue to rise over the wind-blown fields of grain.

9   *Of Bulls and Men*

*It is a long one to write because it is not to be just a history and
text book or apologia for bull fighting—but instead, if possible,
bull fighting its-self. As it's a thing that nobody knows about in
English I'd like to take it first from altogether outside—how I
happened to be interested in it, how it seemed before I saw it—
how it was when I didn't understand it—my own experience with
it, how it reacts on others—the gradual finding out about it and
try and build it up from the outside and then go all the way inside
with chapters on everything. It might be interesting to people
because nobody knows anything about it—and it really is terribly
interesting—being a matter of life and death. . . . I think a really
true book if it were fairly well written about the one thing that
has, with the exception of the ritual of the church, come down to
us intact from the old days would have a certain permanent value.*
—EH to Maxwell Perkins, 6 December 1926

Even before *The Sun Also Rises*, Hemingway had probably
begun taking notes for a work on the art of toreo. In the
spring of 1925 he was already speaking of a "bull book on
bullfighting" with photographs and illustrations by Picasso,
Juan Gris, and others. That project turned out to be a
bubble, but Hemingway was determined to compose a work that would
open the world of toreo to the English-speaking public as Doughty's
Travels in Arabia Deserta had opened the uninhabited Middle East. Many
other foreigners, especially English, had written about the bullfight. Out
of religious prejudice or moral squeamishness, all had failed to present
toreo integrally. Even the British painter-writer Richard Ford, one of
Hemingway's favorite authors on Spain, had admitted that "we turn away
our eyes during moments of painful detail which are lost in the poetical
ferocity of the whole." Hemingway wanted to write a book (and he did)
with his eyes wide open, which would tell what he actually saw and felt
at the corrida, not what he was supposed to see and feel. This was the

well-known sequence of fact-motion-emotion-word he was striving to get in his writing and he had gotten it most consistently from the bullfight, leading to the creation of his rhythmic, ecstatic prose.

When Hemingway finally completed his book on toreo in 1932, it had been nearly eight years in gestation and some two-and-a-half in the writing —more than *The Sun Also Rises*, *A Farewell to Arms*, or any other work he would publish in his lifetime. Not his best book, *Death in the Afternoon* was his most personal, and the most important for understanding his views on the corrida, Spain, art, life and death. So much that is hopelessly wrongheaded has been written about this work that one despairs of being heard among the chorus of owls and popinjays. Hemingway himself put all future commentators on guard by warning them against too much abstraction and an "overmetaphysical tendency in speech," commonly known as horseshit. Anyone who wants to discuss *Death* feels afraid, almost as much as a torero smoking his last cigarette in the *patio de caballos* before a bullfight. But the trumpet sounds, the matadores stride into the ring, and there are a few practical things to be said.

First of all, why did Hemingway spend nearly three years writing his only real book of nonfiction, one which he himself and most critics have considered inferior to his novels and short stories? Like Doughty, he realized his subject was one that "nobody knows about in English," in Britain or America. The situation was similar in France: Mérimée had included toreo amid the local color of Andalusia in *Carmen* (1845), but it was only with Henri de Montherlant, Hemingway's contemporary, that bullfighting entered the mainstream of French letters. Even in Spain, serious writers did not turn to toreo as a subject worthy of literature until the late nineteenth and early twentieth centuries—Blasco Ibáñez, Ramón Pérez de Ayala, García Lorca, Rafael Alberti, José Bergamín.

Hemingway was correct when he said, in his "Bibliographical Note" at the end of *Death in the Afternoon*, that there had been no book in English or Spanish that explained the spectacle "both emotionally and practically." Such a book was especially necessary in the Anglo-Saxon world, where people approached bullfighting burdened with centuries of prejudices born from the Black Legend, portraying Spain as the country of religious hypocrisy, oppression, and brutality. In his own manner, Hemingway, who had "converted" to Catholicism in 1927 in order to marry his second wife, Pauline, rewrote the legend and gave a new view of toreo from the Anglo-Saxon perspective, but with a deep understanding of Hispanic culture. The bullfight could exist only in the Catholic countries of the Western world, where there is a clear distinction between human beings with immortal souls and soulless animals. Since the bulls who die in the plaza do not have souls according to the Church, it is not morally wrong for men to kill them, nor to allow horses to suffer from goring by the bulls. In the Protestant world by contrast, the line between human and animal life is less neat; only there could the people Hemingway mockingly calls "animalarians" have originated. He realized from the beginning, with his almost unfailing instinct, that the corrida could not be judged by the notions of sport and fair play—in large part creations of the English-speaking peoples. He knew that the only way to appreciate toreo was to see it as a tragedy uniting many arts: music, dance, painting, sculpture. The very word "bullfight" is of course a misnomer ("corrida" literally means "running" of bulls), implying an adversarial relation between man and animal rather than a mutual participation in a prescribed ritual, or as some matadores have suggested, a kind of lovemaking between toro and torero. Although Hemingway's original intention was not to write an apology of toreo, *Death in the Afternoon* evolved into a subtle, implicit defense of the spectacle and the mentality that makes it an acceptable form of public entertainment among the Hispanic peoples alone. In this way, what had begun as a book on the bullfight grew outward to include Spain, Spaniards, Spanish life, and the whole culture. Like his partly autobiographical protagonist of *For Whom the Bell Tolls*, Robert Jordan, Hemingway wished his book to contain "what he had discovered in Spain in ten years of travelling in it, on foot, in third-class carriages, by bus, on horse- and mule-back and in trucks."

The bullfight had been the magic key that unlocked many of the secret things in Spanish life for Hemingway. Although the so-called *fiesta nacional* involves only a small minority of Spaniards directly, and some detest the spectacle as an embarrassing, degrading relic of a primitive and "African" past, innumerable aspects of Spanish culture are tied to images, memories, and idioms of the bull and toreo. Antonio Gala, a Spanish writer known more for his dramas and love of animals than for his afición, could still write in 1980: "In Spain, from its centuries-old traditions to its very geographical shape in the form of a bull's hide; from its racial virtues to the joyous impudence of its language, almost everything is connected . . . to the attributes and the figure of the bull. There is no other totem that grips us so tightly. In its double mode, cultured or popular, almost all our creations are steeped in that theme and its related expression." Hemingway had learned for himself what Queen María Cristina had advised her son, later Alfonso XIII and King of Spain during the novelist's early trips to the peninsula: one must go to the bullring in order to understand the Spanish nation and her people.

The Culture of Death

Hemingway's original interest in bullfighting extended to all of Spain, her inhabitants and their ways of life. The best example of this process in *Death in the Afternoon* is the proverbial Spanish concern for death. Contrary to what Hemingway once said, the bullfight is not always a tragedy—in modern times the bulls and the toreros often do not have the dignity required by tragedy—but it always contains death: of the bulls inevitably, of the horses sometimes, of the men occasionally. *Death in the Afternoon* can be seen as the culmination of Hemingway's absorption with mortality, made more immediate by his father's suicide about a year before he began to write the book. The reader who is unaware of the proximity between the doctor's death and the composition of the book must be taken aback by its apparently gratuitous references to suicide—and in particular to that of one's father. The discussions of death (as in "A Natural History of the Dead" inserted in Chapter Twelve), of killing (Clarence Hemingway had taught his son the virtues of killing animals cleanly), of doctors and bullfight surgeons must have brought memories of his father teeming into Ernest's mind. The writing of *Death in the Afternoon* was his own peculiar way of overcoming the shock of his father's suicide and of approaching the Spanish concern for death through the corrida. Hemingway's personal experience, his afición for bullfighting, and his fascination with Spain all coincided and overlapped in the composition of the book.

Ernest's father was the one parent he really "cared about." He resented his mother because of the way she had raised him and because he believed she was partly responsible for Dr. Hemingway's suicide. In the bullfight book, he metamorphosed her to an extent into the wacky, despised "Old Lady" whose conversations with the author-narrator provided comic relief from the tragedy of the corrida and from all the technical material. As H. L. Mencken noted with more accuracy than he may have guessed, the reader to whom Hemingway seemed to address his book was "a sort of common denominator of all the Ladies' Aid Societies of his native Oak Park, Ill." This kind of reader, embodied in the Old Lady, could be scandalized by the more visceral elements of bullfighting and provide a foil to the world-weary, cynical aficionado who is the narrator and to a large degree the author himself.

One of the problems of *Death in the Afternoon* is in fact the confusion between Hemingway's public and private personalities, and the beginning of what Carlos Baker calls the "Narcissus principle"—the writer's assumption that the details of his life could engage the reader's interest as they engaged his own, and that they could be incorporated in his books without the same amount of invention he had used in *Sun, Farewell,* and the short stories until 1932. Although there is no doubt that the Narcissus principle is one of the major flaws in Hemingway's later novels, it might be argued that it contributes to the unique, idiosyncratic appeal of *Death,* which after all is a nonfiction book where the personality and opinions of the writer need not be transformed as in a work of fiction. It could also be argued that Hemingway's need to join his private and his public images, his life and his writing, was comparable to the recurrent tendency in Spanish culture called "integralism" by Américo Castro. It can be found in the works of such diverse figures as Cervantes, Lope de Vega, Velázquez, Goya, and Picasso, where there is usually no clear separation of the creator's life from its expression in artistic form.

So Hemingway's afición for bullfighting and the memory of his father's recent suicide converged in the typically Spanish preoccupation with death. The corrida is only one example of what the poet and critic Pedro Salinas has termed his country's culture of death. Other manifestations are the religious processions on Holy Friday in most Spanish towns and cities, and the moving *saetas* or songs addressed to Christ on the cross during Easter week in Andalusia. El Greco and Goya in painting and Jorge Manrique, Quevedo, and Lorca in literature are examples of the phenomenon; all of these artists were known and some of them admired by Hemingway. When he speaks of the culture of death, Salinas does not mean a kind of Thanatophilia or obsession with mortality as the Black Legend would have it—a morbid dwelling on the gruesome details of the grave or on the afterlife at the expense of life on earth. He refers rather to a vision of man and his existence in which the awareness of death is a positive force, a stimulus to living and acting which enables us to understand the full meaning of our lives. An existence in which the awareness of death is hidden or suppressed is lacking in the dimension that gives life its edge, its intensity and drama. "Man can only understand himself, can only be entire, by integrating death into his life; and every attempt to expel death, to take no account of it, in order to live, is a falsification, a fraud perpetrated by man on himself."

Hemingway recognized immediately that the Spaniards' refusal to ignore death was in actuality a way of sharpening life, of living more intensely. In the important chapter on the killing of the bull in *Death in the Afternoon*, he explains the Spaniards' commonsensical acceptance of mortality as part of the life process and mocks the hypocritical English and French attitude of living for life alone—only to discover death too late, when it arrives. Hemingway could have mentioned America too, where more than anywhere in Europe, discussion of dying was considered to be in bad taste. He found the Spaniards' attitude much wiser and more consistent with his own experience during and after the war.

The cardinal difference between Hemingway's tragic vision of life and death and that of most Spaniards lies in their virtually opposite views of immortality. For example, in the work of Unamuno—the modern Spanish writer who has written most trenchantly on the theme—the inevitability of death leads to a hunger for life beyond the grave and to a hope for the resurrection of the body and the individual personality according to Catholic doctrine. In spite of his conversion to Catholicism, Hemingway never mentions this kind of personal immortality in his published or unpublished work. In an important sentence deleted from *Death in the Afternoon*, he says "Men search consciously or unconsciously for some sort of immortality." In contrast to Unamuno and most Catholic thinkers, immortality for Hemingway does not mean an eternal life in heaven, but rather a feeling of timelessness transported to life on earth, such as the matador feels when he deals death to the bull, and this feeling is communicated to the public. Hemingway's achievement was to give death and immortality the religious overtones of the great Catholic writers like

St. John of the Cross and the less orthodox Unamuno without mentioning God, heaven, or an afterlife. *Death in the Afternoon* and his other works on toreo have retained their freshness largely because they are not burdened with religious, historical, and cultural references. One critic has noted that Montherlant, the only other major author with a comparable knowledge of the bullfight, "ransacks anthropology and comparative religion for references to bulls, a violation of which Hemingway would have been incapable." When one of Ernest's matadores goes in over the horn for the kill, he does not think of Mithra's sacrifice, like Montherlant's toreros, but of where to place the sword with the right arm and how to cross the muleta in the left hand so that the animal passes out and away from his body. Hemingway had a few practical things to say.

The very title of *Death in the Afternoon* reflects the author's preoccupation. The letters he wrote during the composition of the book also contain frequent allusions to mortality and cite appropriate lines from writers like Andrew Marvell and Baudelaire. When the typesetter for Scribner's slugged the galley proofs of the book with the abbreviation "Hemingway's Death," the writer wired and wrote angrily to Max Perkins, asking him to "raise hell with the son of a bitch." Ernest's reaction showed his superstitiousness, a characteristic of his personality reinforced by years of close contact with bullfighting, where the constant potentiality of wounding and death makes virtually all toreros religious and sensitive to good or bad omens.

The title of *Death in the Afternoon* should warn us, even before we begin reading, that this book was intended to be much more than a manual on the modern Spanish bullfight. By calling his book in this way, Hemingway conveyed not only his vision of toreo as a matter of life and death, but also the subjective, emotional, and symbolic approach he would use, working both from the "outside" and from the "inside," as he put it. Let us see how this method functions in the book.

"Secret Things": Blood, Wine, and Duende

With the deaths of some 1,000 bulls in his memory, and the general assumptions of the work clear in his head, Hemingway began to write in his usual spontaneous way. He allowed the prose to create its own momentum, to find its own way without formal divisions; only later did he go back and divide the material into the chapters of the published version. In general, Hemingway followed his intention, announced to Perkins in the prescient letter of 1926 (epigraph to this chapter), of taking the bullfight first from the outside—how he came to be interested in it, his preconceptions and initial reactions—building it up until he finally went "all the way inside." But this process was not a steady one and the author made many digressions, some of them triggered by unconscious associations of images and ideas that give the work a vital, organic structure and its unique, compelling nature. This is in many ways his most poorly organized, confusing book, but it also possesses a strangely living quality that makes it his most revealing work.

During its largely sporadic, improvised composition, *Death in the Afternoon* acquired a loose structure which Hemingway was oddly reluctant to rework, as he had revised the first draft of *The Sun Also Rises*, for example. The real structure of the book is to be found deep below its surface, in a profound, irrational undercurrent of primordial images and symbols embedded in the rhythmic, ecstatic prose. It is useless to expect here an orderly progression of well-organized chapters which might have been called for by the bullfight itself—an extremely orthodox art whose three *tercios* or acts are almost as rigidly codified as the liturgy of the Mass. In fact the great Andalusian poet and playwright García Lorca called the corrida a liturgy, an "authentic religious drama in which a God is worshiped and sacrificed in the same way as in the Mass." The bull has been sacred among the Hispanic peoples from the earliest times; research has shown that the remote origins of the animal's sacrifice probably lay in nature and fertility rituals. Hemingway was intuitively aware of the mythic, religious dimension of the bullfight, but his training as a writer of fiction, his iceberg theory, and his anti-intellectual temperament led him merely to suggest this dimension rather than state it openly.

In the first chapter of *Death in the Afternoon*, for example, Hemingway begins by taking bullfighting from the outside: how he happened to be interested in it, how it helped him as a writer, his expectations before seeing his first corrida and his reactions afterwards; the most sensational aspect of the spectacle for most foreigners, the goring and killing of the horses; the definition of the bullfight as a tragedy strongly disciplined by ritual. So far nothing seems unusual about the book, except perhaps the narrator's very personal tone and his emphasis on the one aspect of the corrida whose significance he is attempting to deny (he protesteth too much)—the suffering of the horses. After this visceral introduction to the bullfight, the narrator makes a long digression about wine drinking, which he admits is "far-fetched"; yet he goes out of his way to justify it. Wine, he intimates, offers a great range of enjoyment and appreciation for the palate, as the bullfight does for the eye; a trained palate wants its wine unwatered and unsweetened, as the eye of the true aficionado wants his bullfights unadulterated by fancy tricks or protection of the horses by the *peto* (quilted mattress).

It must be confessed that part of Hemingway's motivation for including several extensive paragraphs on wine probably derived from the Narcissus principle—his unwillingness to exclude his minor passions from his writings; also from his constant urge to prove himself an insider—on wine, food, bullfighting, fishing, shooting, war, loving, etc. But there is a deeper, secret justification for this passage: the country where bulls are fought and killed in the ring is also wine country, and the libation of wine is an integral part of the whole ritualistic world of bullfighting. At the *tientas* or testing of calves for bravery on bull-breeding ranches, there is always much eating accompanied by wine. At the *sorteo* or sorting of the bulls in the corrals at noon on the day of a corrida, sherry is often served; afterwards one goes to the café to drink an aperitif in order to whet the appetite for lunch. Before entering the bullring in the afternoon, one may visit a bar for a glass of sherry brandy, wine, beer, or coffee with aficionado friends. At the corrida itself, leather wine bags make the rounds, especially on the sunny side of the plaza. Afterwards, the cafés are filled once more with aficionados drinking and discussing the performance of bulls and men.

Due to the amount of liquor, especially wine, that is imbibed as a necessary part of life in and around the bullring, alcoholism can be one of the occupational diseases of toreros. Hemingway discreetly silences this fact, perhaps from having known personally several cases of careers destroyed by the sauce. (Cayetano Ordóñez, Niño de la Palma, is the most obvious example.) To live in the tradition-bound, masculine world of bullfighting and not to partake of wine would be considered odd and unnatural. At a deeper level, wine is connected to the religious dimension of the bullfight, as in ancient rituals of sacrifice and fertility. The body of the slain god—bull or Dionysus—was torn to pieces by the worshipers, who then ate the raw flesh. There are still survivals of this kind of totem banquet in many parts of Spain, such as the celebration of Midsummer or the *Día de San Juan* in Soria, where the dead bull's meat is cooked and eaten. A Catholic writer like Anthony Burgess, never an aficionado, has admitted feeling an emotion of sacramental participation, as valid as communion in the Church, after eating the roasted meat of a fighting bull. If the bullfight is a liturgical sacrifice, then wine corresponds to the blood of the animal as it stands for the blood of Christ in the Catholic Mass. This association between wine and blood is reflected in the popular imagination by the name of the famous wine-punch sangría (the word also means "bloodletting") and by the well-known red wine "Sangre de Toro."

Hemingway's apparent digression on wine drinking may not be defensible on the surface, but we can see how it begins to build, from the inside, the deep, irrational, mythic dimension of the bullfight. Of course the author does not tell us so; the reader must make this perception from the association of words and images. It does not matter if the reader does this consciously, because Hemingway himself may have been working unconsciously here, making an intuitive connection between wine and blood after his visceral discussion of horses in the preceding pages. In the first paragraph after the passage on wine drinking, he creates, with a long sentence of rhythmic, ecstatic prose, the emotion of a slow, sculptural faena by the gypsy Cagancho, which produces a kind of drunkenness and ecstasy in the bullfighter and in the public. This passage was added to the original draft of the manuscript, as if Hemingway realized that something was missing from the first chapter—the bullfight "its-self," what makes his book different from all others on the subject.

So after evoking the hidden, religious depths of the corrida with the passage on wine in the first chapter, he shows the irrational, Dionysian ecstasy of a faena by Cagancho—an emotion as profound as any religious experience, he will tell us later. This emotion is related to the Spanish word and feeling of *duende*, a power nearly everyone can feel but nobody can explain satisfactorily. Its basic meaning is inspiration in the root sense, yet no foreign word can convey the wealth of connotations evoked by the

Spanish. It may refer to a bullfight; to the singing of *cante jondo*, the traditional song of southern Spain; or to any moment charged with feeling and
enveloped in grace. Duende should not be confused with mere artistic
skill or technical competence: the catalyst of inspiration must be present.
In the most lyrical treatment of the subject by any writer, the poet Lorca
says that duende is not rational, but is linked to the dark realm of the
unconscious. It does not descend from Aristotle but from the Dionysian
Greeks, later from Nietzsche. Literally a spirit or demon, it cannot be
summoned at will. When it does arrive, it shakes the man it possesses
like an electric charge. Duende reveals itself most readily in the temporal
arts—music, dance, spoken poetry, bullfighting. It depends on an actual
present, being a perpetual baptism of the moment. Its appearance is received with a kind of religious ecstasy. In Arabic music, Lorca says that the
participants cry "Allah! Allah!"—an exact parallel to the *"Olé!"* shouted
by the public in spontaneous acclaim of a bullfighter. At this instant,
those who are present feel a kind of communion with the supernatural
through the senses.

Hemingway knew all about this experience, and he may have been
familiar with Lorca's beautiful description of the phenomenon (written
about 1929–30), which in fact uses Cagancho as an example of a bullfighter who performs with duende. In *For Whom the Bell Tolls*, duende
is expressed as "La Gloria." Robert Jordan says, as his creator suggests in
the bullfight book, that he is no mystic, but to deny the mystic experience
would be "as ignorant as though you denied the telephone or that the
earth revolves around the sun or that there are other planets than this."
Death in the Afternoon evokes the sense of duende or gloria through the
mythic dimension of the bullfight buried in the secret structure of the
book.

Secret Things: Sun, Sacrifice, Cojones

After the discussion of wine and the feeling of Dionysian
ecstasy produced by a great faena, Hemingway concludes his first chapter
with another apparently gratuitous passage, this time about the sun. Like

the evocation of Cagancho's magical faena, this passage was added to the typescript in longhand by the author. Rather enigmatically, the narrator says that the best bullfight for a beginner to see would be on a hot, sunny day, because the entire spectacle has been built on the assumption that the sun will shine. If it does not, "over a third of the bullfight is missing." Of course the other two thirds are the matador and the bull, completing the triad of man, animal, and nature. Hemingway does not attempt to explain his cryptic words, allowing the sun, like the blood and wine earlier, to reverberate in the reader's mind. Here his prose begins to resemble lyric poetry in its preference for showing over telling, for image over explanation, for implication over statement.

The absolute importance of the sun in the bullfight is well known to anyone who has attended corridas. The ring itself is divided into two halves, *sol y sombra*, sun and shade. The bullfight season in Spain, from April through October, corresponds to the warmest, sunniest part of the year. Every plaza de toros is oriented so that about half of the arena will be in the light, the other half in the shade at the hour when most bullfights begin—usually sometime between four and seven in the afternoon. As Montherlant has noted, Spaniards have an acute sense for the subtleties of sun and shade. In his novel *Les Bestiares* (translated as *The Bullfighters*), probably checked out by Hemingway at Sylvia Beach's lending library in Paris in 1926, Montherlant related the bull to the ancient worship of the sun. In the plaza, the sun or the life-principle illuminates the giving of death by the man and the loss of life by the animal. The substance of the bull's life-force, his blood, is also the sign of his wounding and death. Without the sun, the bull's blood—dual symbol of life and death—does not shine on the animal's neck. It has been said that one of the few times the sight of blood does not repel human beings is when it streams from the hump of muscle in the bull's neck during a corrida. In fact, far from being repulsive, the blood may even have an esthetic quality for the aficionado as it flows and gleams in the sunlight, the bright red against the black of the bull's hide.

So in the first chapter of his book, Hemingway has approached the bullfight from the outside through an explanation of facts, but more important, from the inside through an apparently arbitrary evocation of three fundamental images or symbols—blood, wine, sun. They are important elements in most religions, from primitive nature worship and fertility rituals to Catholicism, in which the eucharistic wine represents the blood of Christ and the host recalls the solar circle. All three symbols converge around the potent, central figure of the bull, whose blood is spilled inevitably, and to a lesser extent around the matador, who will perhaps shed his own blood in the sacrifice of the animal that was worshiped as a god for thousands of years. The spectators, like the public at the performance of an ancient Greek tragedy or the community of the faithful at the celebration of a Mass, will participate in the rite through their necessary presence, and ideally will achieve a sense of ecstasy, catharsis, and renewal. The remainder of *Death in the Afternoon* will develop this symbolic, mythic undercurrent through the subtle use of primordial symbols expressed in rhythmic prose. This is the deep, hidden structure of the book, the source of its originality, power, and meaning.

Now that we have seen Hemingway's secret method in the opening chapter, let us follow it briefly through the most significant parts of the book. The beginning of the next chapter reverts to the tone of a treatise on bullfighting, defining the spectacle again as a tragedy, not a sport or equal contest in the Anglo-Saxon tradition. In contrast to the corrida, sports do not deal with death but with victory; they replace the bullfight's avoidance of death with the avoidance of defeat. The narrator says that it "takes more cojones" to be a sportsman when death is part of the game. This is the book's first mention of testicles or *cojones*, a word that frequently interlards the discourse of Spaniards (as it did Hemingway's, whether he was speaking in English or Spanish). The valor of a matador is popularly believed to reside in his testicles, like the fierceness of the fighting bull. When castrated, the bull becomes a *manso* or mild, tame animal. The manso is concerned only with avoiding danger, while the great fighting bull actually prefers danger and even death to escape or surrender. Thus Hemingway associated cojones not only with courage, daring, and masculinity, but also with a sense of death. He once called critics the mansos or eunuchs of literature because they do not have or understand the writer's tragic sense of life and death. Cojones, whether the bull's or the man's, are another one of the recurring images in the deep structure of *Death in the Afternoon*.

Since the technique of toreo is more readily discernible in a state of

imperfection, Hemingway now advises novice aficionados to attend a
novillada, or apprentice fight, before they see a corrida with fully grown
bulls. Accordingly, he launches into an apparently logical description of
a novillada he saw one very hot Sunday in Madrid. The clumsy Basque
novillero Hernandorena suffered a massive horn wound that day because
of his suicidal insistence on receiving the bull's charge from a kneeling
position. The declared purpose of this lengthy description is to give the
reader an instructive example of faulty technique at a novillada, yet a
paragraph inserted into the original typescript of the book, preserved in
the final printed version, reveals a more subtle, deeper purpose. In this
paragraph Hemingway tells how he awoke in the night, trying to remember what it was that he had really seen in Hernandorena's goring that was
significant and eluded his memory. Then he got it: it was the dirtiness
of the man's breeches and underwear and "the clean, clean, unbearably
clean whiteness of the thigh bone that I had seen, and it was that which
was important." In other words, Hemingway denies his own proclaimed
purpose for including this episode here—to show how a bullfighter's imperfect technique can be instructive for a novice spectator. The real purpose of this passage is not pedagogical but esthetic and psychological: the
problem was one of the writer keeping his eyes wide open, looking un-
flinchingly at the act, preserving it in his memory somewhere between
the conscious and the subconscious, and depicting it truthfully in words.
Hernandorena's bloody wound, revealing the depth of bone beneath the
surface of clothing and skin, belongs to that irrational undercurrent of the
book which attempts to reach the deeper layers of the mind.

As if he were testing the reader's stomach, Hemingway proceeds with
a discussion of the *capeas*, informal bullfights or bull-baitings in village
squares; they usually contain more violence and cruelty than formal corridas. If the village or town can afford to buy the bull, the animal may be
killed by the male populace swarming over him with rocks, sticks, dag-
gers, and knives until he sways and goes down. This kind of collective
brutality is disappearing from most of Spain, but still survives in some
rural areas.

If a town or village cannot afford to purchase the bull, an older animal
who has been fought before is used; he may be so knowledgeable of men
on foot that he is said to know Latin. Hemingway tells the story of one

such bull in the province of Valencia who killed sixteen men and boys and wounded over sixty. In order to avenge the death of their brother who had been killed by the animal, a gypsy boy and his sister followed this bull for two years, hoping to assassinate him in the village capeas. When bull baiting was temporarily abolished by government order, the animal's owner sent him to the slaughterhouse in Valencia. The two gypsies followed him there, and the boy was given permission to slay the bull that had killed his brother. While the animal was still in a cage, the boy dug out the bull's eyes, spitting into the sockets, and killed him by severing the spine with a dagger between the neck vertebrae. He then cut off the bull's testicles, which he and his sister roasted on sticks over a small fire "at the edge of the dusty street outside the slaughterhouse."

The anecdotes of the village capeas and of the bull in Valencia round out Hemingway's introduction of the ancient, sacrificial dimension of the bullfight. The capeas are the closest modern survivals of the primitive rituals of sacrifice in which the god, horned or human, was slain and eaten by his worshipers. The gypsy boy and girl who slay the bull and eat his testicles are responding to the same primordial instinct as the participants in the ancient mysteries of sacrifice and communion with the dead god. It is not by chance that the brother and sister are gypsies, a people who have managed to preserve the old ways of life more than any other in Europe. We can be almost certain that Hemingway invented or at least embellished this anecdote; he gives no source and tells the story from the point of view of an omniscient narrator in a work of fiction. By having the gypsy boy and girl consume the bull's testicles, the author implies that they absorb the animal's life-force as the worshipers in remote sacrificial rites supposedly acquired the strength of the dead god, bull, or man. If Hemingway awakens echoes of ancient religions here, these are always masculine and pre-Christian: the bull represents the generative, male power. The ancient cults of bull-gods in the Mediterranean basin were replaced in Christianity by the worship of the lamb and the Virgin Mary, symbols of meekness and femininity. Unlike other twentieth-century artists who believed the creative instinct was mainly feminine—Joyce and D. H. Lawrence come to mind—Hemingway, at this stage of his career, expressed the male principle.

The first two chapters of *Death in the Afternoon* form a kind of rite of passage for the reader. The visceral accounts of horses slain by bulls, the stories of Hernandorena's terrible goring, the bloody village capeas, and the brutal assassination of the bull in Valencia by the gypsy boy are so many tests of the reader's fortitude. If he has survived the trial, he is prepared to learn the technical facts of the corrida. He has proved his mettle and he knows that the bullfight is not sport but a tragedy demanding blood and death. He has passed through a labyrinth, a subtle initiation into the irrational, mythic ritual of the corrida, revealed through a secret structure of primordial symbols—blood, wine, sun, cojones.

Secret Structure: From the Bullfight to Spain

After describing the plaza de toros and the sorting of the animals in the corrals, Hemingway tells the reader where and when to see bullfights in Spain. He ends up by following the book's general trajectory from toreo to Spain and Spanish life. When he says that Aranjuez would be a good place in which to see one's first corrida, for example, he soon forgets about bullfighting and proceeds to recreate the town's life and scenery. Although he has been accused of sounding like a cross between Baedeker and Duncan Hines in these sections, he does much more than merely describe the monuments and cuisine of Spain. In a wonderful, revealing passage on Aranjuez, Hemingway does not call it the Spanish Versailles as so many travel writers have done, nor does he depict the royal palaces and gardens. On the contrary, he reduces all of the historic and cultural background of the town to one magnificently scornful sentence: "You can find the sights in Baedeker." Instead of describing the sights, he tells us how to live in Aranjuez and penetrates directly into the actual, present life of the town—its swift river, tall trees, and rich gardens, the succulent strawberries and thumb-thick asparagus for which the area is famous in spring, the booths where chickens are roasted and steaks are grilled over charcoal fires and washed down with Valdepeñas wine. But all is not pleasure in Aranjuez; the author remembers to include the Goyesque army of cripples and beggars who follow the ferias throughout the peninsula. Hemingway's Spain: a land of contrasts.

The sensual atmosphere in Aranjuez is deepened by an evocation of the beauty of Spanish women, observed in the "girl inspection" with opera or field glasses at the bullring in Aranjuez, or during the evening *paseo* in the town square. Here once more there is a spontaneous association of ideas— between the sensual imbibing of food and wine and the sexual attraction of women, all related to the erotic undercurrent of the bullfight. In the original manuscript of this section, Hemingway wrote a telling passage which he later deleted, perhaps because it was too personal and may have offended his wife Pauline (who often typed for him during this period):

> I have seen at least six girls in Spain so beautiful that it would tear your heart out and let you realize your life had been wasted to see them. I saw a girl one evening at Escorial . . . who was so beautiful it made the ribs in back of your lungs ache to see her. . . .

In his myth-making fashion, Ernest concludes the passage by suggesting, ever so ambiguously, that he might have spent the night with this beautiful girl.

Under the pretense of telling the reader where to see bullfights, Hemingway continues his search for the deepest core of Spanish life with an evocation of Madrid. Although some of his favorite bullfighters—Maera, Juan Belmonte, Cayetano Ordóñez—were from Andalusia, by this time he had acquired a predilection for the heartland of the Iberian Peninsula: Castile and the capital of Spain, Madrid, located in the precise geographic center of the country. While nearly all other foreign writers on Spain have preferred the sunnier, more "exotic" Andalusia, Hemingway detested the picturesque costumes, local color, and exploitation of tourists in southern Spain; he did not feel as comfortable with the facile Andalusians as he did with the more austere Castilians, Navarrese, Basques, and Aragonese. He also favored the higher average elevation of central and northern Spain, the invigorating contrasts of heat and cold, and the mountain climate of cities like Madrid and Pamplona. If the Navarrese were his favorite people in Spain, he also felt that the *madrileños* were fine and that Madrid alone contained "the essence" of Spain. With its tonic climate of high cloudless sky and clear mountain air (polluted by smog since Hemingway's death), some of the best bullfights and the most knowledgeable afición in the world, the Prado museum, and the city's proximity to such good towns as El Escorial, Toledo, Ávila, Segovia, and La Granja, "it makes you feel very badly, all questions of immortality aside, to know that you will have to die" and never see Madrid again.

When he first traveled there in 1923, Hemingway did not understand the city because it had none of the picturesque look he had expected to find. Everything seemed too simple and unadorned. He compared the Prado, for example, to a naked woman, because of the accessibility of the paintings and the simplicity with which they were hung; he thought there had to be a catch somewhere. Hemingway was also befuddled by the madrileños' habit of staying up most of the night, then rising from bed late in the morning—the reverse of his own daily habit of waking at dawn. But as he returned to Madrid each summer, he began to be accustomed and to acquire an affection for this "strange place." By the time he wrote *Death in the Afternoon*, it had become one of his favorite cities, a good town for working and living. In his imagination, Madrid was related to the sun because of its cloudless skies and dry heat, and because so many of its inhabitants stay up most of the night in the summer "until that cool time that comes just before daylight." This thought triggered Hemingway's memories of postwar Constantinople, where people also exhausted the night then drove out to the Bosphorus to see the sunrise. One memory awakened another, more recent, of the time he was driving in the country late one night near Kansas City and saw the glow of a great fire on the horizon. He drove toward the fire, only to discover that it was the sunrise. By following his memories, writing spontaneously with a free association of images, Hemingway thus expressed the nature of Madrid— the "essence" of Spain—through images of the night, heat, fire, and sun.

It was appropriate that he concluded this section on Madrid with a condemnation of those overwritten, one-visit books with a false epic tone, like Waldo Frank's *Virgin Spain*. In a letter several years earlier, Hemingway had said that Spain lost its virginity before any other country. By this he did not mean that it had been spoiled by the forces of modernization and progress, like America and other Western European countries. On the contrary, Spain had lost its virginity in the sense that it was the most ancient, sensual, "pagan" country in Europe despite its official veneer of orthodoxy and Catholicism. To know Spain, one cannot use the "bedside mysticism," the "pseudo-scientific jargon," and the "false epic quality" employed by intellectual authors in a state of sexual frustration and sublimation—Hemingway called their work "erectile writing." In order to know Spain one must use all the senses, the cojones and the whole body as well as the mind: one must immerse himself in the life of the fiesta, imbibe the wine of the country, eat the abundant fruits of the earth and seas, exhaust the night, love women, participate in the ritual of sacrifice in the bullring beneath the sun in the high cloudless skies. And to write about this experience, Hemingway tells us that an author should use clear, unadorned language. By implication, we can add that the writer should prefer a lyrical to an epic tone, using the expressive rhythms of prose and concrete images to imply rather than declare his meaning, much like a poet.

Hemingway, Torerista

By now the author assumes that his reader has seen a bullfight, and the tone of the book changes. Instead of continuing directly with a formal description of the corrida, Hemingway introduces the Old Lady, who will serve as a foil to the narrator. First he goes back in time to recall the golden age of toreo during the competition between Joselito and Belmonte (1914–20), which led to the present state of the spectacle. Then he recalls the young "phenomenons" who raised great hopes but ultimately failed to regenerate bullfighting. This section of the book is chatty and journalistic, dropping enticing details about the matadores' private lives; it would have benefited from intelligent editing. Here Hemingway commits the sin of which he was very critical in other aficionados—being a *torerista* or worshiper of bullfighters rather than a *torista* or admirer of the fighting bull as the center of the fiesta. In a sentence deleted from the manuscript, he had said that there are two loose groupings of aficionados: "those who care most for the bull fighters and those who care most for the bulls." The situation is similar if not identical to horseracing, where the most knowledgeable and passionate are those who love the horses, not the jockeys, trainers, or owners. The deterioration of toreo derives from human beings, not from the animals. For his part, the matador soon learns from experience that the real beast in the plaza is not the animal but the public, as in the famous ending of Blasco Ibáñez's *Blood and Sand*. Because the danger of painful wounding and death is always on the points of the bull's horns, toreros, their managers, the breeders, and all the supernumeraries of the taurine world have customarily done as much as their cunning, influence, and power have enabled them in order to lessen risk and increase profit. For this reason, many of the best aficionados have normally reserved their greatest interest, respect, and admiration for the fighting bull and not for the man, who is often a mere intermediary, like the priest in a Mass. Hemingway tried to emulate such aficionados, but tended inevitably to fall back into an almost puerile adulation of matadores which became more dominant as he grew older. The reasons for this tendency may have lain in his original identification with the torero as a man who must learn to live with fear and death, as the young ambulance driver in Italy had been forced to learn; in his recognition of the terrible solitude of the matador with the bull before the implacable crowd, as a parallel to the writer's loneliness with a sheet of paper before the unpardoning judgment of history.

So in these middle chapters of *Death in the Afternoon*, Hemingway prattles on about bullfighters who have nearly all been forgotten, while the figure of the bull practically disappears. This part of the book has aged more than any other. The overemphasis on the personalities of toreros is a major flaw relieved occasionally by a memorable portrait, like the one of Hemingway's greatest hero at this time of his life, Maera. The writer paid this matador the highest compliment he would ever offer to any man: "Era muy hombre." In a curious sentence deleted from the manuscript, he went even further in his praise by saying that after Maera's death, "I felt the worse I've felt after any man dead so far." Since Dr. Hemingway had died by this time, we can understand the force of the writer's statement and his reasons for removing it from the book. Most bullfight critics and aficionados who were around in the 1920s believe that Hemingway exaggerated Maera's value and importance in toreo, perhaps because he knew the man personally and because the matador died in 1924, before the young, impressionable Ernest had become an experienced connoisseur.

Hemingway goes on with his treatment of the "personal element" in bullfighting, turning to a pair of toreros who had appeared early in his fiction—Nicanor Villalta and Cayetano Ordóñez. Describing Ordóñez's short, happy life as the new messiah of toreo, and his shameful fall into ignominy after his first serious goring, the author is led by an association of ideas to discuss the theme of honor in and out of the bullring. When Cayetano showed cowardice truly and unmistakably, he lost his honor. Pride is the strongest characteristic of the Spaniard, Hemingway tells us, and it is a matter of pride to keep one's honor. Here he confuses two Spanish words, *honor* and *pundonor*. *Honor* is an inner, moral quality or virtue, while *pundonor* is a point or state of honor which involves one's reputation and depends to an extent upon the opinion of others—as in the hundreds of classic Spanish plays by Lope de Vega, Tirso de Molina, Pedro Calderón de la Barca, and other dramatists of the sixteenth and seventeenth centuries. Although he gets the words wrong, it is clear that Hemingway is always concerned with the inner quality, not with its social manifestation. As in so many aspects of Spanish life, he goes directly to the heart of his subject.

Only a few years earlier, in the famous passage of A *Farewell to Arms*, the narrator Frederic Henry had said that "abstract words" like honor, glory, and courage sounded obscene beside the concrete names of villages, roads, and rivers where soldiers had fought and died. Unlike his creator and his fictional brother Jake Barnes in *The Sun Also Rises*, Henry was not able to heal his wounds after the war in Spain, nor to meet bullfighters and other men for whom courage, honor, and glory were real qualities to be lived by, not empty slogans of chauvinistic propaganda and war-time rhetoric. For a Spaniard, no matter how dishonest, Hemingway tells us, honor "is as real a thing as water, wine, or olive oil." *Death in the Afternoon* and later works, like *For Whom the Bell Tolls* and *The Old Man and the Sea*, are the stories of men and women—toreros, guerrillas, or a fisherman—who succeed or fail in various degrees to keep their sense of honor in times of stress and danger.

Hemingway, Torista

After all the gossipy chatter on toreros, Hemingway dedicates the following, central portion of his book to *El Señor Toro*, the real protagonist of the bullfight. The fighting bull, he tells us, comes from a

Spanish fighting bulls in the open country at a ganadería. *Photograph chosen by*
Hemingway for Death in the Afternoon *but not included in the book.*
(Hemingway Collection, John F. Kennedy Library, Boston)

strain that descends directly from the wild bulls that used to range over the
peninsula, and is as different from the domestic bull as a wolf from a dog.
The bravery of the bull is the root of the whole corrida; it is "unearthly
and unbelievable." People who have not been close to the fiesta, or have
never faced an animal with brave blood in a ring, find it difficult to understand the seemingly preternatural speed, power, and ferociousness of the
fighting bull. Unlike nearly all other animals, he will attack and destroy
even when not motivated by hunger. He is more fierce than predators and
also more deadly, as was proven in barbarous spectacles of former times
when bulls confronted elephants, lions, and tigers in the plaza. Hemingway tells anecdotes of bulls who have charged motor cars and stopped
trains, slaughtered as many as seven horses in a single corrida, jumped
the barrera and maimed or gored spectators to death.

The purpose of these taurine horror stories is to build up the under-current of fear that flows throughout the book; the bull is surrounded by such an aura of terror that he nearly comes to represent all of the dark, destructive forces of nature, as in much of Picasso's work. Yet the true fighting bull also possesses a quality, called nobility in Spanish, "which is the most extraordinary part of the whole business." Unlike the lion and the tiger, for example, he does not use stealth against his enemies: he is frank, simple, and straight in his charges, and thus easily deceived. Be-cause of his nobility we could say of the fighting bull, more truly than of the lion, that he is the king of beasts. This quality, combined with his fierceness and power, give an atmosphere of seriousness, dignity, and fear to the corrida which justifies its tragedy of necessary death.

The description of the bulls' potency awakens the Old Lady's curiosity about their "love life." Animals destined for the ring are not allowed to breed, the narrator tells her, but a seed bull can service more than fifty cows. The very first photograph at the end of *Death in the Afternoon* shows a mighty seed bull who has fathered 822 sons for the ring; his "hind quarters are light as a calf's," the author says in the caption, "but all the rest is built into the bull's own monument" of his penis and testicles. The Old Lady's frivolous question leads to a development of the book's underlying themes of sexuality and the traditional religious dimension of the bull, long worshiped as a male divinity.

Amid his treatment of the breeding, raising, testing, and fighting of the bull, Hemingway inserted his "Natural History of the Dead," which has always been a source of confusion to readers and critics. In it the author describes, with the cold detachment of a naturalist describing animals or plants, the gore and cruelty of war, especially during the bloody Austrian offensive of June 1918. Why did Hemingway include this extensive piece —without a single reference to bullfighting—in a book about toreo? As we have seen, *Death in the Afternoon* is a work about death anywhere, not only in the plaza de toros. As Hemingway had observed the corrida with his eyes wide open, he wished to observe and describe warfare with the same forthrightness. The various references to Goya, in the sections of the book on both bullfighting and war, show that Hemingway was attempting to do in words what the Spaniard had done in the etchings of *La Tauro-maquia* and *The Disasters of War*. "A Natural History . . ." would also be included in Hemingway's collection of short stories, *Winner Take Nothing* (1933), yet he preferred to print it first in the bullfight book for a good reason. In a letter written between the publication of the two works, he said that he used the piece not "directly, but indirectly . . . to make a point." The point was that war is far more terrible and cruel than bullfighting. While death is partial to bulls, horses, and men in the plaza, it is indiscriminate in war—as shown by Hemingway's paragraph on the explosion of a munitions factory whose employees were women. Even outside of war, most humans die like animals. In spite of Hemingway's intention of not writing an apology for the corrida, the point of "A Natural History of the Dead" was in fact to show the relatively unimportant amount of cruelty and bloodshed in bullfighting when compared to modern war.

In the last pages dedicated to the bull in this central portion of the book, Hemingway gives the best treatment I have ever read of the querencia, or the place in the ring where the fighting bull tends to go and where he feels most comfortable. The writer was intrigued by the mentality of animals and considered himself somewhat of an expert on the subject. To him the development of querencia was the most interesting change in the bull's brain during the unfolding of a corrida. The animal can develop a querencia for a cool spot in the ring on a hot day, for a place where he has enjoyed success or can smell the blood of a wounded horse, for a location where he feels secure—like the *toril* from which he entered the plaza, or the barrera where he has a back-to-the-wall sense of protection. From his love and understanding of the fighting bull, I believe Hemingway himself began to sympathize with the animal's feeling for a querencia or a place where he felt secure and confident. From his experience as a fisherman and hunter and as a soldier with a knowledge of tactics and terrain, he had already acquired a feeling for the importance of location. Spaniards always have a knack for detecting whether or not a place has *ambiente*—the complex, indefinable balance of light and shade, comfort and naturalness, visibility and inconspicuousness, human presence or absence which makes a location habitable at a given moment or at any time. A place either has or does not have ambiente, and Hemingway knew this as intuitively as the Spaniards. All the places where he lived and worked had it; his favorite bars, cafés and restaurants had it, and within those locales, his favorite stool, table, or window. There he was just as strong, confident, and dangerous as a fighting bull in his querencia.

Secret Structure: Appearances versus Reality

After the well-placed discourse on the fighting bull in the center of his book, Hemingway defines his own stance in relation to the decadence of modern bulls and toreros. If an aficionado makes the error of placing himself in the bullfighters' position, he will condone their disasters and their failures to work with all kinds of animals, as some of the old matadores could do. By seeing the fiesta from the toreros' point of view, the aficionado becomes an accomplice to the decay in standards that characterizes the modern spectacle. On the other hand, if he is more of a torista than a torerista, if he stands for the real fighting bull and for the complete bullfight, the individual spectator becomes a kind of moral arbiter who knows what is good and what is bad, who lets nothing confuse his standards. A bullfighter, Hemingway says, will not be superior to his audience for long. If complete toreros are to return to the ring, there must be a nucleus of spectators who prefer honesty to tricks, real danger to the appearance of danger, the integral corrida to partial brilliance of cape or muleta. Of course Hemingway's definition of the true aficionado could also serve as a code for the reader of literature or the spectator of drama, cinema, and television.

The true aficionado must learn how to distinguish between what is real and what seems to be real; he must be both an esthetic and an ethical witness. Like so many aspects of Spanish life, the corrida has an attractive, official exterior which often conceals a seamy side. One example is bullfight journalism, which frequently reports the fiesta with inflated rhetoric while sustaining itself on the gratuities given by toreros to the newspaper critics. The venality of journalists and the pervasive use of the *propina* or baksheesh at every level of the business are two examples of the economic corruption of the bullfight. Hemingway knew it from the inside, since he used to prepare the envelopes, containing money and the torero's card, from his friend Sidney Franklin to the critics of the Madrid papers. (He did not admit this in *Death*, but in a passage deleted from his last work, "Dangerous Summer.") As he once said, a corrida is not always art, but "it is always business."

In the final chapters of the book, leading up to the epilogue, Hemingway treats in an orderly way the progressive *suertes* of toreo from the time the bull enters the ring to his death by sword, always telling the reader how to distinguish between real and simulated danger. After the technical sections, he lightens the tone with digressions. In one of the last, the Old Lady asks the narrator to tell another story, this time about the living, not the dead. As before, she shows her preference for erotic stories and requests a tale of homosexuals. The narrator complies by telling her what he called, in a marginal note to himself in the manuscript, a "Story of 2 fairies. . . ." In Paris, a newspaperman friend of his had met two "fine, clean-cut looking" American youths. The older of the two forced the other to comply with his sexual advances, perhaps because of superior strength and certainly because of his money. From a distraught victim, the younger man quickly became a willing accomplice, a kind of male prostitute maintained by his wealthy friend.

In order to understand the meaning and function of this story within the context of *Death in the Afternoon*, we should remember that for Hemingway, homosexuality was a kind of ultimate in degradation. Partly because he had rejected his mother and the artistic, cultural qualities she represented for him, he detested men in whom feminine aspects prevailed. This story of people who are alive makes an indirect point, like the "Natural History of the Dead": the cruelty of man to man is immeasurably greater than the cruelty of man to animal in the bullring. The Paris story carries the point even farther, because the psychological suffering inflicted by the wealthy homosexual on his helpless friend—we remember the younger man's sobs and despairing scream—surpasses even the terrible physical pain portrayed in the piece on wartime Italy. Hemingway knew from his own experience at Fossalta that death and the actual wounds of war cause less suffering than the aftermath of nightmares, insomnia, and the feeling of nada. He called death "a sovereign remedy for all misfortunes"; the agony of the living is more prolonged, and it lacks the finality, the dignity of death.

Finally, the Paris story develops the important theme of appearances versus reality. When the narrator (possibly Hemingway himself here) saw the two youths sitting on the terrace of the Café des Deux Magots, wearing well-tailored clothes, they looked as clean-cut as ever except that the younger man "had had his hair hennaed." After this story representing the extremity of sexual and moral corruption, Hemingway threw the Old Lady out of his book.

Since his foil was gone, the narrator had to create his own digressions now. He took advantage of the opportunity to answer a recent criticism of his work by Aldous Huxley in an essay entitled "Foreheads Villainous Low," where the English novelist accused Hemingway of consciously avoiding the appearance of education and culture in his work. The accusation was largely true: Ernest's rejection of his mother included the values she represented—formal education, socially respectable art, high culture. In his reply to Huxley, Hemingway did not admit this; perhaps he was not entirely aware of how much his mother had influenced his life and writing. Instead, he defends his own method in fiction and implicitly in *Death*. He accuses Huxley of being a solemn intellectual writer who creates his characters out of his head alone, while a greater novelist projects the people in his work "from his head, from his heart and from all there is of him"—including his cojones, we could add with Hemingway's approval no doubt. Unlike the intellectual author who overanalyzes experience, the great novelist writes so truly that he can leave out things that he knows and yet give the reader a feeling of those things: the iceberg theory. In a famous sentence, Hemingway says that "Prose is architecture, not interior decoration, and the Baroque is over." Although he is ostensibly discussing fiction, his words are even more applicable to *Death in the Afternoon* than to his novels and short stories. The bullfight book is architecture because its meaning is revealed more by the deep structure than by the surface decoration. The work is like an iceberg whose tip consists of a manual on the bullfight and whose submerged body contains the deeper levels of life, death, sacrifice, and renewal, expressed in primordial symbols and rhythmic prose.

The final digression in *Death* is Hemingway's best piece of prose on Spanish art. After so many allusions to the Prado and to Goya, it was only a matter of time before he compared this painter to the other classic Spanish artists, Greco and Velázquez, whose major works are also housed in that museum. Hemingway recognized the greatness of all three, but preferred Goya for reasons consistent with his own personality and art. Ever since he had first seen the artist's hundreds of oils, cartoons, etchings, and lithographs at the Prado in 1923, Ernest had been under a spell. He perceived the parallels between his own life and the painter's: both were born in the provinces and gravitated to metropolitan centers of artistic activity

—Madrid or Paris; both were self-educated men who felt uncomfortable in the intellectual circles of the court or city. Each was a revolutionary in his art, defying the accepted rules and working against the grand manner of his predecessors. Both Goya and Hemingway were anticlerical and liberal in politics, and supreme lovers of the bullfight. One of the Spaniard's nicknames was "Don Francisco de los Toros"; he was the first man to consider the corrida worthy of treatment by a serious artist. In the etchings of his *Tauromaquia,* he portrayed what he saw and felt, as Hemingway would do in the later miniatures of *in our time,* with a similar taste for the more violent, visceral aspects of the fiesta. Both Spaniard and American lived in periods of crisis and were profoundly marked by the great wars of their times, of which they were two of the most honest, moving witnesses. The wartime interchapters of *in our time,* like A *Farewell to Arms,* "A Natural History of the Dead," and *For Whom the Bell Tolls,* were Hemingway's equivalent of the *Disasters of War.*

More than almost any modern painter, Goya was a "narrative" artist who held a natural attraction for a writer of fiction: with the exception of his portraits, his works tend to depict episodes caught at the moment of maximum tension. His subjects are usually drawn not from classical or Christian tradition but from the life and events of his time, like Hemingway's. If Velázquez painted from the head and Greco from the spirit, Goya painted from all the senses, his body, heart, head, spirit, and cojones.

In one of the fullest, most revealing sentences he ever wrote, the writer offered this personal tribute to his favorite painter:

> Goya did not believe in costume but he did believe in blacks and
> in grays, in dust and in light, in high places rising from plains, in
> the country around Madrid, in movement, in his own cojones, in
> painting, in etching, and in what he had seen, felt, touched, handled,
> smelled, enjoyed, drunk, mounted, suffered, spewed-up, lain-with,
> suspected, observed, loved, hated, lusted, feared, detested, admired,
> loathed, and destroyed.

If we substitute "writing" for "painting" and "etching," we would have Hemingway's most forceful expression of his own artistic convictions and methods in *Death in the Afternoon.*

The Art of Killing

The last regular chapter of *Death in the Afternoon* deals with the final suerte of the bullfight; it is the longest and one of the most significant chapters in the book. The actual kill used to be considered the supreme action performed by the torero in the ring, as indicated by the very name of matador. But since the golden age and the later decadence of bullfighting, with its almost exclusive emphasis on the esthetic use of cape and muleta, the art of killing has declined. Hemingway shows his adherence to the old ways and to the integral bullfight by granting more space to the sword than to any other aspect of toreo.

The kill is the most dangerous part of the corrida. If he is performing properly, the man must expose himself to the bull's horns more than at any other moment: this is the *momento de la verdad*. The true killer must have more courage, pride, and honor than the ordinary torero. As a soldier and hunter, Hemingway identified himself with the strong, manly swordsmen more than with the graceful, "feminine" artists of cape and muleta. When a man is still in rebellion against death, he tells us, he has pleasure in taking to himself the divine power of giving death. A man kills from pride—a pagan virtue but a Christian sin. It is pride that makes the bullfight.

Hemingway was one of the few writers with the courage to discuss the "spiritual" qualities of killing. Since most of those who enjoy the kill have been simple men, and those who do not enjoy it have been more articulate, there has been little fair treatment of the subject. Hemingway, who was both simple and articulate, makes one of his most eloquent statements on the esthetic enjoyment of killing in this section of *Death in the Afternoon*. His father had taught him to kill cleanly and never to kill more than he could use to eat. Since Ernest was in rebellion against death more than Dr. Hemingway, he did not always follow the second part of his father's advice. Although he never went in over the horn for the kill himself, he witnessed the deaths of hundreds of fighting bulls in his lifetime, caught countless fish in rivers and seas, and shot thousands of animals ranging from jack rabbits to lions and water buffaloes. His indiscriminate killing of animals is difficult to excuse; it will not be pardoned easily by future generations more aware of life's fragility. Hemingway walked across the earth like a giant, leaving behind a trail of blood and carcasses. His need to kill was a measure of his pride, anxiety, and unhappiness. He killed well, with enjoyment but also with desperation, as if the giving of death postponed his own mortality.

After describing the technique of the kill in the bullring, Hemingway ended this last regular chapter with a treatment of the culture of death in Spain. Whereas most foreign writers on the country lump all Spaniards together when attempting to analyze the national character, Hemingway knew the peninsula too well to make that mistake. For him, the Spaniards' interest in death was based on a common sense as hard and dry as the plains of Castile, and he believed that common sense diminishes in hardness and dryness as it moves away from Castile. The Castilian peasant lives in a country with a severe climate: *Nueve meses de invierno y tres de infierno*, as the proverb has it ("Nine months of winter and three of hell"). He lives austerely, with little comfort and few possessions. He knows that death is an unescapable reality, and he has a religion that says life is much shorter than death. Therefore he can afford to risk his life with an impracticality that would be difficult to understand in the countries of northern Europe. In his lucid analysis, Hemingway coincided with other modern Spanish writers such as Unamuno and Lorca, who saw the Castilian as a man with an acute sense of death and a tragic sense of life.

The Navarrese and Aragonese in the north of the peninsula also have a bravery that comes from pride and honor. The Andalusians, who have given the country many of her best toreros and fighting bulls, have a strong sense of death too. But unlike most foreigners, Hemingway did not worship the *andaluces* as being the wittiest, most daring, and characteristic Spaniards. Although he revered the name of Joselito, admired Belmonte, and worshiped Maera, he believed that southern Spain was becoming less important as a center of toreo; his belief turned out to be mistaken. He thought the bravery of the Castilian to be tragic and that of the Navarrese and Aragonese "romantic," while the southerner's is "picturesque." Bull-fighters from the south, especially those who follow the Sevillian school of toreo, tend to have a varied, flowery style that gives more importance to cape, banderillas, or muleta than to the kill. Many of the gypsy toreros are Andalusians, and Hemingway was not a great admirer of the *gitanos* either in or out of the ring. (El Gallo, Joselito, and Cagancho were notable exceptions.) While they could be brilliant with the right kind of bull, he believed they did not have the simple, steady bravery nor the sense of duty to the public possessed by the fighters from central Spain whom he preferred, like Marcial Lalanda and Nicanor Villalta.

For one reason or another, the peoples from the remaining areas of the country do not have the special feeling for death required by the bullfight, according to Hemingway. In Galicia on the Atlantic coast, death is not "a mystery to be sought and meditated on"—as in central Spain—but rather a daily peril to be avoided. In Catalonia, life is too practical and businesslike for there to be much feeling about death.

As we would expect, there is a direct proportion between the sense of death in the various regions of Spain and Hemingway's admiration for the inhabitants. The Basque-Navarrese and the Castilians were his favorite peoples in Spain, followed by the Aragonese and Andalusians. In this as in so many other things, he was different from most of the foreigners who have traveled in the Iberian Peninsula over the last several hundred years.

The Tragic Sense

In a sentence deleted from an earlier chapter of *Death in the Afternoon*, Hemingway said: "To get Spain into a book is very hard." He believed his friend Joan Miró had managed to get Spain into a painting, *The Farm*, which the writer had purchased in 1925 and considered one of his most cherished possessions. Since nearly everything in his Spain had to do with bullfighting in one way or another, Hemingway tried to get the whole country into his book. Of course he failed, but in Chapter Twenty —his epilogue or coda, one of the best things he ever wrote—he would try to condense all of his thronging memories of Spain into a few pages. He knew that if you could see one part of the world clearly and wholly, it would stand for the rest.

The secret structure of *Death in the Afternoon* culminates in the last chapter. Since most of the epilogue does not deal directly with the bullfight, we realize that this has been a book about many things besides the corrida. In a letter to Arnold Gingrich, written soon after the publication of *Death*, Hemingway said:

Am glad you liked the last chapter in the last book—it is what the book is about but nobody seems to notice that. They think it is just a catalogue of things that were omitted. How would they like them to be put in? Framed in pictures or with a map?

What the book is about is of course Spain, its land, peoples, food, drinks, ways of life and death of which the bullfight is a supreme example; it is also about the writer's experience in a country he loved very much. As Robert W. Lewis has said, *Death* is really about Hemingway and "his love affair with Spain and all that passed between them."

In the epilogue, the secret structure of the book reveals itself in some of the primordial images and symbols that have been embedded in its prose —sun, heat, wine, blood, sacrifice, death, woman, sex. To take only one of these symbols, wine or alcohol in general, Hemingway recalls the year everyone drank so much at Pamplona (1924); drinking wine on picnics along the Irati River during San Fermín; the leather wineskins of Navarre; a boy carrying wicker-bound jugs of wine and everyone getting drunk on the train from Pamplona to Madrid (1925); the sweatbeaded pitchers of cold beer in Valencia; hard Asturian cider; "the beer place on the cool side of the street" beneath the Hotel Palace in Madrid; the earthen wine jars, twelve feet high, each with a different vintage, set side by side in a dark room of Miró's house at Montroig, then drinking the wine of that year (1929) and of the year before and so on; whisky in an earthen crock at Sidney Franklin's house; the cafés where the saucers pile up and drinks are tallied in pencil on the marble tabletops; riding back from Toledo in the car at night, washing out the dust with Fundador.

The sacramental use of wine or alcohol is accompanied by related images of death, blood, and sacrifice. For example, there is a cryptic reference to the death of the novillero Pedro Carreño, killed by a bull in 1930 (Hemingway was not in Spain at the time). According to some friends of the writer, people carried the dead torero's body through the streets, surrounded by torches, into the church where they put him naked on the altar. There are references to other gorings and deaths of bulls, horses, and men, but they are absorbed in the overwhelming affirmation of life contained in these pages: the fertility, abundance, and beauty of the Spanish earth, evoked just as powerfully here as in *The Sun Also*

Rises; the immersion of all the senses in the fiesta sense of life embodied by the ferias of Pamplona, Madrid, Valencia, and so many other towns; the warm camaraderie of friends and aficionados, like the bullfight critic Rafael Hernández and the owner of the hotel in Pamplona, Juanito Quintana ("Que tal Juanito? Que tal, hombre, que tal?"); the sexual presence of women, always in the background. *Death in the Afternoon* is a book about tragedy and death, but even more, it is a book about a still greater mystery, life.

The last chapter of the work is a symbolic trip through Spain and through time—all of Hemingway's experience there between 1923 and 1932. The trip begins where it should: at the Prado in Madrid, the heart and essence of Spain. With the same organic, spontaneous association of images, memories, and ideas that has guided him in the body of the book, the narrator moves back and forth from Madrid to the provinces, and backward and forward in time from the past to the present. He remembers the places he loved most in the capital: the Prado, the streets and cafés full of people after midnight, the bullrings, the old Pensión Aguilar, the bare white mud hills looking toward Carabanchel from Luis Quintanilla's house, the Manzanares River along the Pardo road where he and Franklin swam with the toreros and their cheap whores. Then the towns near and around Madrid: Toledo; La Granja where they practiced capework on the gravelled paths between the shadows of the trees; Barco de Ávila with storks nesting on the houses or wheeling above the mountains.

From Madrid, Hemingway's memory naturally leads him to his other main querencia in Spain—Pamplona. He recalls the first two ferias of San Fermín when he had such a good time and "no one was nasty"; the cafés on the main plaza with all the bootblacks and the fine girls walking by; the Hotel Quintana with its friendly owner, good food, and all the rooms full. Then outside of Pamplona toward the Pyrenees, the landscapes of *The Sun Also Rises*: the countryside the color of ripe wheat; villages with churches and pelota courts; clouds coming across the mountains from the sea; the beech forests of the Irati with "trees like drawings in a child's fairy book"; the water of the river as clear as light; the hot days of summer and the cold mountain nights; the early morning smells and always trees with shade. Then there were all of the simple, natural things with the nobility of objects in a still life painting—the loops of twisted garlic, leather wineskins and saddlebags, rope-soled shoes, earthen pots, wooden pitchforks with branches for tines. If you had all of that, Hemingway said, "then you would have a little of Navarra."

Although Madrid and Navarre dominate this symbolic trip through Spain, other favorite places also appear: Valencia with its ice-cold beer and *horchata*, the smell of burnt powder, the flash and explosion of the *tracas* or fireworks during the feria each July; Saragossa at night on the bridge over the Ebro, the hills of baked clay, the red dust, and the small shade beside the dry rivers in Aragón; Santiago de Compostella in the rain, fishing for trout in the Tambre, the hills and pines of Galicia; the green country of the Basque provinces. Among the major regions of Spain, only Andalusia, Asturias, and Extremadura shine because of their absence.

Since the technical part of the bullfight has been dispatched, the prose of the final chapter is liberated: the sentences become longer and freer, the language more rhythmical and poetic. It is not by chance that portions of the epilogue to *Death in the Afternoon* have been included in an anthology of modern verse, since its language is as concrete, lyrical, and musical as a poem's. Entire sections of the prose can easily be arranged in metrical units. The language is tied together by the repetition of certain key phrases functioning like refrains: "If I could have made this enough of a book," "If it were more of a book," "it should have . . . ," "There ought to be . . . ," "Make all that come true again." These refrains bind together the dozens of memories from the past, evoked in an actual present. Hemingway "makes" the country by recreating all of the specific, sensual images in a living present, as if they would never change; this is the eternal Spain of *The Sun Also Rises*. As in the novel, human beings act out their brief lives against the enduring background of the Spanish earth.

By using the present tense predominantly to recall the past, Hemingway makes it "come true again" for himself and for the reader—in the same way he had recreated the movement and emotion of cape, banderillas, and muleta earlier in the book. Whereas he employed his rhythmic, ecstatic prose to make the bullfight itself in the previous works and in the main chapters of *Death in the Afternoon*, he uses it now to create the emotion of time. Nearly ten years had passed between Hemingway's first visit to

Spain and the writing of the epilogue. He had gone through one marriage and a divorce, remarried, begotten two sons, lost his father, grown from an unknown young journalist to a famous, mature writer. Through a few subtle references, the narrator suggests that things have changed in the world and for him. He admits that he could not get all of the people and places he knew into his book, "nor all of us ourselves as we were then." Pamplona has changed for the worse; modern apartment buildings block the view of the mountains. Some of the trees in the forest of the Irati have been cut down by loggers, polluting the streams and killing the fish. The writer's friend Rafael Hernández says things are so changed that he won't return to Pamplona. Hemingway is wiser than his friend when he says toward the end of the epilogue: "Pamplona is changed, of course, but not as much as we are older." After a drink, things get much the way they were before.

Neither Hemingway nor any other writer can capture all of the complexity of life and death in a single work: "No. It is not enough of a book. . . ." He accepts the limitations of art and the inevitability of change in his own life and in Spain. Although the past can be recreated—in Miró's *Farm* or the epilogue he is writing—it cannot be erased. He, his friends, and family will grow and change, and they will "all be gone before it's changed too much." Even when they are dead, it will rain again in the summer in the north and hawks will nest again in the Cathedral at Santiago. The author will be gone, but the Spanish earth will last; the sun will also rise. Individuals pass on, the species and nature endure. Life does not end; it renews itself.

In the epilogue, the tragic emotion of the bullfight, always related to death, becomes the more universal emotion of human life, whose law is also mortality. The elegiac rhythm of the prose slows to a decrescendo. *Death in the Afternoon* has been transformed, by the music and rhythm of its language, into Hemingway's most personal expression of the tragic sense of life.

Madrid, 1983

"Our father opened in 1931. His father was also a bootmaker. We are the last generation. *Joder*, our children don't want a damn thing to do with this shop."

Félix García Tenorio looks like the photos of his father on the wall—square jaw, shiny black hair, an ironic gleam in his small brown eyes. He works standing up behind the scarred wooden counter in his smock, stenciling a pair of high *polainas* or leggings from a piece of calf skin. His brother Carlos takes a pack of cigarettes from his shirt pocket and offers you one.

"*Tabaco negro*," he says. You do not smoke often, but you know enough to accept the Spanish male's token of friendship.

Carlos lights your cigarette, then his own. He is quieter than his brother, more pensive. He has whitening hair and he wears rimless glasses on a cord around his neck. The dark-tobacco smoke smells good mingled with the odor of fresh tanned leather.

"Hemingwáy," Félix sighs, placing the accent on the last syllable like most Spaniards. "How much has changed since he first walked through those doors."

"When was that?" you ask him.

"Not long after we opened here. My father made the hunting boots for the first African safari, then much later for the other wife and the other safari—after the Civil War. Madrid was very different in the early days."

"How?"

Félix makes a flicking motion with his wrist, as if to say That is a long, long story. "Why don't you sit down, Eduardo?"

You walk across the small room, the floor creaking under your feet, and sit in a chair against the wall.

Félix takes a deep breath. "Madrid was like a large village then—*la real villa*, the royal village. Everybody knew one another. Our clients were friends—always keeping the proper distance, of course. Hemingwáy was a friend too. He would come in to order a pair of boots, we would

Carlos and Félix García Tenorio, Madrid, 1983. Hemingway called their father,
Félix Sr., "the best shoemaker in the world."
(Photo Gonzalo de la Serna)

take his measurements, then go out for a drink together next door. A few days later, he would return to see the progress of the boots and to exchange impressions. The uppers would be cut, notched and pinked by then, wetted and placed on a mold to stretch the hide. And so on. By the time the boots were ready for their inauguration, we had become friends. Can you believe it, our best boots cost around 150 pesetas in those days. Like these, in for repair."

He holds up a two-foot high boot, the leather worn smooth and almost black, with a zipper up the side and a delicate but simple filigree along the top. Félix gives you the boot. It is as soft as a glove and waterproofed with grease.

"How old is this pair?"

Carlos whistles through his teeth as he taps a pair of soles with a hammer: "Who knows, maybe fifteen years?"

"And how much does a pair of boots like this cost nowadays?"

"Too much. Twenty-seven thousand pesetas."

You calculate silently: almost $400.

Félix lights up a small cigar. "All that is gone now, the low prices and Hemingwáy and the old Madrid. It had already changed when my father died thirteen years ago. He would tell the story of a man who rushed in here one day around 1965, saying 'Hurry up and take my specifications because I am double-parked outside.' You couldn't tell if he had come to order a pair of boots or to pull a holdup. '*No puede ser!*' my father would cry, 'This cannot be! One must be more gentlemanly, *Hay que ser más caballeros!*' But it is that way and it has become much worse."

A man enters, saying "Buenos días." He lights a cigarette and talks about a soccer match on television last night. As he talks with Félix and Carlos, you fondle the leather of the old boot. The man finally says "*Hasta mañana*" and walks out.

"That is what Hemingwáy found in Madrid—*la convivencia*," Félix says. "The living together with others, the conviviality. It has almost disappeared with him."

Carlos says "Come here, I want to show you something."

He leads you through a low archway toward the inside of the building. You pass into a small room with limestone walls, a weak light, an odor of time and moisture. Shelves on the walls are full of wooden shoe molds, outdated telephone directories, boxes and supplies.

"We call it the cave," Carlos says. "It was the kitchen when we used to live in the shop." He points to a stack of huge, flat, black, leather-bound volumes that look like old atlases. "In these books are the feet of half a century." He takes one tome and carries it back to the front of the shop where there is more light.

Carlos drops the book with a smack on the counter and begins turning the yellowed pages. Each has the outline of a foot on it, with specifications scribbled around the margins. Carlos turns the pages slowly as he remembers: "Ex-Minister of the Interior . . . the Marquis of Villaverde . . . a horsewoman from California . . ." He comes to a page and stops. You see the familiar signature: "Ernesto Hemingway / Hotel Florida / Madrid."

"The feet of kings, nobles, politicians, actors, bullfighters, hunters from all over the world are in these books," Carlos says. "We even make boots for Japanese customers now."

Félix laughs and a picaresque smile forms on his face. "They are all equal when they walk in here, from the king on down. Two feet with corns and toenails."

You both laugh. "In America," you tell them, "you would have expanded your business with more shops and employees."

"We don't want that," Carlos says quickly, almost snapping. "*Eso no es vida*—that is not life. Already we have more than enough work to keep us and one helper busy, and we do not starve. My brother has a car but I am one of the rare birds—a madrileño without a car. Félix only drives his Seat on weekends. We are much happier on our feet. We live in the Plaza de la Paja just five minutes away. We walk to work in the morning at eight, close around one o'clock, walk home for lunch and a rest. There is nobody on earth who can take my siesta from me—nobody. We walk back here to reopen about four-thirty in the afternoon, then close at eight. In the old days my father stayed open until ten or eleven at night, and he never closed except Sundays, Easter, and Christmas. Now we close on Saturdays, Sundays, holidays, the whole month of August."

The electric light in the ceiling flickers for a second.

"Fluctuation in the *puñetera* current," Félix says. "The landlord lets it happen so we will leave and he can raze the building to put up a high-rise. Speculation."

You think about it: three generations of craftsmen whose work is admired all over the world, yet they still do not own the shop where they have worked for fifty years.

You remember what Félix said about their children. "Your kids don't want to work here?"

"*Coño*," says Félix. "In a way I can't blame them. They might change their minds some day when they find out how difficult it is to get a job in Spain now. But it will be too late. You have to suck this trade with your mother's milk as we say. Sorry for the vulgarity."

He puts down the knife he has used to cut the leggings. Walking out from behind the counter, he asks: "Would you like to go next door for a little glass of wine?"

A Clean,
Well-Lighted Place

---

nly six months after *Death in the Afternoon*, Hemingway published one of the best short stories he ever wrote. Set in a Spanish city, perhaps Madrid, it had been fermenting in his head ever since he read a newspaper article in Valencia, during the summer of 1925 or 1926, about a widower who had thrown himself off a tower because he was getting old and because his granddaughter considered him to be a bother. Hemingway had included the episode in a satirical poem about Dorothy Parker, "To a Tragic Poetess," using the old man and several Spanish bullfighters as examples of authentic suffering and despair in contrast to the literary posturing of tragedy by the New York writer. Characteristically, Hemingway changed the granddaughter to a niece, and omitted the suicide or "wow" at the end of his story.

"A Clean, Well-Lighted Place" is closely related to the themes of death, pride, and honor developed in the bullfighting book. It is Hemingway's most concise fictional expression of the Spanish sense of nada and the tragic feeling of life.

Late one night in a café, an elderly man is seated alone at a table, slightly drunk. The younger of two waiters is anxious to get rid of him so that he can close the café and go home, where his wife is waiting for him in bed. The older waiter is more sympathetic: he explains to his companion that the customer has lost his wife, and has recently tried to hang himself; he was cut down by his niece, who feared for the well-being of his soul. The gentleman conducts himself in the café with pride and dignity in spite of his anguish and drunkenness. Against the wishes of his senior, the younger waiter makes the customer pay and leave. Then the older waiter walks to a bar himself, thinking about the man, understanding his feelings of loneliness, despair, and nothingness, making the well-known parody of the Lord's Prayer and Hail Mary: "Our nada who art in nada . . . Hail nothing full of nothing . . ." As he drinks a glass of wine, the waiter has become the last customer himself at another establishment, taking on the role and identity of the old man: he too likes staying up late, knows the comfort of drinking at a well-lit café with a certain cleanness and order, and dreads returning to his lonely room where insomnia will keep him awake until daylight.

In an essay written many years later, Hemingway would recall this story and realize he had gone as far as possible there in applying his iceberg theory of fiction. "I really had luck. I left out everything. That is about as far as you can go. . . ." In order to approach the piece, we should know what it was that Hemingway left out.

To begin, the scene of the story and the central metaphor of the title, the clean and well-lit café, is an obvious example of the Spanish concern for ambiente—the atmosphere or ambiance that makes a place livable or acceptable at a given time. In one of the best treatments of ambiente by a foreigner, James Michener says:

> A Spaniard would willingly travel an extra fifty miles to find a spot with ambiente. . . . What bestows ambiente upon a place? I don't know. But I have often been with Spaniards who have walked into what outwardly appeared to be a rather ordinary place and have been struck instantly by its charm. "This place has ambiente!" they have cried, and in that split second I have known that it did.

In Hemingway's story, both the old man and the senior waiter know their café has ambiente. Not only is it immaculate and well-illuminated; it also has a terrace with tables under a tree where the man sits. He knows, with the sixth sense of so many Spaniards, that even his table has a particular ambiente. He receives pleasure from the breeze and from the shadows made by the leaves against the electric light. In the daytime the street in front of the café is dusty, but in the evening the dew settles the dust. Although he is deaf, the old man feels the difference between the hum of activity and the quiet peacefulness of the night. From his table under the tree on the terrace, he can dominate a view of the street. He is like a bull in his querencia, or like his creator—Hemingway at his strategically located tables in bars and restaurants in France, Italy, Spain, Key West, later in Cuba.

The rather stupid young waiter does not understand that a place with ambiente can help a man preserve his sense of dignity in times of pain and duress. He suggests the customer could go to one of the bars or bodegas that stay open all night, or buy a bottle and drink at home. The older waiter tries to explain that drinking alone or at the other places is not the same: they do not have ambiente, they do not give the human comfort or the esthetic pleasure of a well-situated, airy, light, clean café. The hurried young waiter is too overconfident to perceive what his colleague and the customer understand so well. "We are of two different kinds," says his friend. The young waiter seems to belong to another age, to a generation of the future—one that has, in fact, inherited the earth.

If the reader does not see the cultural context of ambiente in "A Clean, Well-Lighted Place," the story lacks much of its resonance. Following his iceberg theory, Hemingway did not bother to make it explicit. Almost the same could be said of the Spanish word and feeling of nada, the other central metaphor in the work. Against the neatness, light, and order of the café stands the dark chaos of the night, despair, nothingness, death. Like his characters, the old man and the middle-aged waiter, Hemingway had experienced insomnia, nightmarish fears, feelings of anguish and death after his wounding at Fossalta. When he became acquainted with the etchings of Goya during his first prolonged stay in Spain, all of these dimly felt emotions probably crystallized in the Spanish word and sense of nada: one of the painter's famous pieces from his *Disasters of War*, entitled "Nada" or "Ello dirá" ("The event will tell"), shows a specter apparently flying out of the grave, despair on its cavernous face, carrying a white page or book with the word "Nada" inscribed on it. In the background, grotesque faces of people and animals appear in a gloomy atmosphere that recalls the "black paintings" from Goya's country house outside Madrid, known as *La Quinta del Sordo* ("The Deaf Man's Villa"; like Hemingway's gentleman in the short story, the painter was deaf toward the end of his life). The specter's message in the etching could refer to the nothingness beyond the grave or to the nada of life on earth.

Hemingway probably became familiar with the existential sense of nada through Goya's etching, but he must have learned around the same time the word's importance at other levels of Spanish life. Walking down the streets of Madrid, Gerald Brenan noted:

> One will hear, like shots fired off at intervals, a stream of *no no no nada nada nada*. These people seem to be always refusing or rejecting

something. If the language of Provence used to be known as the *langue d'oc* and that of France as the *langue d'oïl* and that of Italy as the *langue de si,* then decidedly Spanish should be called the *langue de no.*

Hemingway captured this colloquial presence of negation in the older waiter's parody of the Lord's Prayer: "he knew it all was nada y pues nada y nada y pues nada. . . . but deliver us from nada; pues nada."

Like the word cojones used in *Death in the Afternoon* in the Spanish rather than in translation, nada has a sound and meaning that are different and more forceful than its equivalent in other languages. In addition to its everyday use as a pronoun and adverb described by Brenan, when used as a noun the Spanish has an abstract or philosophical meaning of "not being, or the absolute lack of all being." Hemingway is dealing in fictive terms with the greatest of all existential and philosophical questions here, that of being and non-being. It was the question treated more formally and systematically by Heidegger in his monumental *Being and Time,* published six years before "A Clean, Well-Lighted Place."

Hemingway did not like to use too many foreign terms in his English prose, but in the case of nada he knew that no word or expression in his own language could render the sound and sense of the original. At least since Spain's great religious writers of the Golden Age opposed the nothingness of life without God to the fullness of divine communion in the mystic experience, nada has had a uniquely poignant meaning in Spanish. Spaniards seem to have an almost physical sense of the word and the feelings it evokes. At the Diego de León subway station in Madrid, I saw this graffito in the spring of 1984:

Vida
Libertad
Amor
Locura
Muerte
NADA

("Life Liberty Love Madness Death NADA.") The six words form a trenchant commentary on human existence which we might see as a hypothetical summary of the old man's life in "A Clean, Well-Lighted Place."

After the vitality, freedom, and love of youth and maturity, he is alone in a kind of living death that will end in suicide. The loss of his wife; the young girl and the soldier who pass by his table outside the café; the hurried waiter's insinuation that "A wife would be no good to him now" are so many reminders that the old customer will no longer enjoy love. It makes little difference. The man and the middle-aged waiter know that love and the other things of the world may help to distract a man from his awareness of nada, but once he has felt it, he will never be the same. As Carlos Baker has said, it is "so huge, terrible, overbearing, inevitable, and omnipresent that, once experienced, it can never be forgotten." Many lesser men, like the hurried waiter, live in the midst of nada, surrounded by it, without ever feeling its presence. They are those who, in Heidegger's terms, forfeit their authentic being to the petty concerns of everyday existence. They are those who live in constant flight from themselves, in self-betrayal of their human destiny as creatures who will die. In short, they lack the tragic feeling of life.

On the other hand, there are some men, like the old gentleman and the middle-aged waiter, who have seen death and nada in themselves and in the world, who have confronted their own authentic being with honesty and directness. In solitude and silence they have come face to face with their own nothingness, and have shaped their lives in the light, or the darkness, of that encounter. Like the old gentleman, they may have committed the official sin of attempted suicide; like the middle-aged waiter, they may have blasphemed and parodied consecrated prayers. But they are the true seekers, they are the daring ones who are not afraid to see death and nada as the ground and end of life. For this reason they must be so demanding about the kind of place where they spend the evening. It must be quiet ("Certainly you don't want music," thinks the older waiter), and it must have a certain neatness, order, and light. If Hemingway has been criticized for failing to deal with the introspective, meditative realm of human experience, he came very close to it in "A Clean, Well-Lighted Place": the old gentleman and the middle-aged waiter are mystics of the senses in a dark night of the soul whose only illumination is not the divine flame but an electric light. They embody the tragic sense. As Heidegger would say, they are "on the track of the holy"; they are not the lost souls but the saved, in a world without salvation.

Critics have argued about how to classify the main characters of "A Clean, Well-Lighted Place" with regard to Hemingway's other protagonists. In contrast to most of his previous fiction, it has not one but two central characters. The old gentleman and the sympathetic waiter belong to the group of those early Hemingway characters, like Nick Adams and Jake Barnes, who "need a light for the night." Both the old man and the good waiter also have much in common—nearly everything I would say —with the writer's other Hispanic heroes. We need to remember that the model for the gentleman, the eighty-year-old suicide from Valencia, is aligned with Maera (one of Hemingway's earliest code heroes) in "To a Tragic Poetess." Like Maera and like Pedro Romero in *The Sun Also Rises*, the old man and the middle-aged waiter are more intuitive than cerebral: at his table on the terrace, the gentleman feels "the difference" between the day and night, while the waiter, for his part, understands but cannot explain the difference made by the light and the shadows of the leaves. At the end of the story, he goes to another bar for a drink, in this way identifying himself with the old man, who will go home "without thinking further" and will be kept awake all night by insomnia. The gentleman and the sympathetic waiter may seem to differ from the bullfighter-heroes in that they do not display their courage in public, but the old man has faced death as much as a torero by attempting to hang himself; more important, he and the waiter have an inner courage that enables them to face the nada of their own lives. Because they rely more on intuition than on reason, both characters are men of few words (of course the gentleman's deafness inhibits conversation). Like most of Hemingway's heroes, they are suspicious of too much talk; it is not for nothing that the older waiter's monologue on nada is unspoken.

Finally, these two brothers of the night possess that other necessary quality in the writer's Hispanic men—dignity. Hemingway would say a few years later that "decorum and dignity rank above courage as the virtues most highly prized in Spain." As he had done with the feeling of nada, he locates and pins the idea of dignity to the map by a sort of triangulation process. The corners of the triangle are the gentleman and the two waiters. The younger thinks "An old man is a nasty thing." "Not always," responds his middle-aged companion. "This old man is clean. He drinks without spilling. Even now, drunk. Look at him." But the hurried waiter does not want to look; unlike the other two, he does not know how to live right with his eyes. He is too confident in his youth, too self-sufficient in his ignorance, too rushed to stop and look, to see. Unlike his colleague, he does not see or care that the gentleman drinks without spilling a drop in spite of being "a little drunk." The old man is clean, he dresses well and walks "unsteadily but with dignity." He retains his self-possession, treats the insolent waiter courteously, and like all the Spaniards admired by Hemingway in life and fiction, he practices the ancient virtue of generosity. Even after being mistreated by the waiter, he leaves a half-peseta tip. (In the early 1930s, one could live well in Spain for about eight pesetas a day.) In contrast to his dignified, polite, generous customer, the younger waiter is sloppy—he angrily spills the brandy when serving the old man—discourteous, and stingy of his time. Unlike his older colleague, he feels no compassion for the gentleman nor for the other brethren of the night who may need a clean, well-lit place.

What is the source of dignity in a person like the old man who has lost so much and even attempted suicide? This too is what Hemingway left out of the story, but he had put it in *Death in the Afternoon*. In that book he called pride the strongest characteristic of the Spanish people. It is a matter of pride and pundonor—a point of honor—not to show weakness or cowardice. Although the old gentleman would rather die than live, he has such a great sense of self-respect that if he must continue living, it will be with a certain pride. More important than pundonor or the social manifestation of pride is the intimate, inalienable sense of honor which resides within a man or woman, and which the old gentleman and the sympathetic waiter possess. They know that honor "is as real a thing as water, wine, or olive oil." They know that the real nada is not oblivion after death, but the emptiness of life on earth when everything has gone, including honor. Like bullfighters, they too exhibit a kind of "grace under pressure."

Just a few years after publishing "A Clean, Well-Lighted Place," Hemingway wrote to John Dos Passos:

> I felt simply awful . . . about six weeks ago so started fishing and hell in no time felt wonderful and full of juice. . . . I felt that gigantic bloody emptiness and nothingness like couldn't ever fuck, fight write and was all for death. . . .

The old gentleman in the story also feels the great emptiness and nothingness, but he cannot go fishing in the Gulf Stream to recover his juice. He has lost his youth, but Hemingway, in middle-age like the good waiter, recognized the dignity and beauty of a venerable man. In France, Italy, and Spain he had seen old gentlemen, often well dressed within their means, who frequented a favorite café to have a drink, read the papers, talk to friends, or simply to be there. When he read the Valencia newspaper article in 1925 or 1926, he identified his own experience of such habitués with the eighty-year-old widower who had committed suicide, as the sympathetic waiter identifies himself with the customer in "A Clean, Well-Lighted Place." Even at thirty-four, Hemingway had the imagination to "always think of other people" and to "get into somebody else's head." Unlike the younger waiter and the youth-seeking Scott Fitzgerald, Ernest believed that guns, saddles, and people are not peaches: they get better when they are worn and without the bloom. If continued far enough, any story must end in death, but only when a man retains his dignity can his death be tragic. "I've known some very wonderful people who even though they were going directly toward the grave . . . managed to put up a very fine performance enroute," he once said. "A Clean, Well-Lighted Place" tells of two such people. Hemingway's next great novel, *For Whom the Bell Tolls*, would tell of others.

Sierra de Guadarrama, 1984

It is good climbing in the cool fresh morning. The trail is used by woodcutters and forest rangers and the dirt is worn smooth, now lightly moistened from the dew. You have left La Granja behind with its long gravelled paths between the shadows of the trees. Ahead the mountains look very clear with timber up their slopes, outcroppings of granite, and meadows above the timber. There is still snow on the peak of Peñalara, highest in the Guadarrama. The sky is empty now and high and clear.

The old man stops and points to the foothills sloping down toward the town of San Ildefonso de la Granja. You can see the slate roof of the royal palace above the green of the pine trees.

"Down those hills came the attack of the 14th International Brigade on the 31 of May."

"In 1937, no?"

"Yes, in '37. How shall I ever forget it?"

Ángel Pérez Escudero is a short and solid old man in a black peasant's smock and grey corduroy trousers. He has thick white hair combed straight back from a low forehead; the wrinkled, wind- and sun-burned face of a man who has worked in the open air all his life; small, sunken brown eyes; black eyebrows; a prominent, aquiline nose; a few teeth. A fine head. If you should take him to a barber and a tailor in Madrid, Ángel would resemble a diplomat. He has the natural nobility of so many humble Spaniards.

"With luck we shall reach the cave in a quarter of an hour," he says. He is breathing heavily from the climb.

You take the military map from your pack and spread it on the ground. The Cueva del Monje is marked at the end of the forest trail, about four kilometers from La Granja.

"Is this the only cave in the area that you know, Ángel?"

"Yes, without doubt," he says. "I was born in these mountains and I have climbed them since much before the war. My father was a wood-

Ángel Pérez Escudero, veteran of the battle described by Hemingway in
For Whom the Bell Tolls, *San Ildefonso de la Granja, 1984.*
(Photo Gonzalo de la Serna)

cutter and I would accompany him and his donkey into the sierra for firewood."

You fold up the map and begin to walk again. There are wildflowers along the trail—red poppies, daisies, purple thyme blossoms. In the meadows higher up you can see splotches of yellow gorse and broom. Poplar trees that leafed out more than a month ago in Madrid still have the new yellow green here.

"How is the life of the people in La Granja?" you ask him as you climb.

"Something barbarous," he answers. "Much disemployment until the rich arrive from Madrid in July and August. Then for sixty days of the vacations there is much concentration of the automobile and the people. When the madrileños depart the cold returns, always the cold. Some years the snow never melts on the peak of Peñalara."

"You never go to Madrid?"

"Uniquely when my sons take me for a baptism or a burial. In Madrid rules nothing but greed and money and the most grand *carajo*."

You have come out in a high meadow. You ask him: "The new democracy has not changed the life of the people?"

"Nay, not even in joke. I have lived under the old monarchy and the Republic and Franco and now the democracy. The life of the people continues the same. Here it is, the Cave of the Monk."

You look around for the large opening in the rock that you have imagined, but there is none. The old man is pointing to a small granite ledge at the base of a hill, only large enough for one or two men to crouch in.

"But *viejo*, I am looking for a cave with space for people to live and sleep and cook in."

"Nay, there is no such cave in these mountains, not now nor never."

You know he is telling the truth. Hem invented Pablo's cave for the *Bell* the way he invented so many other things in his life and in his books. You can't work too close to the world. The only writing that is any good is what you invent, what you imagine. That makes everything round and whole and solid, he said. Don't describe it, create it, make it.

You laugh at yourself, taking the wineskin off your shoulder. You unscrew the tit and offer it to him.

"Many thanks," he says, lifting the bota to let the wine spurt into the back of his mouth. He hands it to you and you drink the slightly tar-tasting wine from the leather bag.

You ask the old man: "If there are no caves, where did the guerrillas in the mountains live during the war?"

"Wherever they could. In the houses of those who sympathized, in empty farmhouses and barns, in shepherds' huts, in the abandoned forest stations."

"Do you wish to continue hiking to the bridge?"

"Let us continue. From here the bridge is uphill. There is the only badness."

You begin to climb in the late May morning. The sky is still high and clear but clouds blow in from the north and great shadows darken the pine groves. The old man leads with sure feet.

When you reach a rise above a creek, he points up the hill on our right. "*Inglés*," he whispers.

There on the hillside, head-on, wide, black, looking straight toward us, big, thick-necked, ears twitching, wonder-eared, swaying as the nose searches for the wind, is a rabbit. He looks huge, no more like a domestic rabbit than a bunny is like an old, tawny-hided, horse-built-in-the-flanks jack rabbit. We stand there perfectly quiet, Ángel holding his hand on mine, watching him, only eight feet away, poised, beautiful, fullnecked, a dark ruff on his neck, his ears up, trembling all over as his nostrils widen with our scent.

Ángel whispers, "In my life have I seen such a hare. It is a cathedral of a hare."

The rabbit turns and scurries into the woods.

"Would that we had carried a shotgun, Inglés."

"I am not inglés, old man. I am American."

"But you speak the English, do you not?"

"Yes."

"Then you are inglés."

"Let us commence to climb again."

"In accord."

You climb up through the pine forest that covers the mountainside. There is no trail, but you are working up and around the face of the mountain with the old man ahead. Big white and gray clouds move across the sky from Old Castile.

"It could rain on us," he says. "Less bad that we have come thus far before the raining."

You hear the remote sound of an engine, look up and see the tiny silver plane, fast-moving across the mountain sky.

"Do many airplanes fly around here, *Español?*"

"Few" he answers, turning his head to look at you.

"And during the war?"

"Many. The Nationalist aeroplanes used to pass directly over here on their bombing runs from Segovia to Madrid. Now must we climb in seriousness to reach the bridge. In this of the bridge there is much climbing uphill."

You pass great boulders of moss-covered granite among the pines. The climbing is now more difficult and your thigh muscles are twitchy from the steepness. Suddenly you have reached the pass.

You look at the valley below, stretching from the dark pine-covered peaks down across the high meadows to a stream rushing between gray rocks. You both breathe deeply of the clear air that smells of pine needles. You offer him the wineskin and he drinks deeply. He returns it and you drink. The wine feels cold against your throat.

"Let us now descend, Inglés. With luck we shall reach the bridge shortly."

It begins to rain.

"There has only lacked this," the old man says. "I defecate in our luck and in the milk of the Great Whore who has brought this rain."

The weather has made a sudden mountain change and you are in the shadows now, feeling the new cold in your bones as you walk down into the valley, the wind blowing, it getting colder, through yellow gorse in the high meadows in the thin rain, then great outcroppings of granite as the steepness lessens, some of the slabs leaning together to form shelters large enough for several men to stand in—this is what Hem had in mind in the novel, you think. Then you hear the stream and ahead through the trunks of the pines you see a flash of water.

"There is the stream of the bridge," the old man says. "Now we have only to follow the course of the stream down to the bridge in the gorge where the road passes over."

The water rushes down between grassy banks through gray rocks and boulders from the peaks of snow above. You look at the water of the stream, where Pilar washed her feet. Nearby Robert Jordan made love to María the day the earth moved under them.

The old man leads you down the gorge along the bed of the stream through the pine trees and poplars that grow down to the edge of the rushing water. Then you see the granite of the bridge ahead and it is large and tall-arched against the steep emptiness of the gorge.

"The bridge," says the old man. "Puente La Cantina."

"How do you know that this is the bridge of which I spoke to you before?"

"I know what I know," he says. "This is the only bridge over the road from Madrid to La Granja and Segovia which was here during the war and which can support the weight of the camions and of the tanks and of the artillery of which you spoke to me, Inglés."

"But I spoke to you of a steel bridge."

"Not now nor never has there been a bridge of steel over this stream nor along this road, Inglés."

"So Hem made up the steel bridge too," you say in English.

"What tongue do you speak, Inglés? What does that signify in Christian?"

"Never mind, Español. I am going to pick some of the watercress and wild mint on the stream bank."

"In accord."

You place your wineskin and your pack on the grass. Then you step onto the slippery boulders to cross the stream, pick a double handful from a thick bed of watercress, wash the muddy roots clean in the clear coldness of the current, and return to the bank where the old man sits on the grass.

You offer him a handful and you both eat of the clean, cool green leaves and of the crisp, peppery-tasting stalks.

"Now shall I harvest some wild mint on the bank of the stream for the use of your wife in her cooking, viejo."

You step on the mossy boulders again and you are slipping sudden and going down, completely wet, water achingly cold on your behind, rising to your feet now and stepping out of the stream, wiping off glasses, Ángel worried, you soaked and your boots squelching water.

"Inglés, you will catch a pneumonia of the *Gran Puta* if you do not return rapidly to my house."

You follow him up around the bridge to the road where you commence walking fast downhill along the shoulder, you ashamed at having fallen

Doña Ciriaca, wife of Ángel Pérez Escudero, San Ildefonso de la Granja, 1984. (Photo Gonzalo de la Serna)

in the stream, your back cold against the sticking wetness of the shirt, he more worried than ever and feeling responsible, swearing by the milk of the Great Whore, it getting better as you walk faster on the asphalt of the road, the socks and boots no longer squishing, it still raining thinly but no longer cold, Ángel ahead of you, down the winding curves of the road toward the bottom of the valley with the River Eresma on the left where the trees are heavy and tall and the pass, which above had been a narrow gash, opens to a plain and the town of Valsaín and the sawmill until you see, ahead on your right, the slate-covered roofs of La Granja.

Ángel leads you through the big wrought-iron gates of the town, walking on the cobbled streets to his whitewashed house at the end of the Calle de los Guardas.

"Welcome to your home, Inglés."

You have reached home, all right. Doña Ciriaca, four feet six inches tall and named after a medieval saint, receives you with consternation and wringing of hands. You have never seen a face as lined and grooved by wrinkles as hers; there are no such faces in America anymore. Her hands are red and tender-looking from constant washing and cleaning with cold mountain water. Doña Ciriaca stokes the old iron stove, brings you a towel, telling you to dry off while she goes to prepare a hot meal, and you hear her calling on God, Jesus, the Virgin, and all the saints.

Your clothes are heavy in their wetness and you rub yourself hard with the towel by the warmth of the stove. Ángel brings what must be his best clothes for you, the wedding-baptism-funeral, Sunday walk-in-the-plaza suit of a small-town Spaniard—baggy boxer shorts, wool slacks five sizes too big bulking loosely around your butt, tight around the ankles like a zoot suit of the 1950s, a starched white shirt with damascene Toledo cuff links, pointed black shoes like a Pachuco or a mafioso. Doña Ciriaca puts your clothes out to dry on the balcony, it sunny outside now in the afternoon light, you and Ángel sitting down to eat while the woman serves, drinking two bottles of Valdepeñas *tinto* with hot *cocido* made of small pieces of veal, ham, chicken, blood sausage, garbanzos, potatoes, cabbage, you feeling warmer, the two of you eating, not speaking, in the Spanish way.

He wants you to stay for brandy but you must catch the last bus to Madrid, saying goodbye to Doña Ciriaca and thanking her, she giving you the almost dry clothes in a bundle and saying, Be careful and may you not catch a pneumonia, you promising to bring back Ángel's clothes next Saturday, then out in the too bright sun of the plaza with the old man barely in time to get on the bus.

You embrace him and climb aboard, feeling stupid but not caring a goddamn in your zoot suit, opening the window to say goodbye.

"Viejo, you were enormous in the climbing."

"It was nothing," he says. "You were immense in the falling in the stream. Never would I tire in saluting you nor in giving you farewell. Take much care of yourself, Eduardo, Ten cuidado."

The driver starts the engine of the old bus and you see Doña Ciriaca running to the window, holding aloft your still wet socks, "These had you forgotten," you reaching out to take them and holding her cool hand for a second in farewell, the bus moves slowly, and you turn around to see the old couple alone in the plaza of the town, waving goodbye to you.

That was how it was on May 31, 1984, forty-seven years to the day after the Republican offensive on the Segovia front in the Spanish

Civil War. If you don't believe it, you can always go to the town of San Ildefonso de la Granja, forty-eight kilometers northwest of Madrid. Go to Calle de los Guardas number 10, the last house on your right. You'll find Ángel Pérez Escudero and Doña Ciriaca there, living on his government pension of $114 a month.

11   *The Undiscovered*

           Country

The men of my generation have Spain in their hearts . . . they bear it like a bad wound. Because of it . . . they have discovered . . . that one can be right and yet be vanquished, that force can subdue the spirit, that there are times when courage does not have its reward. It is this, no doubt, which explains why so many men all over the world feel the Spanish drama as a personal tragedy.
—Albert Camus

There is a truth that overpowers the fastidious judgment.
—Richard Ford

Before the outbreak of the Spanish Civil War, Hemingway was one of the few well-known writers who had not been affected by the polarization of international politics in the 1930s. He held that there was no right or left in literature—"only good and bad writing." Privately he admitted that he couldn't stand "*any* bloody government," no matter how worthy its goals. His sole political belief was in liberty. First he would look after himself and his work, then his family, finally his neighbor. For the state he cared nothing. This individualistic, almost tribal set of priorities was very similar to that of many Spaniards. Gerald Brenan has noted that the people of Spain "live by a tribal or client system, which makes it a moral duty for them to favor their friends at the expense of the State. . . . That is the first law of this country, and it was as much observed during the rule of the Republic as it is today."

Strangely enough, it was also the "Spanish thing" that motivated Hemingway to take a clear political position for the first time in his life. Some of the writers and intellectuals who traveled to Spain during the conflict underwent religious conversions, among them W. H. Auden and Simone Weil. Hemingway had already undergone his quasi-religious "Spanish conversion" in the spring and summer of 1923. During the first year of the Civil War he experienced another sort of conversion—to political and social consciousness—at the same time turning away from the Catholic Church and ceasing to believe in personal salvation. He soon realized Spain was a proving ground for international fascism and that if the democracies did not act, there would be a world war to pay. He joined a political cause for the first time, contributing and collecting money for the Republic, traveling to and from Madrid, to Paris, New York, Washington, D.C., and even Hollywood, giving the only speeches of his entire career, writing articles in favor of the Loyalists against General Franco and his German-Italian allies.

Just as Scott Fitzgerald said half-seriously that Ernest needed a new wife for each of his major novels, so might we say he needed a new war. When the Spanish army revolted against the legally elected government of the Republic in July 1936, Hemingway had not published a novel for almost seven years. His marriage to Pauline was already foundering. He was now a prosperous man of letters, and his hobnobbing with the rich in Key West had begun to nag his conscience. Then the Spanish war came along. It gave him a reason for returning to his favorite country and committing himself to a political cause without selling out to the "ideology boys." His dedication to the Spanish Republic was as much an expression of his love for the people, and an attempt to save the experience of his young manhood in Spain, as it was a political commitment.

Hemingway's involvement in the Spanish Civil War produced dozens of newspaper articles, five or six short stories, a play, a novel, and a film. So much did the peninsula and the war dominate his life that a decade later he would refer back to the period as "the Spain years." His experience in the country since the early 1920s had made him an old Spanish hand. He would have hated to miss a major campaign in the peninsula "worse than anything in the world." Hemingway realized that experience in war, especially of the civil variety, was invaluable to a writer. He had participated in the other major international conflict of his time, World War I, and he did not want to let this one go. As Cyril Connolly said, Ernest was the one person who could write the great book about the Spanish war. Hemingway knew it; most of what he did between 1936 and 1939 was a preparation for that book—*For Whom the Bell Tolls*.

Unlike other famous authors, such as André Malraux, Hemingway did not pull out of Spain to write "gigantic masterpisses" before the outcome of the war became clear. He did everything in his power to aid the cause of the Republic without compromising his work. He stuck it out for the duration, being careful to separate politics and journalism from his fiction, salting away enough experience for a book that would have the real "old stuff." He called it the most important thing he had ever done. It was the time in his career when he had to write a "real one." It was a real one, *For Whom the Bell Tolls*, possibly his best, surely his fullest, deepest novel.

Because Hemingway has been accused by Francoist historians and sympathizers of not knowing the terrain or the facts of the war, it should be established right away that he had traveled the Guadarrama Mountains on foot, on horseback, and by motorcar, and that he based his novel on an actual Loyalist offensive of May 31, 1937. When I hiked the scene of the book in late May 1984, more than forty years after the publication of the novel, the accuracy of the book's depiction of terrain, vegetation, and weather was uncanny. Of course Hemingway invented Pablo's cave and changed the stone bridge over the Madrid-Segovia road to one of steel, but nearly all other details tally with the *Bell*: a brook joins the main stream of the pass at the bridge where it leaps in white water down a deep gorge through rocks and boulders; the road makes a turn and swings out of sight around a curve below; there are roadmenders' huts above and below the spot, and even a sawmill—not at the bridge but several kilometers down the pass. Hemingway based his scenery meticulously on a real place with specific weather and flora, which he had engraved on his memory in precise detail. Wherever necessary, he invented to enhance the scenery and the action—the cave, a steel-girdered bridge, the displaced sawmill. He followed his own advice of writing only what he knew about, while leaving the imagination free to recast and invent on the basis of experience in order to "make it round and whole and solid." As Ramón Buckley has said, the country depicted in *For Whom the Bell Tolls* is neither Republican nor Nationalist, fantasy nor reality, but an original synthesis, a "third Spain."

The setting of the novel on the northern slopes of the Guadarrama, with snow-covered peaks and bracing air, looks back to other mountain retreats: Burguete in *The Sun Also Rises* and the Alpine sanctuary where Frederic

Henry and Catherine Barkley enjoy their short happiness together in *A Farewell to Arms*. As in those novels, there is a contrast between the highlands and the cities of the plain pointed out by Carlos Baker—Pamplona, Milan, here Madrid. In the *Bell*, Guadarrama is a clean, well-lighted place where nature has not been spoiled, in contrast to besieged Madrid, a city of which the protagonist Robert Jordan has fond memories but also the scene of the international intrigue and espionage Hemingway showed in his play *The Fifth Column*. In the mountains, time seems to pass more slowly, marked only by the movement of sun, stars, and moon. Here the guerrillas of Pilar and Pablo's band live in contact with the earth and sky as men and women have lived for centuries. The mountains present an ennobling scenery appropriate to the innate dignity of the Spanish peasants who have sought refuge there in wartime. Except for their modern weapons, many of them manufactured by the industrial countries outside of Spain, the characters in the novel lead a simple, primitive life. (One of the partisans is in fact named Primitivo.) Like the Indians of Hemingway's early fiction, these people are noble savages surviving in the twentieth century. The American dynamiter Robert Jordan will teach them something about military discipline and the techniques of modern warfare; in turn, they will teach him how to live in greater touch with nature, with his own body, senses and mind, and to achieve a more spontaneous, integrated vision of the world.

We should not neglect at the outset the most obvious difference between *For Whom the Bell Tolls* and Hemingway's other great novel of war, *A Farewell to Arms*. While the earlier work describes a major campaign between large armies, the *Bell* depicts nonregular, partisan action. Hemingway knew that the word and the practice of guerrilla warfare were given to the world by Spain, and that this had been the characteristic military expression of the Iberian peoples at least since the Romans, through the Napoleonic and the Carlist wars. *For Whom the Bell Tolls* is what Unamuno would have called *intrahistoria* or inner history of the Civil War on the level of individual Spaniards rather than anonymous battalions, brigades, and divisions. Hemingway wrote a novel that deals more with men and women, Spaniards and Spain, than with war itself, just as *Death in the Afternoon* was about the country and her people as much as it was about the bullfight.

Anselmo or the Old Man and the Mountain

When the book begins, we see Robert Jordan prone on the pine-needled forest floor—a position that will recur throughout the story. Soon we learn that he knows well this earth upon which his body rests and his heart beats: he has been fighting for the Republic since the beginning of the war, has traveled all over the peninsula for years, has written a book on Spain, and is an instructor of Spanish at a university in Montana —a state whose terrain and weather remind him, and Hemingway, of Castile and Aragón.

The American protagonist is accompanied by Anselmo, an elderly partisan from Barco de Ávila, a town Hemingway visited and praised in 1931, during the hope-filled early days of the second Republic. The old Spaniard embodies everything Hemingway had admired in Barco de Ávila that summer—the clean, simple life, close to animals and nature, of a kind, "damned intelligent" people with an innate spirit of democracy. Anselmo is the most impeccable character in the novel, a man with the natural nobility of the Castilian peasant. Both the old man and Robert Jordan are dressed in peasant trousers and rope-soled shoes; from the beginning they are a pair in harmony despite their obvious differences—old and young, illiterate and educated, peasant and teacher, Spaniard and American. They are bound together by their dedication to the Republic, their sense of self-sacrifice for the good of the cause, their unwavering sense of loyalty.

Anselmo is a kind of paternal figure and a spiritual as well as geographical guide for Jordan, to whom he imparts his deep belief in the sanctity of human life and the problematical nature of any taking of that life. But the old man is in many ways subordinate to the American, from whom he takes commands and learns the techniques of firing weapons, observing the movements of troops, and blowing bridges. Although some critics have tried to convert the humble Anselmo into the Hispanic code hero of the *Bell*—parallel to Villalta, Maera, and Pedro Romero in Hemingway's earlier fiction—the difference here is that the American protagonist gives as well as receives from the old man, who will influence him less than the Spanish women of the partisan band, Pilar and María. In other words, there is no single code hero in this novel, but several Spaniards who will serve as different models for Robert Jordan, and teach him various aspects of life in the next three days. Moreover, by this stage in his career, Hemingway had given his American protagonist many of the qualities acquired in the earlier works from the Spanish heroes—pride, a sense of honor, the enjoyment of alcohol, a grace under pressure, courage in the face of death. In his final Hispanic novel, *The Old Man and the Sea*, he would join the protagonist and the Spanish hero into one character, the Anselmo-like Santiago.

Pablo or Mala Leche

After leaving Jordan at the stream where he eats wild watercress, Anselmo returns to the spot with Pablo, chief of the guerrilla band. Scrambling down the ledge above the stream, Pablo looks like a goat. At one time or another he will be compared to a fox, a hog with red eyes and swine-bristly face, a boar, a cat, a bull, and a he-goat (cabrón)—one of the greatest insults for a Spanish male because of its suggestion of cuckoldry. He is the shrewdest member of the group, with the raw intelligence and the lack of scruples of an animal. Pablo was a brilliant and daring fighter for the Republic at the beginning of the war, but now he has lost his spirit, his cojones, his sense of duty and camaraderie with the others. He is a character who can be best understood in terms of the Spanish idiom *mala leche*—"bad milk," with the figurative sense of bad sperm or seed. Originally the expression referred to a person who was nursed by an unworthy woman with diseased milk, then was extended metaphorically to a man's semen. The idiom is almost impossible to translate into English, but if you have read the book and observed the character of Pablo you know what mala leche is: ill humor, bad intentions, a bitterness, an evil so deep that it has tainted what Spaniards conceive as being the center and source of manhood—the sperm, the very generative power in the testicles. The repeated allusions to milk in the novel refer to semen: "obscenity them in the milk of their filth," "I obscenity in the milk of science," etc.

Pablo is a literary brother of the xenophobic soldier from Extremadura in Hemingway's fine story of the Spanish Civil War, "Under the Ridge." The guerrilla chief feels a natural hostility to Jordan and to all strangers:

"What right have you, a foreigner, to come to me and tell me what I must do?" Pablo asks the American. Jordan answers, revealing a secret wish of his creator: "That I am a foreigner is not my fault. I would rather have been born here."

As if Pablo's animal-like appearance and hatred of foreigners were not enough to make him the bête noire of the *Bell*, Hemingway tells us that he worked as a horse dealer in the bullfights before the war. We remember from *Death in the Afternoon* that horse contractors were the only people in bullfighting who the author believed had been brutalized by their job; they furnished more "filthy cruelty" than even Hemingway had ever seen. So Pablo's evil is apparently extreme, like Anselmo's goodness. The husband of Pilar has "the complete Spanish lack of respect for life"; the old man believes in the absolute sanctity of human life. Together the two characters embody the extremism of the Spanish people recognized by thinkers such as Américo Castro and by Hemingway too: "There is no people like them when they are good," thinks Jordan, "and when they go bad there is no people that is worse." Yet the matter is not so simple. In the course of the novel, Pablo fluctuates between evil and good, between hostility to Jordan's mission and a willingness to cooperate. The guerrillas know the depth of their leader's mala leche, but they also realize that they cannot succeed without him. Unlike his opposite, Anselmo, Pablo is not old enough to be Jordan's father, but he too will teach the protagonist: nothing is simple among this ancient people in whom a darkness and malice can be mixed with the greatest generosity and kindness; it is an old world where men live and survive by their wits. Pablo is a survivor, like the peoples in the peninsula who have survived invasions over the centuries by Carthaginians, Celts, Greeks, Romans, Visigoths, Arabs, French, English, and now by Franco's Germans, Italians, and Moors. He also represents the worst in the Spanish people, in a line of "sons of bitches from Cortez, Pizarro, Menéndez de Avila all down through Enrique Lister to Pablo."

When Pablo shows his reluctance to help Anselmo carry Jordan's heavy sacks of dynamite up the hill to the camp, the old man vilifies him: "I this and that in the this and that of thy father." These and other expressions, like the archaic *thous* and *thees*, reveal we are in a foreign world where the characters are speaking an assumed Spanish rendered into English

dialogue. This translated or transposed dialogue is the most obvious difference between the *Bell* and Hemingway's other works, as well as being
the most innovative and controversial aspect of the novel. The book cannot be understood without a grasp of what the author has done with the
language, the very warp and woof of his style.

Language as Destiny

When he began the novel, Hemingway had been speaking
Spanish for more than fifteen years. He never studied formally, but his
nearly perfect ear had picked up the idioms, intonations, and rhythms of
the language. His Spanish friends have attested to his ability to speak to
their compatriots in a tone appropriate to their social class and education.
Hemingway's later boast, in a letter to William Faulkner, that he knew
Spanish as well as English was not true of course, but he had learned
plenty, especially the argot and notorious obscenity of the bullring. Like
Robert Jordan, he harbored a secret wish to have been born in Spain and
to write Spanish as a native instead of feeling that he was hunting on
posted land or fishing out of season. He realized that Spaniards do not
have to distrust their everyday language because it has not been divested
of its poetic qualities as much as English, French, German, and Italian,
the other languages to which he had been exposed. "If I had been born
in Spain," he told a friend, "I would have written in Spanish and been a
fine writer I hope." As it was, he had to make do with English, "a bastard
tongue but fairly manoeverable."

Hemingway believed Spanish had retained the primitive echoes of ancient speech more than other modern tongues, more double and "secret
meanings from the talk of thieves, pick-pockets, pimps, whores, etc." He
was impressed by the apparent similarity between Spanish and Kamba
(M'Wakamba), one of the African languages he dabbled with during his
safaris. According to Hemingway, whose amateur opinions on linguistic
matters should not be taken too seriously, in Kamba the word *Tu* means
"you alone, you only, you who I love, you who I see again, you with who
I share a tribal secret." Of course *tú* is the second-person familiar pronoun
in Spanish, corresponding to the archaic English *thou*. For Hemingway,

"Spanish is a language Tu" because it also is ancient, secret, intimate, tribal. For this reason he instinctively spoke Spanish to his Masai companions in a great drunken scene after the kudu hunt in *Green Hills of Africa.*

Hemingway had another *idée fixe*, that Spanish was "the roughest language that there is." He was partly right. In the nineteenth century, one of his and Robert Jordan's favorite writers on Spain, Richard Ford, had remarked that few peoples could surpass the Spaniards in cursing and blasphemy: their language of vituperation was limited only by the extent of their anatomical, geographical, astronomical, and religious knowledge. To the blasphemy common in Catholic nations, Spaniards add the family and ancestor insults typical of the Middle East, and the allusions to sex and body functions characteristic of the Protestant countries. Hemingway loved and attempted to imitate the Spanish flair for cursing in his own speech and in many of his writings on Spain. We could not expect the rough-talking veteran of World War I, author of a "Defense of Dirty Words" in *Esquire*, to follow the priggish advice of Richard Ford: "More becoming will it be to the English gentleman to swear not at all; a reasonable indulgence in *Caramba* is all that can be permitted. . . ."

For Whom the Bell Tolls is Hemingway's attempt to incorporate into his own prose the profanity, grammar, syntax, idioms, secret meanings, and rhythms of the Spanish language. The novel was the culmination of his experiments, begun in his early days of journalism in Paris, in transposing dialogue from one language to another. He realized that he could not recreate the Spanish people truly in his book without their language. The mostly illiterate members of Pilar and Pablo's band belong to an oral rather than a written culture. They have the fertile imagination and the lively sense for proverb and metaphor typical of peoples who must rely on their memory for the transmission of knowledge. Their thoughts have been shaped by spoken language rather than by print. Hemingway's publisher, Charles Scribner, Jr., observed that it would have been difficult for the author to render these characters authentically without attempting to imitate their manner of speech. As we see in the hilarious passage in which the guerrilla Fernando fails to understand how a native English speaker like Jordan can be a teacher of Spanish, language is an equivalent of nationality for these simple people. Thus they call Jordan *"Inglés"* until he proves himself to be a knowledgeable insider and a comrade-in-arms. Hemingway was accurate in his use of this nickname; in Madrid during the winter of 1980, my son's Spanish schoolmates at the Colegio Estudio called him "Inglés" until they accepted him as a member of the group. To paraphrase Napoleon's words to Goethe ("Politics is destiny"), in the world of Hemingway's novel, language is destiny.

As in his previous work, Hemingway often incorporates Spanish words directly into the text of the *Bell*. If he had translated expressions like "cojones" into English, they would have lost much of their resonance, force, and coherence. But Hemingway was aware of the dangers in overloading his dialogue with too many foreign words, so he transposed other Spanish expressions into English. The result often sounds unnatural—"much horse," "less bad," "a rare name." The reader with a knowledge of Spanish realizes these phrases have been translated literally into English. For the reader who does not know Spanish, they create a foreign, primitive tone that contributes to the remote, heroic atmosphere of the novel.

In a superb article written soon after the publication of the *Bell*, Edward Fenimore observed that complete familiarity no less than complete ignorance of Spanish would probably take away from the reader's appreciation of certain passages. Hemingway wrote his book neither for scholars nor illiterates. The reader with a knowledge of Spanish who is aware, for example, that *"conejo"* or rabbit can be used to refer to the female organ finds it difficult to read without smiling those passages in which Jordan uses the assumed Spanish word as an endearing nickname for María ("little rabbit"). Either Hemingway himself was unaware of the figurative meaning of the word, or he used it as a kind of private joke, unconcerned about the reaction of the few readers who might understand the sexual connotations. Failing to see the forest for a single tree, some critics have gone to the extreme of claiming that María's nickname ruins the entire novel. As Peter Lisca has said, no matter what "little rabbit" means in Spanish, the phrase sounds marvelous in English, the language Hemingway wrote in, after all. It did, however, create problems for Spanish translators of the novel. They were occasionally forced to "correct" the original in order to avoid an obscene interpretation, as when Pilar, playfully jealous of Robert Jordan and María's love, says: "Now if I could take the rabbit from thee and take thee from the rabbit." One of the Spanish translations of the *Bell* tactfully avoids the ribald by changing "rabbit" to another, more innocent nickname, *gatita* or "little cat."

Hemingway's translators were also obliged to change the original when the author used his *thees* and *thous* inconsistently. His letters in Spanish show that he did not "dominate" (as a character in the *Bell* might say) the use of the formal and the familiar pronouns which can produce so many delicate nuances of meaning. In the opening scene between Jordan and Anselmo, for example, Hemingway correctly has the American, younger than his companion and a foreigner, use the formal "you"—corresponding to the Spanish *Usted* derived from "Your Mercy"—in order to show respect for the older, dignified man. On the other hand, Anselmo uses the informal "thou" construct ("How do they call thee?") with Jordan, although he may mix it with the formal "you." It is doubtful an illiterate Castilian peasant would take the liberty of using the familiar second-person with an educated foreigner in a situation like this; Hemingway's translators amend the original by having the old man address the American in the more respectful "you." On the other hand, the translators leave the familiar *thees* and *thous* later in the novel when Anselmo and Jordan become good friends and comrades.

Hemingway's inconsistent use of pronouns may derive in part from his own imperfect knowledge of Spanish, but more often than not he was concerned with overall effect rather than precise detail. "I have made the thees and the thous as accurately used as possible without giveing the book an archaic-ness that would make it unreadable," he told Perkins. The novel might indeed have become unreadable if the author had used the Biblical pronouns in every case. When he does decide to use them, they produce a kind of Elizabethan tone appropriate to this Spanish tragedy. Often they are employed with great beauty to create a sense of intimacy, as in the love scenes between Jordan and María.

Other techniques also create an ennobling, heroic tone—the elimination of contractions ("I do not remember") and the use of the prepositional possessive ("the woman of Pablo" instead of "Pablo's woman"). The same could not be said of Hemingway's practice of repeatedly substituting an offensive Spanish word with "this," "that," "obscenity," "unnameable," "unprintable"—no doubt the most artificial and harmful device of all. Of course he was constrained to a certain degree by the taste of the period and the fears of his editor and publisher that the novel might offend some readers. As it stands, the *Bell* is one of the most daring books of its time in the extent of its profanity.

By besprinkling his dialogues with oaths, Hemingway did more than merely imitate the Spanish tendency to blasphemy. As any veteran of the American army knows, foul language is not unique to Spanish soldiers. In the *Bell*, the characters' cursing reveals their rebellion against the enemy, against their own government and high command, against the suffering and injustice of war, against God and destiny. (It has been observed that only a people with such an intimate sense of religion as the Spaniards could blaspheme so much and so well.) Hemingway came to consider the Spanish war as a betrayal on many levels: betrayal of friends by friends as in his short story "The Denunciation"; betrayal of Spaniards by their compatriots as in *The Fifth Column* and the movie which he narrated, "The Spanish Earth"; betrayal of Spaniards by foreigners as in "The Butterfly and the Tank" and "Under the Ridge"; betrayal of foreigners by Spaniards as in "Night Before Battle"; betrayal of all men by war. Hemingway has Robert Jordan ask himself, "Was there ever a people whose leaders were as truly their enemies as this one?" In the novel, the partisans sense they are being betrayed both by foreigners and their own leader Pablo. Their use of oaths is a way of expressing discontent while preserving their own individuality and honor. When Primitivo says, during the fascists' attack on El Sordo, "Oh, God and Virgin, obscenity them in the milk of their filth," there are no bombs or bullets that could destroy his sense of rightness and honor. Obscenity stands as the spontaneous idiom of the people against the hypocritical language of propaganda and bureaucracy. In the great scene of the attack on El Sordo's hill, when the naïve boy Joaquín mouths the Communist slogan *"Resistir y fortificar es vencer"* ("To resist and fortify is to win"), one of Sordo's men replies—*"Mierda"* ("Shit").

The constant use of oaths is connected to the secret, tribal nature of language in the *Bell*. The characters on both sides, Republican and Nationalist, have a superstitious belief in the power of words—especially profanity. In the same scene of the attack on El Sordo's band, the fascist Captain Mora shouts filth and blasphemies at the guerrillas on the hilltop while his comrades, Lieutenant Berrendo and the cavalry sniper, dissociate themselves from their commander, not wanting "to have that sort of talk on their consciences on a day in which they might die." The captain's curses are indeed contagious: all of Sordo's men will be killed and decapitated within a few hours, while Berrendo himself will come into the sights of Robert Jordan's submachine gun the next day. As the Spanish proverb says, *"En la casa del que jura, no falta desventura"* ("In the house of the man who curses, ill fortune will not be lacking").

Even in the rare scenes with no use of profanity, there seems to be a connection between language and destiny. When Robert Jordan tells Pilar that he will take María to the Republic if they are still alive after blowing the bridge, the woman answers, "That manner of speaking never brings luck." The dynamiter will in fact never be lucky enough to escape to the Republic, although María may. Coincidental or not, there is often a relation between the way people speak in the story and what happens to them. It is not a matter of cause and effect but of a more ancient principle: language is reality, words are things; they must be used with care and reverence. There is a taboo against speaking about death before a battle because speech is believed to have a reality of its own with the power to influence the future.

The connection between language and reality in the novel could be dismissed as superstitiousness in the Spanish characters if it did not affect the prose narration also. From the very first scene, when Robert Jordan interprets his own failure to remember Anselmo's name as a "bad sign," *For Whom the Bell Tolls* contains a steady, complex series of omens that accumulate in a "pattern of tragedy." To mention only a few of the most obvious—Pilar's reading of death in Jordan's palm, the fascist planes that roar over the mountains like "mechanized doom," the untimely snowfall that will reveal the partisans' tracks, the destruction of El Sordo's band, Pablo's betrayal. There are many more such signs or omens foreshadowing Jordan's death, the failure of the Loyalist offensive, and the eventual defeat of the Republic. The signs do not cause death and defeat; they form part of a pattern integrating man, woman, nature, and time into the most complete, organic relationship to be found in any of Hemingway's novels. Through the use of primitive language, with the speakers' belief in taboo and the connection between words and things, the author has arrived at a mythic conception of life in which all things are interrelated. The operating principle of the novel is not the scientific, Western concept of causality but the ancient, Eastern sense of synchronicity as described by Jung. Diametrically opposed to causality, "synchronicity takes the coincidence of events in space and time as meaning something more than mere chance, namely, a peculiar interdependence of objective events among themselves as well as with the subjective (psychic) states of the observer or observers."

Of course the supreme example of synchronicity occurs when the earth moves as Robert Jordan and María make love in the high country coming down from Sordo's camp. The joining of the lovers' bodies, the harmony of their wills, their contact with the Spanish earth and the high sky above, their simultaneous orgasm do not "cause" the earth to move. All these conditions coalesce at a given moment to create the ecstasy in which there is a perfect balance between man, woman, and nature. Spain, home of Middle Eastern peoples for eight centuries and a bridge to Africa, was one of the final redoubts of this acausal, mythic view of life embodied in the language and the action of Hemingway's novel.

When Robert Jordan feels exasperated by the unpredictable, irrational behavior of the Spaniards, he lapses into his native tongue. Talking with the partisans in Spanish about their machine guns for example, he suddenly says in English, to the bewilderment of his listeners, "they jam, run out of ammunition or get so hot they melt." Speaking in his native language, even if it is to himself when alone, gives Jordan a reassuring sense of comfort. In some ways, English is more real to him than Spanish. Remembering his father, who committed suicide, he thinks of him as a *cobarde*. But no foreign term can mean as much to Jordan as "coward" in his own tongue. Perhaps it could be ventured that English is the bridge-blower's "paternal" language—like Hemingway, he has rejected his mother because she bullied his father into cowardice—while Spanish, with its warmth, earthiness, and sexuality transmitted by Pilar and María, comes to be a kind of "mother" or female tongue. It is the language of love and of the tribal family in the novel, while English is largely the language of reason and technology. Not until he wrote this most Spanish of all his novels did Hemingway have one of his American protagonists relive his past and come to terms with his own patrimony, his parents and grandparents, his childhood and youth—his own culture and tribe.

Language is character as well as destiny in *For Whom the Bell Tolls*.

Although Hemingway did not have a perfect knowledge of Spanish, he had an intuitive ability to grasp the deeper structures of the language. This is especially true in the use of dialogue, where he identifies with his foreign characters in his imagination at the moment of their speaking, then renders their thoughts into English. We have seen that Hemingway valued the ability to "always think of other people" and to "get in somebody else's head." Many writers have gotten into a character's mind in their own language, but few have done it as well as Hemingway in a foreign tongue.

One example of how he got into a character's head in the *Bell* is corroborated by his unpublished manuscripts. On the day before the attack on the bridge, Anselmo prays "Help me, O Lord, to comport myself like a man." The sentence translates the Spanish expression "*comportarse como un hombre,*" which had fascinated Hemingway for years. A deleted passage from the manuscript of *Death in the Afternoon* reads: "He [Rafael el Gallo] drank six bottles of Manzanilla on his wedding day and afterwards comported himself as a man" (by consummating the marriage). The phrase looks like this in the manuscript:

afterwards comported himself as a man
~~despues ha comportado como un hombre~~

The passage shows that Hemingway was *thinking* in Spanish (even if it was slightly incorrect), then translating directly into English in order to give the expression an unidiomatic tone suggesting the Hispanic sense of what it means to act like a man: for the bullfighter Rafael to drink heartily with his male friends according to the fiesta sense of life as he had always done when a bachelor, but also to comply honorably with his new duty as a husband by deflowering his bride. For Anselmo in the *Bell*, acting like a man means executing Jordan's orders and fulfilling his responsibility to his comrades-in-arms, dominating his fear by performing bravely in the battle. "To comport oneself like a man" is an expression with a wealth of cultural echoes and secret meanings, which Hemingway achieved by identifying with his character and thinking with him in Spanish before projecting the character's thoughts into English. The result is a new kind of language balancing Spanish rhetoric with English understatement.

Many critics have commented on the fact that Spanish has influenced the dialogue of the *Bell*, but few have noticed that the prose narration is also informed by structures and rhythms of the author's second language. Fenimore perceived a similarity of tone between dialogue phrases such as "the wife of Pablo" and narrative sentences like "The wife of Pablo was standing over the charcoal fire on the open fire hearth in the corner of the cave." But he went on to deny that the dialogue shapes the narrative or vice versa. What in fact shapes much of the dialogue is the Spanish language or Hemingway's rendering of an assumed Spanish, as when Jordan says to Agustín, "I know not." The important thing is not linguistic veracity but a tone of formalized dignity appropriate to the setting and characters.

As for the narrative, it is shaped above all by Hemingway's own style, whose characteristic rhythms we know were strongly influenced by the bullfight (see Chapter 3). We have only to look at the beginning of the first sentence of the *Bell*—which could also be the last—to see how the elegiac rhythm of the author's prose has been integrated with the narration: "He lay flat on the brown, pine-needled floor of the forest. . . ." Hemingway's preference for the prepositional possessive, typical of Spanish ("the woman of Pablo," "the floor of the forest"), had not been so obvious until he wrote this novel. If we substitute the normal English possessive, "the forest floor," we see the change in rhythm and tone:

the fŏrest flŏor

compared to

the flŏor ŏf the fŏrest.

The first construction would have been monotonous in its mechanical alternation between stressed and unstressed syllables. The second has the dignity produced by the prepositional possessive and shows Hemingway's usual pattern of several unstressed syllables between the accents—the elegiac rhythm befitting a book about men who must learn to die, about a Spanish culture threatened by "mechanical doom" and the technology of modern warfare. Of course the relentless heaping up of omens also contributes to the inevitable sense of tragedy.

Years after *For Whom the Bell Tolls,* Hemingway's friend Janet Flanner remarked that *The Old Man and the Sea* was written as if it were translated out of Spanish. She perceived what all the critics had failed to notice in the earlier novel. The assumed Spanish of the guerrillas and of the old fisherman bestows on them what Flanner called an "unfair nobility." Hemingway's own confession, that the secret of *Old Man* is "poetry written into prose," could also be applied to the novel of the Spanish Civil War.

Ernest knew he had to understand the Spanish language and incorporate it in the *Bell* if this was to be a true book. Others had written "phony" works on the war because they had not been in the peninsula long enough, or they didn't comprehend the language well enough to "know how things *really* were in Spain." Hemingway knew all right, and he showed it in his novel through the employment of Spanish words and expressions with their secret, tribal meanings; in his translated dialogue with its heroic tone; in the scatological richness of Spanish displayed in his characters' use of profanity; in their sense of taboo and the magical power of language leading to a mythic conception of the world in which all things are interrelated by a tragic pattern of doom; in the elegiac rhythms of his prose, deepened by echoes of the language he knew better than any other except his own.

There is no doubt that Hemingway's use of language in the *Bell* is not perfect—a daring experiment that worked most of the time in this novel but could not have been extended to all of his work. It quickly became a mannerism easy to imitate by the author himself or by those who could not resist the temptation of parodying his style. The parodies always touch the surface only, not the mythic, tragic depths of the language that is destiny in *For Whom the Bell Tolls.*

Pilar or Duende

When Anselmo leads Robert Jordan up to the partisan camp, Pablo's wife emerges from her cave. Pilar seems to dwarf the others. Almost as big as her husband, dressed in black, with thick dark hair and gray eyes in a brown face like the model for a granite monument, she has a presence unmatched by any other character in the novel. Although she is part gypsy from another province of Castile, Pilar seems almost to have grown from the granite-strewn terrain of the Guadarrama. We realize soon that she has taken her husband's place as the real leader of the band. Since Pablo lost his cojones and bravery, Pilar has become the only authority among the partisans. She remains faithful to the Republic; she controls María, the food and hearth. The situation at the guerrilla camp is a microcosm of Spanish society: as many writers have observed, Spain is a nominal patriarchy controlled beneath the surface by women. Most critics usually refer to "Pablo's cave" and "Pablo's camp," but we know it is the woman who dominates there. In many ways Pilar dominates the book too; *For Whom the Bell Tolls* would be Hemingway's most "feminine" novel. Its world is vastly different from that of his previous collection of short stories, *Men Without Women*.

Robert Jordan and Pilar get on with each other at once. He trusts her instantly and she says, "We will understand each other." As María's adoptive mother, the older woman sees in the American a possible mate for the girl and a means for getting her back to safety in the Republic. Pilar belongs to the long tradition of matchmakers or *Celestinas* in Spanish life and literature, but unlike most of them, she does not seek personal gain. She will feel only a kind of motherly pride and a vicarious sexual satisfaction in the love between the two young people who are the closest thing she will ever have to a son and daughter.

When Jordan breaks the taboo against mentioning the possibility of death in battle, Pilar asks to see his hand; she reads the lifeline in his palm and finds death there. Her certainty that the American will die is another reason for matching him with María; in this too, she acts with the absolute compassion of a mother. Robert Jordan will receive the girl and many other less tangible gifts from Pilar. He has rejected the inheritance of his American mother, but will accept most of what the Spanish matriarch teaches him in the course of the next three days, which will be as important to him as his whole childhood and youth.

Pilar's role in the *Bell* is that of symbolic mother and a kind of witch or shaman who possesses an ancient, secret knowledge of the world— a knowledge of the most secret things which Hemingway had intuited in Spain and which he did not express so openly in other books. His character's name comes from the *Virgen del Pilar*, the patroness of Aragón and all of Spain, whose shrine and annual feria in Saragossa he had discovered in 1925 and 1926. No longer a practicing Catholic, still less a virgin, Pilar nevertheless embodies some of the collective qualities of the Spanish people and their religion. She has turned away from the Church because of her devotion to the secular ideals of the Republic. Her devotion is also to something much more ancient and enduring than either the Church or the state—to a religion of the senses, the body, sex, the dark forces of the blood, the subconscious, the Spanish earth. Her wisdom is older than science, which she despises: "I obscenity in the milk of science." All of Robert Jordan's preparations for blowing the bridge, all his knowledge of military techniques can do nothing to prevent the fulfillment of the terrible, implacable future read in his palm by the woman of Pablo.

Like the figure of the witch or prophetess in primitive societies and myths, Pilar is both a light and a dark figure. She is a compassionate, nourishing earth mother; with her secret knowledge of the subconscious and of death, she also has a shadowy side. She is the most complex, ambiguous character in the *Bell* because she combines, even more than her husband, light and shade, life and death. When she gives María to Jordan, for example, she does not repress the jealousy and the sexual attraction she feels for both of the young lovers. Pilar's morality transcends traditional norms and taboos; there is a kind of incestuous undercurrent in her relationship to her symbolic children. Partly because of this, Jordan is repulsed by her sibyl-like figure, even as she seduces his mind with her irresistible personality and knowledge. The subtle, forbidden relation of attraction-repulsion between the young man and the older woman is one of the great minor achievements of the novel.

Just as Pilar initiates María into the knowledge of a woman's body, she will initiate Robert Jordan into other mysteries. When the novel begins, he is educated, scientific, and "very cold in the head." From Pilar he will acquire a knowledge of the head that is anything but cold; he will learn about the importance of the senses and the rest of his body. When we first see him, Jordan resembles in a way those other puritanic, archetypical Americans evoked by Hemingway in *Green Hills of Africa*—the New England writers like "Emerson, Hawthorne, Whittier, and Company" who had plenty of head but no bodies. Robert Jordan has never granted much importance to sex, for example; he admits lamely that he has always been too busy with his work to pay much attention to women. By giving him María, Pilar enables him to learn the mysteries of the senses, the body, sexuality. Then Jordan is fully accepted by the Spaniards as a member of the band, while he feels himself more "integrated" with the world. As Joseph Campbell has pointed out in his book on primitive mythology, the function of the shaman is to initiate the individual not only to the family, tribe, or society, but to nature and the universe.

With her unerring instincts, her almost supernatural insight into other characters, her ability to foretell the future, her profound sense of death and tragedy, and her possession of secret knowledge, Pilar will introduce Jordan into a realm that is deeper, more ancient and numinous than his limited, pragmatic American world. His previous mental life has been confined almost entirely to the conscious mind—the mere tip of an iceberg compared to the depths beneath the surface. Although Jordan's cold head and scientific cast of mind make him wary of Pilar's "wizardry," he will come to realize, like Richard Ford before him, that there is a truth surpassing the fastidious judgment: "All we know is that we do not know," he confesses. Pilar will teach him to integrate his head and his body, his daytime and nightime worlds.

Not too long before beginning the *Bell*, Hemingway had answered a survey of writers by Eugene Jolas, which asked whether they felt the need for a new language to express the experiences of the "night mind." The novelist replied: "I haven't ever felt this as would like to be able to handle day and night with same tools and believe can be done." The *Bell*, and above all the character of Pilar, might be seen as Hemingway's full acceptance and exploration of the night or subconscious mind in his work.

Although I believe the wife of Pablo may be the most complex character in all of Hemingway's fiction, and a necessary one for understanding his mature vision of Spain, it would be hard to deny that she is somewhat larger than life—this mythic figure with her "head of a seed bull" and "heart of a whore." Readers trained in the same kind of modern rationalism as Robert Jordan find it hard to accept Pilar as a realistic character. She possesses certain qualities long associated by foreigners with a stereotype of the Spaniards as a passionate, colorful, gypsified people. It was no surprise when Hollywood seized upon those qualities in its portrayal of

Pilar in the movie version of the novel. Arturo Barea was correct in noting that she and her horsedealer husband, both involved with the world of bullfighting before the war, are out of place among the Castilian peasants in the Guadarrama. What Barea did not recognize, and like many Spanish liberals what he would refuse to admit, is that the bullfight is a master key to Spanish culture with its tragic sense of life. The former lover of a torero, Pilar is the living link between the ancient ritual of the bullfight with its awe and fear, its feeling of life and death, and the modern war in which men and women must also learn to live gracefully amidst the constant threat of annihilation. In other terms, she is the link between Hemingway's two most Spanish works—his bullfight book and this novel, whose title might have been *Death at Noon.*

Other readers have been even harsher in their judgment, comparing the *Bell* to Mérimée's *Carmen.* Hemingway answered one of these readers, a Spaniard, in words that unveil the origins of Pilar: "I know it is not like Carmen anymore than Pastora Imperio (Pilar) is like Kate Smith. . . . You know how strange and difficult Spain is to write about." Pastora Imperio was a famous gypsy singer of traditional Andalusian music, *cante hondo (jondo)* or deep song, popularly known as flamenco. Hemingway had described her in an unpublished passage of *Death in the Afternoon* as one of the "hard-voiced singers" whose beauty deteriorated before she became famous; he may have seen her perform some time during the late 1920s or early '30s. In one of Pilar's evocations of her youth in the bullfight world, she recalls "Pastora, who is uglier than I am." Just as Hemingway had to include the corrida in any complete novel about Spain, so must he include cante hondo, with its ancient ties to bullfighting through the gypsy people who have excelled in both arts. Some critics believe there may be a common cultural heritage in the two fields: both have a rhythmic nature, spontaneity, and a special communion between performer and public. Walter Starkie has described this heritage as the "Mithraic mystery, with its infinite ramifications and its bonds of interest." The term that best describes the characteristics of a great torero or singer of cante hondo is duende. After making love to María for the last time, Robert Jordan remembers how the girl had spoken of the sexual ecstasy as "La Gloria," closely related to duende: "It is the thing that is in the Cante Hondo and in the Saetas. It is in Greco and in San Juan de la Cruz, of course, and in the others."

Pilar too has felt the earth move beneath her in the ecstasy of orgasm, she too has known la gloria—no doubt the profane rather than the orthodox variety alluded to by Jordan. If her husband Pablo has mala leche, his wife has something far more powerful—duende. In the chapter on *Death in the Afternoon*, we saw the importance of duende in the performance of a faena by the gypsy Cagancho. Pilar is of course not a professional performer, but when she speaks in her deep, resonant voice with her vivid profanity, her unsentimental wit, her lively sense of image and metaphor, she seduces her public as much as any torero or *cantaora* of traditional Spanish music. Hemingway created her character mostly from his own imagination, but he based her in part on Pastora Imperio because Pilar has the ineffable power of duende associated with the famous singer. The music of cante hondo is primitive, perhaps the oldest in Europe, as this character's wisdom is old. She does not have the education of Robert Jordan, but a more ancient "culture of the blood"—a term used by García Lorca in his brilliant essay on duende. In the *Bell*, the American university teacher must admit to himself that Pilar "is a damned sight more civilized than you are." She is an earth mother, and duende is "the spirit of the earth"—the Spanish earth.

Lorca said that duende thrives at the extreme limits of human experience, in ecstasy or in death. Pilar's retelling of her youthful joys in Valencia, the massacre of the fascists in Pablo's town, and her later evocation of the "smell of death" reveal that she has both the fiesta sense and the tragic feeling of life. In cante hondo, the tragic sense is expressed through dissonance and "black sounds." There is a blackness in the wife of Pablo too, as when Jordan compares her to a cobra spreading its hood, or when she says to him in a passage deleted from the novel: "There is a darkness in us that you know nothing of."

Hemingway's most telling statement about the importance of Pilar in the *Bell* is contained in a letter to William Faulkner. He told his contemporary that what he wanted to do in his novel was more than merely give a realistic sense of experience:

I tried to get way past that like when they are fucking comeing back from makeing contact with the other outfit about the bridge, when the Pilar woman knows what the hell it is all about; again where she is talking about her man, before, and Valencia and the fun they had (which think will stand); where she is talking about smell of death (which is no shit) and all the part with her man who was in bull fight business and where we kill the fascists in the village. . . . Anyway is as good as I can write and was takeing all chances (for a pitcher who, when has control, can throw fairly close) could take. (Probably failed.)

Hemingway failed in part, as would any writer or pitcher who took so many chances. But he also threw some great strikes. It is enormously significant that every one of the scenes he mentioned as an example of his best writing is related directly or indirectly to the gigantic figure of Pilar. She is the main presence of the novel, in many ways even more important than Robert Jordan. Through Pilar, and to a lesser extent María, *For Whom the Bell Tolls* brought the night mind and a new feminine consciousness into Hemingway's work. The older woman's dark wisdom stretches back in time long before the discovery of Jordan's America. He will die at the end of the book; she will live. She is Spain, the Spanish earth.

María

During his first evening with the partisans, Robert Jordan goes outside the cave to breathe the cold air. *For Whom the Bell Tolls* is Hemingway's most nocturnal novel: what happens during the three nights between Saturday and Tuesday in that last week of May 1937 is as important as the daytime action. The gypsy Rafael is singing as Jordan looks up at the stars:

> I had an inheritance from my father,
> It was the moon and the sun
> And though I roam all over the world
> The spending of it's never done.

Rafael's inheritance is that of all gypsies, and of all peoples who live in harmony with nature and the rhythm of day and night, the cycle of the seasons of the year. An inheritance that is never done because it is as

inexhaustible as nature herself. For these simple men and women who
have abandoned the official religion of the Church, the sun and moon
are like ancient, tutelary gods of their existence in the mountains. The
partisans live in such close contact with nature that they know and predict
her vagaries: Pilar prophesies the unseasonable snowfall of the second
afternoon and evening. Jordan refuses to believe her because "it *can't*
snow" in June. "These mountains do not know the names of the months,"
Pilar tells him. "We are in the moon of May." The folklore of the Spanish
people is much more accurate than the calendar: "*Hasta el cuarenta de
mayo, no te quites el sayo*" says the Castilian proverb ("Do not take off
your coat until the fortieth of May"). While the rational Robert Jordan
measures time by the abstract units of months, the gypsy woman and her
companions follow the natural calendar of sun and moon. By the end of
the story, they will pass their inheritance onto the American by giving
him a different awareness of time and nature.

 After Jordan dozes off in his sleeping bag, María goes to him in the
night. This part of the novel is not Hemingway's best, but neither is it
"the most absurd love scene in the history of the American novel," as
Leslie Fiedler has claimed. There may be an element of erotic fantasy in
Jordan's love for María, as when he recalls his dreams of Greta Garbo and
Jean Harlow later in the novel. The origins of the Spanish girl's character
explain some of her weakness: Carlos Baker told me that she seems to
be "part M.[artha] Gellhorn (say ¼) and the rest imagination." Hemingway's third wife Martha, the Bryn Mawr-educated daughter of a St. Louis
gynecologist, a novelist and international correspondent like her husband,
could not be expected to have much in common with the daughter of a
village mayor in the Old Castilian province of Valladolid.

 Critics have noticed a discrepancy between the traditionally conservative behavior of middle-class girls in rural Spain and María's sexual
freedom in giving herself to a foreign man on the first night of their acquaintance. Yet such readings are based on sociological criteria peripheral
to the novel. María and Jordan make love in the night partly because of
Pilar's promptings: the wise old earth mother knows that only the love of
a new man can wash away the stain and grief the girl has suffered since
being raped by the fascists on the same day her parents were assassinated.
The wife of Pablo also knows, as certainly as she predicts Jordan's death,

that only the love of a woman can give her adopted son a complete life before he dies. Jordan and María must break the sexual taboos of traditional Spanish society in order to achieve their full humanity and to create a new morality based on nature and instinct, the equality of man and woman, the freedom of choice. Unfortunately, the character of the Spanish girl— it is hard to call her a woman—is too docile and subservient to make that new morality feasible. Nonetheless, it is possible that she will conceive a child as a result of her union with Jordan, and in this way give birth to a new, more complete kind of man or woman: the man or woman of the future, Anglo-Saxon and Hispanic, European and American.

We can find many such objective explanations to justify the love scenes in the *Bell*, but none is more important than their poetic necessity within the structure of the novel. Just as a complex network of forces makes Jordan's death necessary, so his love with María is inevitable both in the novel and in the context of Hemingway's life and work. For most of their adult lives, Robert Jordan and his creator had been attempting to understand Spain, to get "in as far as any foreigner ever could be." In the sexual union with María, the American character and the author finally reach that goal. Of course the girl's name is just as symbolic as Pilar's: she is the embodiment of the religious worship of woman in a matriarchal society. Jordan is fully aware of this dimension: "Maria. There was a name . . . I love thee and I love thy name, Maria." As a teacher and a writer, he is also aware that his love with the girl embodies a reconciliation between two peoples—the Protestant and Catholic, the Anglo-Saxon and Spanish—who have been separated by religious and cultural differences for centuries. A passage from the typescript of the novel makes this clear; in one of his monologues the American says, "Meet Sir Francis Drake Sir Comrade Robert Jordan of the Spanish Armada." By loving a Spanish woman, Jordan and his creator wipe out the Black Legend and centuries of hostility between two religions and peoples.

Although Jordan associates María with the Church, he knows the worship of the Virgin is only the latest historical manifestation of a tendency among the Iberian peoples going back to pre-Christian times. In fact the presentation of the girl is related to the earth and nature more than to Catholicism. When we first see María come out of the cave bearing a platter of rabbit stew, she is closely connected to the natural world and the nourishment of men. If Pablo is constantly compared to ugly, dirty, and clever animals, the "little rabbit" is compared to the graceful creatures of the earth and to the fertile powers of nature: she moves like a colt, her body resembles a young tree, her hair has the golden color of ripe wheat, her face, skin, and eyes are the same tawny brown as the Castilian earth. She is indeed the Spanish earth:

> Maria lay close against him and he felt the long smoothness of her thighs against his and her breasts like two small hills that rise out of the long plain where there is a well, and the far country beyond the hills was the valley of her throat where his lips were.

Her parents have been murdered, her village sacked, she has been violated as Spain herself has been pillaged and raped by foreign and native soldiers for centuries. In spite of the way she has been abused, María manages to regain her strength and her faith in life, just as the Spanish people "will rise again as they have always risen before against tyranny." Robert Jordan, in his double role as lover and soldier, recovers the honor of both the violated woman and her country. By accepting María, by telling her while she sleeps that he is very proud of her family, and by "marrying" her in his natural ceremony without the ritual of the Church, the American has achieved his supreme symbolic union with Spain, the Spanish earth and people.

In many ways, Jordan is more a son of María's parents than of his own. Although he never met the martyred village mayor and his loyal wife, their example will enable him to realize that his own heritage comes from his grandfather, a courageous veteran of the American Civil War, and not from his cowardly father and his bullying mother. María's parents, by their devotion to each other and to the ideals of the Republic, by their heroic deaths, have taught Jordan the greatest lesson of a true mother and father: how to live and die on the suffering earth.

So we must understand the love between the American soldier and the Spanish girl beyond a realistic, sociological level. María softens her lover's shell of aloofness, freeing him from his enslavement to work, teaching him to relax, opening him to the magic of the body. Until he meets her, Jordan has used his work, his knowledge, and his scepticism to protect himself from an intimate relationship with women. When the novel begins, the reader's impression is that this cold hero has never really loved or suffered, nor recognized his own share in the human inheritance of grief and death. As he admits, he is "of those who suffer little." For the other characters, he is "Comrade Jordan" or the "inglés" until María breaks through this formality to call him, with the intimacy of man and woman, "Roberto." In the course of the story, she will teach him to care and to expose himself to the risk and pain of involvement with others. Like Hemingway, he will learn that sooner or later, everybody cries in a war.

In spite of the undeniable weakness of her portrayal, María is more than an "amoeba-like" little heroine, as she was called by Edmund Wilson. She is not as much a woman as Pilar, but give her time. She belongs to the line of European heroines in Hemingway's fiction—Catherine Barkley of *Farewell*, to a lesser extent Brett Ashley of *Sun*, and later Renata of *Across the River and Into the Trees*—who have the tragic sense of life. As a Spaniard whose parents have been shot to death in front of her eyes, María's tragic awareness is the most acute. Death has become an "organized possibility" within her, an awareness that enhances every moment of her life. That awareness is embodied in the single-edged razor she carries in the breast of her shirt so that she can take her own life rather than be captured by the enemy. The end of the novel will show us that her American lover has also learned to make self-sacrifice a possibility in his own life.

María and Jordan love in the night. Her realm, like Pilar's, is nocturnal. In the darkness, without his vision, without the light of reason, depending only on the prescientific senses of touch, taste, smell, and hearing, the man must follow his instincts rather than his mind. While all of Jordan's thoughts have been directed toward a goal in the future—the blowing of the bridge—now he must live in the present. His entire life had been governed by goals: to become a professor, to know Spain, to write a book, to win the war. Now he begins to see life as a process rather than a goal, a means rather than an end. Through the magic of María's body, through the release of orgasm, Jordan discovers that future goals are mere abstractions and that the only real time is always the present:

And if there is not any such thing as a long time, nor the rest of your lives, nor from now on, but there is only now, why then now is the thing to praise and I am very happy with it. Now, *ahora, maintenant, heute. Now* . . .

From María and Pilar, the protagonist will learn how to live so intensely in the present that the next seventy hours will be as full as a life of seventy years.

This is also the lesson Hemingway had learned in Spain nearly two decades before: with their tragic feeling of life on the one hand, their fiesta sense on the other, Spaniards may live more intensely than any other Western people. Because they have always existed on the periphery of Europe, enjoying centuries of contact with Eastern races, they still possess the old, cyclic, or mythic sense of time as opposed to the rational, scientific concept of linear time based on the idea of progress. For the Spaniards in the *Bell*, there is nothing new under the sun that rises and goes down in the sky; the earth abides forever. Life does not reach fullness in an always-receding future but only right here and now. Both María and Pilar know this; from them Jordan will learn to cease postponing his happiness to a future that will never arrive. In the ecstasy of orgasm when the earth moves out and away from the lovers, time is "absolutely still" and they are "nowhere" and everywhere: they have burst the boundaries of time and space to reach what Hemingway would call the "fifth dimension." For the first time in any of his novels, the protagonist has conquered definitively the feeling of nada or emptiness in his life. Robert Jordan and María have achieved religious experience, la gloria, in the root sense of the word: they are bound to each other and to the world around them. Just as all is now, so all is one—"is one, is one, is one." It is the mystic ecstasy evoked by St. John of the Cross but without the old divinity, for María and Jordan have found the gods in each other.

The Sacrament of Death

The next morning Jordan, Pilar, and María hike to the other guerrilla camp, El Sordo's, to engage his help in attacking the bridge. It is a splendid morning with a high, clear blue sky. Jordan of course does not pay much attention to the scenery or the weather; he is anxious to see Sordo and "get it over with." Pilar, who has a different sense of time, wants to bathe her feet in the stream and enjoy the ambiente, this sunny pause in the midst of war. Indirectly, she is teaching Jordan to forget his seriousness for the moment and to enjoy this time with María. She also needs to complete his political education by telling her marvelously spun story of the massacre in her village at the beginning of the war. The flailing to death of the fascists and their sympathizers is based on the metaphor of the capea or bull-baiting described by Hemingway in *Death in the Afternoon* as a "very savage and primitive sport." Like a capea, the massacre is an expiatory rite; the members of the upper classes are the sacrificial victims. The killing progresses, the crowd turns into a mob and begins to resemble an animal. The difference between this mass murder and a real bullfight is that there is no feeling of tragic catharsis afterwards, no genuine purgation of the emotions. Pilar says she felt sick, hollow, ashamed, and oppressed after the killings.

Hemingway does not name the town of Pablo, but his description of the plaza and the cliff over which the dead bodies are thrown recalls Ronda, a city whose tragic quality had intrigued him since his first trip to Spain in 1923. A massacre in fact had occurred there in the first months of the Civil War. Pilar's story is Hemingway's most powerful evocation of the Spanish obsession with death, the strange taste for blood that had appeared in the Napoleonic and Carlist wars before 1936, recurring down to our own time in the separatist terrorism of the 1970s and '80s. The town mob kills for social and political motives, but beyond that they have a grotesque, half-religious, half-sexual passion for blood and death. After the murders, Pablo asks Pilar to refrain from sex that night, partly because the killing itself has given him a kind of religious exaltation and sexual ecstasy. As Robert Jordan will say to himself, death is the "extra sacrament" of the Spanish people, one they had long before Christianity and had "suppressed and hidden to bring it out again in wars and inquisitions." It is also one of the secret things Hemingway had discovered in Spain; it runs like a subterranean stream through *For Whom the Bell Tolls*.

Like bullfighters in a ring, some of the fascists perform well under the danger of death, others badly; some know how to die with dignity, others do not. As Pilar speaks with the rapture of an oracle, Jordan is learning all the time about how to die well. He is entranced by the woman's story, admitting that she tells it even better than the classical Spanish writer most obsessed by mortality, Quevedo. Of course Hemingway is paying a subtle compliment to himself here as the real spinner of Pilar's tale, as well as revealing one of his own sources. Although the massacre is one of the most original and imaginative pieces of writing in any of Hemingway's works, it is also a tour de force that shows how completely he had assimilated and transformed the influences of Spanish literature and art in his writing. Besides the mob brutality and taste for blood of the capea, and the hallucinatory, infernal atmosphere of death reminiscent of Quevedo's prose, Pilar's story recalls unmistakably Goya's *Disasters of War* and to a lesser extent Picasso's *Guernica*—right down to the symbolism of the bull. There is also an absurd, macabre sense of the grotesque that has reminded some Spaniards of two other modern masters of prose admired by Hemingway—Baroja and Valle-Inclán.

The novelist's silent homage to Goya is confirmed by the appearance of the guerrilla leader El Sordo in the next scene; we remember that the painter's deafness in the later years of his life inspired the same nickname for him. Indeed, El Sordo resembles one of those popular heroes who fought against the French in the Spanish War of Independence depicted in Goya's *Disasters*, as Pilar reminds us of the female soldiers who were folk heroes of the time. He and the woman go together in many ways. His Christian name is none other than Santiago, after Spain's patron saint, as hers is that of the country's patroness. Both Sordo and Pilar dedicate themselves to the Republic and to their comrades; Robert Jordan can trust them as he cannot trust the shifty Pablo. Like the woman, the deaf man seems to be a part of the Sierra de Guadarrama where he lives and moves with his followers. He is as dependable as the Spanish earth; he agrees to assist in the blowing of the bridge. Like Jordan and Sordo's namesake, Santiago of *The Old Man and the Sea*, the guerrilla leader is destined for tragedy.

The Sacrament of Love

Jordan, María, and Pilar come down from El Sordo's cave toward their own camp. The older woman leaves the couple alone in the high country where they make love among the heather beneath the high sun. While most of Jordan's previous behavior has been governed by the cold reason of his head, Hemingway emphasizes that his protagonist now uses his senses to *feel*: he feels the sun on his head, the girl's hand in his, her trembling as he kisses her, her small firm breasts. All his senses, and his beloved's, are alive during their intercourse; at the moment of orgasm they feel time stop and the earth move beneath them. This passage is one of the most lyrical in Hemingway's writing: the words "sing" in long, rhythmic sentences of ecstatic prose that recreate the physical motion and the feeling of love as he had recreated the action and emotion of the bullfight in his earlier work.

It is not coincidental that Jordan's and María's love takes place in the same high mountain meadow where Pilar told the story of the massacre only a few hours before. Nor is it by chance that the couple then talk about the razor blade in María's pocket, and about killing each other to avoid being captured alive. Just as Hemingway suggested the relationship between sex and death in the mass murders, he has Robert Jordan tell the girl, "I feel as though I wanted to die when I am loving thee." She answers, "I die each time." Love and death—the two extra sacraments of the Spanish people are revealed on this fatal Sunday afternoon. Both derive from the instincts of the blood and from the night world of the subconscious. "We know nothing about what happens to us in the night," thinks Jordan. But when the earth moves and the unknowable occurs in broad daylight, the conscious mind must yield: there are truths that overwhelm the fastidious judgment.

The Smell of Death

Back in the cave that evening, one of the partisans asks Jordan if he believes in the possibility of seeing into his own future. The American of course says he does not. Pilar disagrees and tells the sceptical protagonist that he is like a deaf man who cannot hear music and therefore denies that it exists. As readers, we tend to agree because we know more than Jordan about the enemy's elaborate preparations for a counteroffensive; his optimism amidst the worsening situation makes him appear naïve

next to Pilar. She has known some men in whom death could be seen as
clearly as if it were sitting on their shoulders, she tells him. The great irony
of her words is that one of those men is Jordan himself. When he tries to
explain Pilar's premonitions in rational, scientific terms as nothing more
than products of fear and apprehension, she tells him how to experience
the smell of death himself: he must breathe it from the mingled odors
of the sea, blood, garbage, dead flowers, semen, soapy water, and cigarette butts in a ship, a slaughterhouse, a brothel, and the Jardín Botánico,
where the cheapest whores work the night in Madrid. All of this should
be done in autumn or early winter with rain or fog—the time of year that
always reminded Hemingway of death.

This passage is by far the most extreme and grotesque in any of Hemingway's works. His publisher feared it might repulse some readers; he
was not wrong. Hemingway defended the passage and insisted that it stay
because it was an integral and valid part of the book: the smell of death
is related to the "whole dark business" of Pilar, gypsy lore and omens.
To make the dark business authentic, he needed to include a naturalistic
passage to give some of the feeling of horror that is in Madrid. Hemingway
told Charles Scribner he could have included anecdotes that were even
worse, like the one about the man who made love to a leper woman, her
face three-quarters eaten away, in order to earn five pesetas.

> No, Charley. There is a goddamned horribleness about part of Madrid
> like no other place in the world. Goya never half drew it. I need that
> to make this book whole.

Although the *Bell* is a novel of the Spanish Civil War set in the Guadarrama, Hemingway needed to include the capital and center of Spain
because this is a book about the entire country, just as *Death in the Afternoon* was about Spain as well as bullfighting. Even more than the story
of the massacre in Pablo's village, the passage on the smell of death is
a tour de force in which Hemingway expressed the paradoxical Spanish
obsessions of love and death—the two major themes of his novel. This
too is a part of Robert Jordan's education: "All right, *Inglés*. Learn," Pilar
warns him. Hemingway balances her ancient wisdom against the American's modern scepticism; Jordan will eventually recognize that the gypsy

woman and the Spaniards see or feel something that is as true as what he sees and feels. Love and death, night and day, the smell that is both the beginning and the end of life: it is all as true as his semen entering María's womb and as true as his blood that will enter the Spanish earth.

The Pattern of Tragedy

As the first idyl with María was broken by enemy airplanes, the second is ended in the early morning by the sudden arrival of a Nationalist scout on horseback. Robert Jordan kills him with a pistol shot aimed at the Sacred Heart of Jesus, an emblem of the *requetés* or Carlist militia on the cavalryman's left breast. The scout's death is poignant to the American because the man turns out to be a Navarrese—the people in Spain whom Jordan and Hemingway admired most. In one of those curious revelations that united his life and his books, Hemingway would later say that the Pamplona youths he had known in the fiesta of San Fermín, and described in *The Sun Also Rises*, became the requetés of the Spanish Civil War and the *Bell*. After shooting the horseman, Robert Jordan thinks, "I've probably seen him run through the streets ahead of the bulls at the Feria in Pamplona." In an even more suggestive revelation of the profound unity between all his Spanish works, Hemingway made the Navarrese town of Tafalla the home of the dead cavalryman; it was also the hometown of another tragic victim of violent death, the farmer Vicente Girones who was killed by a fighting bull in the encierro of *Sun*. To complete this circle of connections, we need only remember that Ernest and Hadley got drunk on wine given them by a boy from Tafalla during a memorable train ride from Pamplona to Madrid in 1925, and that Hemingway recalled the episode nostalgically in the final chapter of *Death in the Afternoon*. *Sun, Death, Bell*; wine, bull, blood, earth; fiesta, life, death—the secret things of Spain that he had discovered and transformed into the material of his art.

The pattern of tragedy in the *Bell* thickens inevitably after Jordan kills the cavalryman. The members of the dead man's patrol will miss their scout and follow his tracks in the snow. Jordan will be riding the scout's big gray horse when he is wounded the next day. As Jordan and his Spanish comrades listen helplessly, the fascist cavalry with Lieutenant Berrendo and their airplanes destroy El Sordo's band on a bare hill. Hemingway contrasts the Hispanic sense of loyalty—Agustín and Primitivo want to go to their comrades' aid—with the American sense of duty—Jordan makes them stick to their mission of blowing the bridge.

The brutal annihilation of El Sordo and his men balances to a certain extent the massacre of the fascists in Pablo's village. As Arthur Koestler said, "only demagogues and abstract doctrinaires with no first-hand experience of the Civil War can deny that a great number of abominable acts have been committed on both sides." One of the most abominable acts committed by the Nationalists, made a part of international consciousness by Picasso, was the bombing of the Basque village of Guernica in the early stages of the war; Hemingway probably had it in mind when he described the merciless, one-sided destruction of Sordo's band on the hill resembling a chancre or syphilitic lesion. Once more the Spanish themes of love and death mingle: when a bomb explodes near him, the boy Joaquín feels the earth roll under him as Jordan and María felt it move in the small death of orgasm.

Life follows death, grows from death once more: the lovers spend their final night together. María tells Jordan the story of her parents' deaths and her rape by the fascists; this also serves to counterweight the massacre of the fascists described by Pilar. As Jordan watches the girl sleep, he thinks about the extremes of the Spanish people. They can be the finest in the world, like María and her parents, or the worst, like the rapists and Pablo. When Jordan falls asleep, Pablo in fact steals the exploder and detonators for the bridge.

After learning of Pablo's betrayal, Jordan makes love to María. The beauty of this scene lies in the contrast between the couple's love and the atmosphere of impending fate that surrounds them. Jordan knows the blowing of the bridge will be even more dangerous without the stolen equipment. Yet he shows his growth by not allowing his preoccupation with work to interfere with his love, by not allowing the future to damage the present, now, by going on with his life, by giving himself to María in the night. The mechanical time of the American's watch, glowing in the dark, is overwhelmed by the human time of love, "now and now and now." A sentence deleted from the book reveals Jordan's emotion: "He felt proud and humble and happy with an ecstasy of fulfillment." He has learned much in these four days and three nights—especially the nights. Before Jordan's life had been a project, a problem; now it is something good to be lived and enjoyed. "You taught me a lot, *guapa*," he tells María.

At the conclusion of this final love scene, there is a splendid contrast with the partisans' preparations for their attack on the bridge: after the smooth warmth and suppleness of the lovers' bodies, the cold, metallic hardness of rifles, bullets, grenades. Each of the three nocturnal interludes between Jordan and María has been ended suddenly by an event of the war. Now the reader knows there will be no more love scenes. This is the time of battle; the moment of truth has arrived.

The Undiscovered Country

Robert Jordan lies once again with his breast against the pine needles of the forest floor on the slope of the hill above the bridge. It is just before daybreak, his favorite time of day, as it was Hemingway's. He feels the dawn gray inside of himself as though he were part of the lightening that comes before the rising of the sun. All the man's senses are alive. He tries not to think but to participate in the daily reborn miracle of life around him: he touches the earth, smells the pines, hears a squirrel chitter and the stream flow, watches the morning light. The squirrel comes down a pine tree close by; Jordan would like to touch it in order to feel integrated with the animal world too. In a passage deleted from the novel, he says to himself, "Mother earth. . . . We don't come to it but we go to it." By now he has accepted the absolute reality of death and is not afraid. He is like a bullfighter who enters the ring to perform bravely despite the possibility of death. In fact, Hemingway gets into his character the same "feeling of life and death" he had found in the bullfight and described in *Death in the Afternoon*.

When the first sound of Republican bombs reaches Jordan's ears, there is almost a feeling of relief as the attack on the bridge begins. Working fast and skillfully as a surgeon, the pragmatic, professional soldier feels the ecstasy of action under danger, a particularly American form of la gloria.

The emotion also resembles that of a bullfighter once the anticipation before a corrida has ended with the entry of the animal into the ring.

Feeling a letdown after the dynamiting of the bridge, Jordan grieves for the death of his comrade Anselmo, who has comported himself as a man to the end; the partisans Fernando and Eladio also have died. When enemy planes come roaring over the mountains from Segovia, Jordan realizes the Republican offensive will be a failure: "There would be no victory now he knew. There would be no break through." (Both of these sentences in the typescript were deleted from the book.) Yet he has achieved another, more difficult kind of victory in the last three days: a victory over himself in his acceptance of death, over the feeling of nada or emptiness; a breakthrough to a new realm of nature, the body, the senses, love, friendship, self-knowledge. When Jordan sees María for the first time after the attack, he embraces and holds her tightly. Never has he known that he could feel emotion for a woman in the midst of battle. He no longer allows his work to shut him off from the fullness of experience. A competent soldier when the novel begins, Jordan has become a complete man by the end—soldier, lover, comrade, friend.

When Jordan is knocked off his wounded horse by an enemy shell and breaks his left thigh bone, he bids farewell to the men and women who have become closer to him than his own family. If Anselmo had been like a father to him, Pilar is like a mother, Agustín the brother he never had, María his wife; she "is also my sister, and I never had a sister, and my daughter, and I never will have a daughter." When Agustín offers to put Jordan out of his misery, the American refuses: he will not follow the tradition of his own family by taking the easy way out in suicide but the example of El Sordo and María's parents, dying for a cause he believes in, head up, facing the enemy.

In his farewell to María, Robert Jordan reveals the change in his character by telling her, "We both go in thee now." These words could not have been spoken by the sceptical dynamiter of three days before. María may carry the seed of a child within her; even more important, her love with the American has healed her wounds and brought her back to life.

The partisans leave Jordan alone and escape on their way to the Sierra de Gredos—an even wilder mountain range where they will carry on their natural way of life and their struggle for the Republic. By staying behind to shoot at their fascist pursuers, the American in effect gives his own life for that of his comrades. As happens so many times in the *Bell*, life comes from death. Instead of portraying the hero's end, Hemingway preferred to show Jordan before his sacrifice, aiming his submachine gun at Lieutenant Berrendo, who heads the charge of the approaching cavalry. As the author said in a small handwritten note inserted in the typescript but deleted from the book, "People are not as they end up (finish) but as they are in the finest point they ever reach." Since Jordan's is a meaningful sacrifice carried out with dignity, his death becomes a tragic one—like that of a matador in the ring who receives a horn wound even as he kills the bull with a thrust of his sword. (To signal the parallel, Hemingway named the enemy Lieutenant Berrendo, a word referring to a bull whose hide is tinged with two colors.) In all his Spanish works—*Sun, Death, Bell*—death is tragic because life is full and beautiful: human pain is integrated with nature and the rhythm of life and death.

The slopes of the mountains where Jordan dies were brown only three days before. Now they have turned green from the snow and the new warmth of spring. As Hemingway said in his elegy "On the American Dead in Spain,"

> our dead are a part of the earth of Spain now and the earth of Spain can never die. Each winter it will seem to die and each spring it will come alive again.

Only in death does Jordan finally know the meaning of his life. In three days of suffering and sacrifice, he has been born to the fullness of life through a knowledge of love and death.

Hemingway's original favorite among many possible titles for his novel was "The Undiscovered Country," probably taken from Hamlet's famous monologue on death. The protagonist of the *Bell* has spent the last few days learning how to die and also how to live intensely in the midst of death. The book has been a struggle between the instinct for life and the obsession with death; Jordan's prone position at the beginning and end of the work suggests his inclination to return to the earth. Just before facing the enemy patrol at the end, he touches the pine needles on the ground and the bark of the pine tree behind him. He feels completely integrated with everything now—earth and sky, life and death.

Robert Jordan has also entered another undiscovered country in the final days of his life. From Anselmo he has learned humility and respect for the absolute dignity of life. From Agustín, Fernando, and the other faithful members of the band he has acquired a deep sense of human sympathy transcending the boundaries of nations, languages, and cultures. From El Sordo he has learned how to die with courage and honor. With María he has entered the magic realm of the senses and the body. Through Pilar he has explored the night or irrational, subconscious mind, which he has managed to join with his daytime consciousness to achieve a wiser, more complete vision. Together, María and the woman of Pablo have opened him to the vast, profound world of the feminine which he had resisted in his youth. Jordan's rational, masculine world was much simpler than the one he comes to know on the slopes of the Guadarrama —the tip of a mountain compared to the deep, complex world of the blood, instinct, the body, sex, duende, earth, night, the subconscious, and a mythic sense of time revealed to him by the two women.

In three days Robert Jordan has learned what it took his creator half his life to learn. In Spain, with the Spanish people, Hemingway and Jordan found the undiscovered country inside themselves.

Ronda, 1980

The plaza de toros is almost two hundred years old. It has a double tier of arcades, a solid stone and wooden barrera around the sand, a roof of red tiles. It stands at the edge of a cliff: they used to throw the dead horses of the picadores over the cliff, and it was probably the place Hemingway had in mind when the Republicans threw the dead fascists into the river in *For Whom the Bell Tolls*. They no longer throw the horses over and the fascists are out of power in the new Spain. This afternoon is September 9, and a Goyesque corrida is being celebrated with eighteenth-century dress.

Pedro Romero was born in Ronda in the middle of the 1700s. He was one of the first and greatest of professional matadores, painted by Goya, an almost legendary torero who is said to have killed some 5,000 bulls. Ronda was also the birthplace of Cayetano Ordóñez, Niño de la Palma, who started to be a great torero until he lost his courage with his first severe horn wound. He ended his career in disgrace as a fat-rumped, bald banderillero—like a major league pitcher who wins twenty games, throws in the World Series, then loses his arm and goes down to the bush leagues to finish his career as a rummy reliefer. Cayetano married a beautiful half-gypsy dancer, Consuelo Araujo de los Reyes, and sired five sons, all bullfighters. One of them committed suicide and three never made it as matadores, earning their livings as banderilleros. The other son, Antonio, was born in Ronda the year of *Death in the Afternoon*; he would become one of the best and most famous and wealthiest toreros of Franco's Spain. He is fighting *mano a mano* with his son-in-law Paquirri in Ronda today. You can see there has been little change in the faces of these men, who could be bullfighters or bandits from the time of Don Francisco. "The modern face had only been produced by the clean shave and the haircut," Hemingway said.

Antonio Ordóñez is forty-eight years old, thin-haired, and overweight. He owns an apartment in Madrid, a house on his ganadería near Seville, other ranches and real estate. He is a millionaire in Spain—Catholic in religion, conservative in politics; the marriages, separations, annulments, and affairs of his daughters appear on the society pages. He and his wife were found guilty of allowing their bulls' horns to be shaved for the important corridas of the Fair in Seville on April 23 and 24, 1979. The government fined them 50,000 pesetas for the first infraction and twice that amount for the second, according to Article 134 of the *Reglamento Taurino*.

Today in Ronda, Antonio Ordóñez cuts ears and tail of the carefully selected bulls with shaved horns. He takes few risks but he fights purely and skillfully, with great knowledge of the animals. One has to admire a man nearly fifty years old who fights bulls, no matter how much they have been tampered with. He has a paunch that bulges from his suit of lights, he slicks long strands of hair straight back over the top of his head, and once he was beau. I guess he was, all right.

Dangerous Summers

---

*When a writer, having written any one thing the way it should be,
writes it again, even though the public may not know that it is the
same thing, then he is usually through as an artist.*
—*Unpublished passage from manuscript,*
  Death in the Afternoon

There are no second acts in American lives.
—*F. Scott Fitzgerald*

When Hemingway returned to Spain after a fifteen-year absence in July 1953, he headed straight for the festival of San Fermín in Pamplona, as he had done in the old days of ferias and fiestas. The bullfights were not very good that year except for what the writer described with exaggeration as "one historic thing": the first time he saw Antonio Ordóñez—son of Cayetano, Niño de la Palma, whom he had recreated as Pedro Romero in *The Sun Also Rises*. Niño had been twenty-one when Ernest first saw him in Pamplona during the Sanfermines of 1925; Antonio was exactly the same age when the novelist saw him at the fiesta in 1953. Hemingway felt strange as he watched the younger Ordóñez perform in what must have seemed like a reenactment of the writer's own life and his first novel. As in 1925, there was a poetic justice in his Spanish experience which seemed to be ruled by fate.

Just as he had met Cayetano Ordóñez for the first time in a Pamplona hotel room on the day of a bullfight, Hemingway met Antonio in a room of the Hotel Yoldi after the corrida. He was impressed by the young man's dignity, charm, and "strange" eyes: "the darkest, brightest, merriest eyes anybody ever looked into." Although he had promised himself never to become friends with a bullfighter again, Ernest knew that he and Antonio were almost destined to be companions. So began a friendship that would have even more bizarre consequences than his relationship with Cayetano Ordóñez, and that would lead to Hemingway's only complete work on Spain after *For Whom the Bell Tolls*.

Six years later, in 1959, Hemingway returned to Spain again with vague plans for collecting material to write an appendix for *Death in the Afternoon*. We can surmise the dearth of his inspiration from his need to depend on such a project: he was doing exactly what he had warned other authors against. (See first epigraph to this chapter). Although the new work turned out to be a separate piece—"The Dangerous Summer"—it marked the end of his career as a writer.

In Madrid for the feria of San Isidro that May, the novelist joined up with Antonio Ordóñez, now called his "pet" by Mary, Hemingway's fourth and last wife. The strangeness of the friendship between the aging winner of the Nobel Prize for literature and the young bullfighter has never been explained satisfactorily; perhaps it never will be. Since the days when he had showed his kid brother Leicester around, Hemingway always enjoyed having a younger friend at his side. "He needed uncritical admiration," Leicester said. "If the kid brother could show a little worshipful awe, that was a distinct aid in the relationship." Antonio showed some worshipful awe mixed with an irreverent Andalusian sense of humor. Ernest could tell him about the old days of bullfighting when Cayetano had been in the ring; he could educate the young torero in the arts of eating, drinking, and living. Since Hadley had been pregnant with John Hadley Nicanor (Bumby) at the Sanfermines of 1923, Hemingway had nurtured a fantasy of having a bullfighter for a son. Antonio Ordóñez was born just a few months after Ernest's youngest child, Gregory. Hemingway admitted to his middle boy, Patrick, that "being around Antonio is like being with you or Bum[by] except for having to sweat him out all the time." In some ways, the young Ordóñez was more like a grandson, since Ernest had "created" his father Cayetano in the character of Pedro Romero in *The Sun Also Rises*. In that novel, Romero can be seen as a prophecy of Antonio as well as a portrayal of Niño de la Palma. Indeed, the description of the torero with the smooth brown skin, the shiny black hair, the dignified manner, and the pure, natural style with cape and muleta seems to fit the son even more than the father. Ernest saw Antonio as the messiah who had come to save bullfighting from decadence as his father Cayetano had done too briefly thirty years before.

The younger Ordóñez must have seemed to Hemingway like a character of his own creation, a living embodiment of his youth in Spain, a part of his imaginative search for a life that would join beauty and action. Antonio offered the devotion of a son, the male camaraderie that the writer had always sought in the Hispanic world, the friendship with "mystery" that he could not find among his American or English companions. During that summer of 1959, Ernest wrote to one of the female admirers who were part of the Hemingway-Ordóñez entourage: "Antonio is absolutely intact inside himself. We have a thing that protects us inside ourselves which we share. It is very complicated and I will explain it to you sometime. Maybe it isn't true but it works. . . ." One of the complicated matters that united the two men was death. Ernest had learned about it in war and in the bullrings of Spain; Antonio had to deal it and face it every day he performed. As a writer, Hemingway attempted to create a "mystery" in his prose; watching Ordóñez in the bullring, the spectators realized that "there was a mystery" in his toreo. For the novelist, his health and talent fading, his judgment flawed, the torero represented the values of his lost youth and the ancient virtues of the Hispanic male—courage, grace, intuition, dignity, honor. Antonio brought Ernest's lifelong gallery of heroes full circle, his American and his Spanish experience: he was like the "great ones" of the old times in Spain, but he also resembled a northern Cheyenne, the tribe from which the writer claimed to have descended on his father's side. Naturally, Ordóñez could not live up to the image his friend created in his mind and in the story of their friendship that year, "The Dangerous Summer." Ernest's overestimation of Antonio as a man and a bullfighter would have sad consequences.

Hemingway exaggerated pitifully the matador's need for his company. He wrote to Carlos Baker: "Antonio Ordóñez wants me with him all the time as we are a winning combination in a lot of ways too complicated to go into. . . ." Ordóñez was flattered to have the famous writer in a first-row barrera or in the callejón at his fights; even his older and wealthier brother-in-law, the matador Luis Miguel Dominguín, could not boast of a Nobel Prize winner in his corner, so to speak. With the ingenuousness of a man of action—he had possibly never read a book except a few of Hemingway's novels—Ordóñez believed Hemingway would somehow make his toreo eternal. The two men had a pact according to which the bullfighter would perform and the novelist would "make it permanent" through art.

Just as Hemingway converted Ordóñez into a kind of spiritual son, the matador idealized him as a creator and symbolic father. Antonio had never enjoyed the security of a stable home; his father had lived a life of squalor

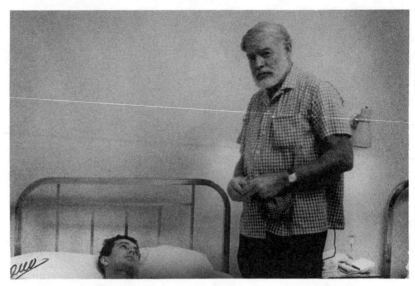

The bullfighter Antonio Ordóñez (son of Cayetano Ordóñez, Niño de la Palma) in the hospital recovering from a horn wound, with "Papa" Hemingway, 1959. (Photo Cano)

and disgrace after a few years in the limelight. It was natural, almost inevitable, for the young Ordóñez to see Hemingway as a paternal figure. Because of Ernest's association with the Republic during the Civil War, it took some courage for Antonio to become his companion in Franco's Spain. Ordóñez has remarked that his American friend had the tact not to discuss politics with him, because they would only have disagreed.

As early as 1955, Hemingway wrote in a letter:

> Antonio has me all mixed up as his father since his father, who was in the Sun Also, spooked out early after the first big wound (and who can blame anybody) but he got on the sauce and really ran for Skid Row.

When Ernest saw Cayetano one day during the 1959 season, he noticed that the ex-bullfighter "looked quite old this morning and oddly shrunken." Hemingway, nearly five years older than Niño and virtually an alcoholic himself by this time, was also beginning to look smaller and feebler to people who met him. The parallel fates of the two men would run their course when the elder Ordóñez died only a few months after Hemingway's suicide.

Ernest followed Antonio all over Spain during what Mary called "that strange summer of 1959." The towns and cities where they stopped read like a Spanish geography—Málaga, Madrid, Cordova, Seville, Aranjuez, Saragossa, Alicante, Pamplona, Valencia, Ciudad Real, Bilbao, Ronda, and so on. Hemingway had to prove to himself that he still could keep the pace that would have exhausted a much younger man. He and his driver, Nathan (Bill) Davis would often arrive in a town on the afternoon of a bullfight, partake of the usual revelry before and after the corrida, then pack into the car to drive all night to the next town. Mary described it better than her husband—a "nonstop circus in which we were, willy-nilly, performing." Meanwhile she began to notice changes in Ernest's behavior. In Pamplona again for San Fermín, she remarked that he was drinking more vodka and wine and that "something was changing in him or me or both of us." As the season advanced, Hemingway admitted to Mary that he had become too involved in the fortunes of Ordóñez; following a bullfighter was nerve-shattering, like "being married to an alcoholic." It was an odd metaphor for a man to choose when his own marriage was falling apart and he was acting like an alcoholic himself.

The photographs of Hemingway during that bullfight season show his change clearly—the thinning white hair now combed forward like an aging Roman emperor's, the suspicious expression, the eyes that look past other people and the camera. The photographer Peter Buckley, who was with the gang that summer, said Ernest acted like a boy of fifteen one moment, like a man of eighty the next. Hemingway shocked his friends by surpassing the Spaniards in the obscenity of his language. Some of his letters of the time, written in a bibulous mixture of English, Spanish, French, and Italian, are added testimony to his condition.

Meanwhile the bullfight impresarios and the Spanish press were exploiting the competition between the brothers-in-law Ordóñez and Dominguín, blowing it out of proportion in order to attract large crowds. When the publicity reached *Life*'s Paris bureau, the Hemingways' old friend Will Lang went down to Spain and persuaded Ernest to sign a contract to cover the rivalry. The writer would regret his decision, claiming he was forced into it by his need for money, calling himself "a fool to have been sucked in to doing that journalism for *Life*."

So Hemingway's abortive final work began. When Ordóñez was jailed, fined, and debarred for infractions of the taurine rules toward the end of the season, Ernest retired to La Cónsula, Davis's villa near Málaga, to begin his article for *Life*. Mary was eager to go home to the Finca Vigía in Cuba, but her husband wanted to begin his bullfight piece within the magical borders of Spain. It was October now; the fall had always been his favorite season for working, the time when authors are moved to write by intimations of death. The first stages of the work went well. After returning to Cuba and driving with Antonio and Carmen Ordóñez to the house he had bought in Ketchum, Idaho, Hemingway found it difficult to continue writing, but back in Cuba in early 1960, he was "working like a steam engine." It seemed that he had to be in an Hispanic atmosphere to write on the bullfight now, whereas he had been able to complete most of *Death in the Afternoon* in the United States.

It is interesting to compare the making of "The Dangerous Summer" to that of *Death in the Afternoon*. Hemingway had used bullfight books and journals, as well as his own notes taken in Spain, to compose the earlier work. Mostly though, he wrote from his own memory and experience to make it "round and whole and solid." In contrast, he depended heavily on newspapers and bullfight journals to reconstruct the summer of 1959. Some passages from his letters to Davis, written from Havana in the first months of 1960, reveal his method:

Right now am up against the problem of missing numbers of [*El*] *Ruedo* [a bullfight magazine]. These are the ones I need. 1 July '59 no.784, 8th July 1959, No. 785, 15 July 1959, no. 786, 22nd July, no. 787. . . . [25 February]

We cabled Juanito [Quintana] in San Sebastian and he was able to dig up the 4 nos. of *Ruedo* but I have nothing on the *corrida* at Burgos. Find that with any sort of detail or even News Agency account, correct or not, I can recall the whole fight but it makes it better if possible to select what you need. . . . It was bad luck to lose the papers that we saved and relied upon. . . . [12 March]

Forgot to thank you for the Burgos clippings. Do you think you could find the one on the fight at Dax where the bull stepped on Antonio's foot? Unfortunately that is all I can remember about the fight except that the bulls had their horns shaved down to the quick. . . . You can see how difficult it is to have only selective recall. [1 April]

These letters show not only Hemingway's problems in composing his article; they reveal the deterioration in his judgment and standards. *Death in the Afternoon* was a work of literature, however much its author would have objected to that description; "The Dangerous Summer" was journalism that relied on secondary sources and "selective recall."

The deterioration in Hemingway's standards of writing was moral as well as esthetic. The letter on the corrida in Dax where the bulls' horns were shaved to the quick is an example. Nowhere in the published version of the *Life* article did he admit that Ordóñez was fighting bulls with such mutilated horns. On the contrary, he made the point that Antonio's rival Dominguín abused the practice of horn-shaving, while fewer than half of Ordóñez's bulls were tampered with that season. We can imagine how scathing would have been Hemingway's denunciation, in *Death in the Afternoon*, of a matador who allowed nearly half of his bulls to have their horns shaved. The author had broken his own rule of not identifying with the bullfighter—and thus stopped standing for "the real bulls, the complete bullfight." In a passage from the manuscript of the article, deleted before publication, he admitted: "I had lost the detachment I had sought in bull fighting and saw it now, daily, from the participants' stand point. . . . You should not be involved. But I had been involved increasingly all year." Because the author was more torerista than torista, emphasizing the bullfighters almost to the exclusion of the bulls, "The Dangerous Summer" lacked the mythic, animal power of *Death in the Afternoon*.

Hemingway had assumed a proprietary interest in his "partner" Ordóñez's career and had ceased being an objective aficionado with his own moral and artistic criteria. The manuscript shows how he changed or deleted passages that would have diminished Ordóñez's image as a torero and a man. "Shaved" horns became "altered" in the magazine. In the manuscript, Hemingway confessed that Antonio fought many of the "half bulls" and "sleepwalkers" that summer, but he did not want his friend's "place in history to be denied him or to be fouled up by the manoevers that were going on."

While Hemingway whitewashed Ordóñez's role in the corruption of bullfighting, he condemned Antonio's "rival" and brother-in-law, Luis Miguel Dominguín. He also condemned Manuel Rodríguez, Manolete—the famous postwar torero who had been killed by a Miura bull in 1947—calling him a "great bullfighter with cheap tricks." Most aficionados and bullfight critics would agree that Manolete had been one of the very best toreros of all time. Why did Hemingway insist on denouncing a man who had been dead for twelve years and whose memory was worshiped by many Spaniards? In order to give his bullfight article the significance and dignity necessary for a work of "permanent" value, he needed to convince himself and his readers that his protagonist Ordóñez, not Manolete, was the real successor to the giants of modern bullfighting, Joselito and Belmonte. For personal and political reasons, it would have been difficult for him to admit that one of the great matadores of the century had arisen and died during his own exile from Spain, which coincided with the darkest years of the Franco tyranny. Hemingway had only seen Manolete in one corrida—in Mérida, Mexico, a few months before his fatal goring—and the torero had drawn the two "worst bulls" of the afternoon. This was hardly sufficient evidence on which to base a total comparison between Manolete and Ordóñez. By the same rights, I have only watched Ordóñez perform twice, and neither performance was worthy of the Manolete I have seen in extensive films shot in Spain and Mexico. More important is the overwhelming consensus of bullfight historians and critics that the "Monster of Cordova" was the greater figure.

Hemingway's unqualified praise of his hero was difficult to accept for those who had seen the torero perform. Ordóñez was clearly one of the best matadores of the postwar period, with a great intuitive knowledge of bulls and a purity of style. He was also a participant in the horn-shaving, the abuse of bulls by the picadores, and the economic exploitation of the corrida that were typical of the 1950s. Even as a torero, he showed a consistent defect in killing. Hemingway admitted to his son Patrick in August 1959 that Antonio's "killing is rapid but is still defectuous except recibiendo" (receiving the bull's charge with the sword rather than going in over the horn). Ordóñez became so infamous for his habit of plunging the sword into the animal's right *brazuelo* or shoulder from the side, rather than high up between the shoulder blades after going in over the horns, that the spot became known as *"el rincón de Ordóñez"* (Ordóñez's corner).

The French bullfight critic Jean Cau, who witnessed the season of 1959, said of the torero's killing: "[His] sword-thrusts are models of craftiness and . . . out of every 100 or 150 bulls that he dispatches in the course of a year, he 'kills' a dozen and assassinates the rest. . . ."

In addition to overestimating Ordóñez as a torero, Hemingway needed to exaggerate the importance of his friend's rivalry with Dominguín in order to enhance his book. There was no doubt some bad blood—mala leche or bad milk—between Antonio and Luis Miguel. Dominguín, scion of a wealthy clan of bullfighters from Castile, friend of Picasso and other artists, writers, and celebrities, may not have been delighted by the marriage of the part-gypsy Ordóñez, son of an alcoholic and a dancer from Andalusia, to his pet sister Carmen. As the two most prominent toreros of the decade, the brothers-in-law competed for the privilege of being *número uno* and receiving the richest contracts. Beyond this, their rivalry was a commercial strategy fostered by their common managers, Luis Miguel's brothers Domingo and Pepe, and by promoters and journalists. Hemingway's comparison of the competition to the other great rivalries in the history of bullfighting, such as that between Joselito and Belmonte, was grotesque. Those two giants had fought together more than two hundred times over a period of six years in the golden age of toreo. The "competition" between Ordóñez and Dominguín lasted only two seasons, they appeared together in a mere four corridas mano a mano (each killing three bulls), and a few times with other matadores. Hemingway saw giants where there were only windmills.

Even Ordóñez and Dominguín smiled at the invention of a "deadly rivalry" between themselves. Partly because it was more profitable, late that season Antonio decided to fight on his own rather than continue with Luis Miguel's brothers as his managers. After the publication of "The Dangerous Summer," he told a journalist:

> Well . . . it's a novel. Of course things did not happen that way. . . .
> But I think this is what the public likes and besides, next year we'll
> have more American tourists. Hemingway . . . it seems to me from
> what I've read, exaggerated the matter of the rivalry.

As the foil to the hero in Hemingway's article, Dominguín was naturally less generous in his appraisal:

The question of the rivalry with Ordóñez makes me laugh. I was
the one who invented it in the first place! The truth is that it was a
good idea: thanks to it, a new golden age of bullfighting has arisen in
Spain. . . . Such full rings and high prices have not been seen since
Manolete's time. . . . It has been a nice business directed by our family
and from which we all benefitted while Antonio was with us. And it
continues to benefit us now that Antonio is on his own. . . .

Hemingway willingly supported the Dominguín-Ordóñez cartel that
was dominating the world of the bullfight. While the two toreros had to
pay Spanish journalists, the winner of the Nobel Prize gave them free
publicity all over Spain and America. It was a "death and money business,"
he admitted. José Luis Castillo-Puche, a witness of that summer, noted
that Ernest was not so much deceived by others as by himself: "he wanted
to live intensely, fictitiously, a great tragedy that only in the end he would
realize had been a great farce."

It is unfortunate that trite journalism and sordid facts need to be cited in
order to understand the background of Hemingway's last piece of writing.
They are a measure of his personal and artistic decline. "The Dangerous
Summer" was a flawed work from the moment of its conception. While
the author had made a clear distinction between journalism and his own
writing before, here the two are confused. Instead of merely covering the
bullfight season of 1959 as he had covered boxing matches for *Esquire*
in the 1930s, he converted his article for *Life* into a full-length book.
The 5,000-word piece he had contracted to write burgeoned into an overweight, 120,000-word manuscript with endless descriptions of faenas that
could not possibly have held the interest of an English or even a Spanish-
speaking audience. When Mary criticized the manuscript, Ernest bristled.
Whereas before he had practiced what could be called an esthetic of exclusion, suggesting meaning through spareness of effect according to his
iceberg theory, now he used the principle of profusion, proliferating words
and images. He had always wanted to be a Spanish writer; now he resembled one in the excessive wordiness called *verborrea* by Spaniards. Never
before had he been so undisciplined.

In "The Dangerous Summer," Hemingway attempted to transform
Antonio Ordóñez into his final embodiment of the Hispanic hero. Not-

withstanding his portrayal of the torero as the messiah of postwar bullfighting, and his exaggeration of the rivalry between the two brothers-
in-law, the subject lacked the dignity required by the tragic vision that
had informed his previous work on Spain. Only the death of Ordóñez
or Dominguín in the bullring might have given Hemingway a suitably
elevated subject. He admitted to Will Lang of *Life* that he had been hired
to write the article when it seemed possible that one of the toreros might
be killed in the ring. When they survived—as the great majority of aficionados could have predicted—his piece lacked a sense of urgency. "The
story is difficult to write and to make of any permanent value," he wrote
to Edward K. Thompson of *Life*. "Would have been easy to write if either
Luis Miguel or Antonio had been killed." As usual, Hemingway had in
mind a great elegiac tragedy that would have made this story a worthy
successor to *The Sun Also Rises* and *Death in the Afternoon*.

In its published form in *Life*, "The Dangerous Summer" is an account
of Hemingway's return to Spain in the summer of 1953, his meeting with
Antonio Ordóñez, and his trips to the country in the mid-50s, leading up
to the bullfight season of 1959. Much of the article is written in the chatty,
humorous, sometimes aggressive manner of his journalism for *Esquire* in
the 1930s—Papa, man of the world. The difference is that he attempted to
give "The Dangerous Summer" a structure similar to his works of fiction
set in Spain: travel in search of knowledge, a series of omens foreshadowing disaster, followed by tragedy and catharsis. Like Hemingway's previous
Spanish code heroes, Antonio Ordóñez is portrayed as a brave, dignified,
honorable man. He also has the "dark side," the duende we saw especially
in Pilar—his knowledge of death and his "pride of the devil." His rival
Dominguín can also be brave, but he is more ambitious and venal. One
of the weaknesses of the work is that Luis Miguel is too much of an artist,
too intelligent and gracious in defeat to represent a true foil to Antonio.
For Hemingway, Dominguín's real sin is the professional one of trying to
surpass his own limits as a torero. He suffers the consequences—two
gorings that bring the last two installments of "The Dangerous Summer"
to a conclusion. In contrast to *The Sun Also Rises, For Whom the Bell
Tolls*, and *The Old Man and the Sea*, there is none of the emptied-out
feeling of cleansing and renewal at the end. The subject lacks the dignity
and the tragedy of loss and death that ennoble the other books. Writing

nonfiction, Hemingway did not have free rein to mold the facts to his vision as he had done in the novels. Nor could he recreate the rough magic of *Death in the Afternoon*, where he had been far less restricted to a specific chain of events. The problem was partly the failure of the world to live up to his ambition, partly his own blindness to that evidence, finally his inability to transform the raw material of his life into a convincing work of art.

A few places show Hemingway's old "alchemy," like his description of the great virgin forest of the Irati River in Navarre that had not changed since the time of the druids. Finding the country unspoiled, the fiesta of San Fermín and the people as great as ever in spite of the overcrowding, the tourists, and the modernization, he felt happy perhaps for the last time in his life. If you know about wine, food, and bulls, the fiesta "is always there and you can find it. . . ."

In spite of a few good passages, most of "The Dangerous Summer" attests to Hemingway's rapid decline. His growing fear of authorities reveals itself for the first time. Although he had struggled to cut the manuscript by 50,000 words, he saw fit to leave in a sentence informing the reader that his and Mary's shotguns were put on the same license when he passed through Spanish customs at Algeciras. Although he prayed constantly for both Antonio Ordóñez and his wife that summer, he tells how he took out memberships in the Jesuit Seminary Fund Association of New Orleans in order to have some "competent" people "with authority" to pray for the couple's well-being. Hemingway's superstitiousness, a trait of his character at least since he became involved with bullfighting, was becoming obsessive. When his money clip with an image of St. Christopher was stolen by a pickpocket in Murcia, he was careful to avoid the bullfighters' capes and muletas so that he would not pass his bad luck to anyone else. The manuscript also contains some cranky ideas, such as the author's belief that the elimination of fireworks in the United States had led to a greater "ratio of crimes of senseless violence." There are countless clichés, beginning with the titles of the three parts published by *Life*—"The Dangerous Summer" (sometimes translated as "Bloody" in Spanish), "The Pride of the Devil," "An Appointment with Disaster."

As the long summer wore on, Hemingway became weary of the endless need for rushing to reach the next town where a bullfight was to be held.

He had written before that it was wrong to live in the world if you did not truly experience it, looking without seeing. Now he recognized that "it was wicked to cross such beautiful country as though you were on a train, passing through towns you should have spent a day in, or a week, without stopping, unrolling the country that you might never see again as though it were a film instead of the place you really loved." There is a sense that his life is coming to an end, threatened by onrushing time. He tells himself that the summer of 1959 was "one of the few you had left to spend." Even as he finished the final pages of the manuscript, Hemingway had a bad conscience about the work. The moral, deleted from the *Life* article in order not to undermine the piece, was that he never should have gotten mixed up with bullfighters again. "I knew that once very well and I should not have had to learn it twice." He had believed the rivalry between Ordóñez and Dominguín would destroy one or the other bullfighter, but the only destruction was his own. That summer was more dangerous for him than for the toreros, since it was consuming the remaining energies of a man who had always seemed to live with boundless vitality.

Just as the long bullfight season of 1959 had worn out Hemingway's body, the pressure of writing "The Dangerous Summer" exhausted his head. When he finished the manuscript late the following spring, he wrote to his old friend, Juanito Quintana, that the forced labor (*trabajando forzado*) of his *Life* contract had tired his eyes and confused his brain. Of course he forgot that nobody had hired him to do a full-blown book instead of a magazine article. His compulsive writing and his own confession that it had affected his mind were signs that he might be losing his reason. As Castillo-Puche has noted, the tragedy that had not occurred in the bullring had been produced over the pages of the manuscript.

Hemingway felt none of his usual elation upon finishing "The Dangerous Summer." He still had enough critical savvy to realize that his work was little more than an overweight piece of journalism: like an old newspaperman, he placed a "30" after the final sentence. He had tried to make something of permanent value from the perishable art of bullfighting, and he had failed.

Although he had ostensibly completed his article, Hemingway convinced himself that he must return to Spain to gather photographs for *Life* and to look after Ordóñez. Since Mary did not want to repeat the experience of the previous summer, he traveled alone for the first time in years, flying to New York, then Madrid. In contrast to every one of his previous trips to Spain, he did not feel any of the old energy and enthusiasm when he touched Spanish soil in early August 1960. Bull-fighting seemed even more corrupt than before. Ordóñez and Dominguín were forcing the promoters to ask huge prices for tickets and creating an "exploitable rivalry." Horn-shaving was flagrant; everyone knew about it. "Plenty sordid stuff—whole set-up bad," Hemingway wrote to a friend in his Choctaw style. There was nothing he or anyone could do about the filth that went on in and out of the bullring. Everywhere in Spain, it seemed that "right and wrong had merged into a kind of greyness."

Hemingway could not reveal the corruption of the corrida in public since he felt partly responsible for it himself. Just as he had assumed a proprietary stake in his friend Ordóñez's career, he seems to have acquired a vested interest in bullfighting as an institution. After all, he was the prophet who had proclaimed the good tidings of courage and grace in the face of death to the Anglo-Saxon world more than thirty years before. He was more responsible for the international vogue of toreo than any other single person. Foreigners, some of them with copies of *Death in the Afternoon* under their arms, were filling the bullrings of Spain in the postwar tourist boom encouraged by Franco's government. In that book, Hemingway had predicted the corrida would die the quicker in Spain as it became more palatable to tourists. He was witnessing the fulfillment of his prophecy, yet to admit this would have lessened the stature of his friend Ordóñez and of his own writings. He had lost his old devotion to the truth and become a moral accomplice to the worst decadence of bullfighting in the twentieth century.

Hemingway even went so far as to suppress evidence of corruption in and out of the ring. When the photographer and aficionado Peter Buckley wrote an exposé of the Venezuelan Girón brothers, Ernest asked him not to publish it because the South American toreros were not "typical" of the Spanish bullfight, their association with Ordóñez might taint Antonio's reputation, and such writing would play into the hands of the enemies of toreo. "If bull fighting were like that there is no excuse for books on it," he said.

Hemingway also neglected to expose the corruption of bullfighting because he feared reprisals, and that he might not be allowed to return to Spain. He was plagued by other delusions during that ill-starred summer. At his favorite restaurant in Madrid, Botín, he took customers for FBI and Internal Revenue agents; to elude them, he would leave by the secret stairway that had been used during the Civil War.

After two weeks in Spain, Hemingway was lonesome for his wife and home. Bullfighting seemed so corrupt and unimportant that he felt it was taking him away from the good work he might have been doing. He loathed the "whole damned bull business"; he wanted to clean up his work and get out. When he helped Ordóñez recover from a concussion suffered during a corrida in Bilbao, he wrote Mary that it "wasn't the blind leading the blind, but the brain fogged shepherding the concussed." More than his family and friends, Hemingway was aware of the danger of his condition. His whole Spanish world seemed to be falling apart. When he visited his beloved Prado one morning, he was distressed to find the museum disordered because the old wooden floor was being replaced by marble; the pictures he had admired for forty years were "scattered as the pages of a torn book." He wrote Mary to tell her he wished she were in Madrid to keep him from "cracking up," using the same expression as his old friend, Scott Fitzgerald, to refer to his breakdown.

When "The Dangerous Summer" appeared in *Life* that September, Ernest felt "ashamed and sick" to have done such a job. The cover portrait with the famous Hemingway grin looked horrible to him. He feared that Dominguín might file suit against *Life* because of the accusations of horn-shaving. Luis Miguel did not take legal action but declared that Hemingway was not a great novelist, only a good journalist at best, calling him "the Nobel [Prize] of the Marshall Plan." Antonio Ordóñez was one of the few Spaniards who approved of the articles—for obvious reasons. The reaction of bullfight critics was generally hostile to the foreigner who had dared to defile the memory of the great Manolete. A few gave a fair appraisal of the piece. Many more, particularly those on the right, took advantage of the opportunity to reopen wounds that had been rankling since the Civil War, expressing their resentment against Hemingway and the liberal, secular Spain he once represented. They even accused him of writing pornography in *A Farewell to Arms*. (There is no telling what they would have said about *For Whom the Bell Tolls*, which was still forbidden by Franco's censorship.) His mortal sin, like the Spanish novelist Pío Baroja's, said one of these critics, was lack of faith.

Hemingway probably would have felt no less ashamed to see the posthumous version of "The Dangerous Summer" published as a book in 1985. Of course he had nothing to do with the final form of this work, based partly on the editing of A. E. Hotchner in 1960 but largely on more recent cuts by Charles Scribner, Jr., and Michael Pietsch. The original typescript of 688 sheets was reduced to a slim volume of 228 pages. The novelist William Kennedy has asked, "Is it half Hemingway? Hemingway by thirds? Should the byline read: 'Words Put In by Hemingway, Words Taken Out by Hotchner and Pietsch'?"

The attacks on "The Dangerous Summer" during Hemingway's lifetime must have hurt him deeply, sharpening the bad conscience he already felt about the job done. He knew the legendary divisiveness of Spaniards: any "group of Spanish speakers will always argue and want to change anything written by anybody," he said at the time *The Old Man and the Sea* was being translated. Yet never had any of his writings been assailed so immediately and so harshly in Spain. Some have granted too much importance to this fact, attributing Hemingway's suicide to the critical failure of the article in *Life*. "The Dangerous Summer" added to his depression, but was only one of many reasons for his impending crack-up.

Epilogue:
All Stories End in Death

People are not as they end up (finish) but as they are in the finest point they ever reach.
—*Unpublished note to typescript,* For Whom the Bell Tolls

At the foot of Ernest's grave there is a simple marker. Beneath it rests the body of a Basque shepherd.
—*Leicester Hemingway*

emingway's suicide in July of 1961 was the crowning example of the unity between his life and his work. Several years earlier the writer had told a journalist in Madrid that he led a literary life—by which he meant one worthy of fiction—and he looked forward to a literary death. His suicide placed him in the neoromantic tradition of authors who lived intense lives and died or killed themselves in a violent way. Like that of the Romantics in the previous century, his tragic end can be seen as a result of his idealization of reality—Spain, Spaniards, and bullfighting, for example—which led inevitably to disillusion and despair. In spite of his hard-nosed pragmatism, Hemingway belonged to the line of artists who created myths to sustain their lives and their work. His Spanish myth reflected the real country profoundly, not exactly, according to the distinction made by Henry James. He had inherited the Romantics' Spain —primitive, exotic, mysterious—but he deepened it, removed the local color, and transformed it into a myth compatible with his own sensibility. Spain for him was a state of mind as well as a physical space.

If we consider Hemingway's death in the light of his entire career, we realize that he not only killed himself as he had lived and written: he died in the only way he could have died. In his suicide there was an inevitability, a poetic justice, a coincidence between life and art unique in literature. On that summer morning in Ketchum, the double-barreled shotgun ended a life in which a man's experience and his writing, his existence and essence became one. Rilke, who also had lived in Spain, spoke of certain men who have their own, characteristic deaths as others have their own lives. Hemingway's death was his own—one he had carried inside himself like a seed. When that death finally blossomed amid blood, bone, flesh, and birdshot, it confirmed the personality that had been revealing itself throughout a lifetime. As a Spanish writer has said, it was fitting that a life as intense as Hemingway's should end with a "similar intensity in death, contemplated, savored like a bitter coffee . . . a rough and inevitable wine."

Hemingway had considered suicide when he was younger, and we can see his life as a history of self-destruction. By pushing himself to the limits of physical endurance and overdrinking for many years, he exhausted his body and his mind. Shooting animals and catching fish were ways of postponing his own end, of taking to himself the godlike power of giving death. As Freud said, some men kill other things in order not to kill themselves. Hemingway desisted from carrying out suicide in the earlier years because he knew "how swell life gets again after the hell is over." By 1961 he realized that another comeback was impossible: his "juices" were not flowing; he could no longer "fuck, fight write." He refused to expire in a slow, humiliating way like Pío Baroja, whom he had visited on his deathbed five years before amid the smell of stale urine and sweaty sheets—nada. Hemingway believed his body had betrayed him so he shot himself, significantly, in the head. The head—the intellect, reason, culture—had always been his enemy. As he wrote to Archibald MacLeish, "Papa probably never could think good with his head but by Jesus he thinks good with his bones."

Hemingway's death repeated a familiar pattern in American literature. Like Walt Whitman, to choose only one predecessor, he began his career with energy, courage, and a hunger for experience. Neither he nor the poet possessed a cultural background in proportion to his vitality. Both placed their faith in the strength of the body and the vision of the senses; their work dealt with the themes of youth and adventure. Only through the full operation of the muscles, the senses, and the imagination could each express a harmony between himself and the world. As the two men aged and lost their vigor, they underwent a crisis in their personal lives and in their creativity. For Whitman, a decaying body was the signature of a corrupt soul. After a painful reevaluation of his youthful thought, he accepted change and discarded the sensual elements in his verse, to the detriment of its power.

Hemingway was unwilling to renounce the beauty of the body and the senses; he was condemned to repeat the themes of his youthful creations in later works like "The Dangerous Summer" and *A Moveable Feast*. The only artistic alternative was silence, which would have been the equivalent of death for him. Hemingway needed to write in order to live with a clean conscience. However much he had rejected his parents, he inherited their Protestant ethic of work, which he applied to artistic creation rather than commercial labor. "I missed not working," he wrote not long before he died, "and I felt the death loneliness that comes at the end of every day that is wasted in your life." When he could no longer work well, unable to make the alchemy and mystery in his writing, he killed himself. Like Whitman, Fitzgerald, and so many American authors, he had the misfortune of outliving his talent.

In the character of Santiago in *The Old Man and the Sea*, Hemingway had been able to project the wisdom of age, acceptance, and renunciation. Published nine years before his death, this novel was the true culmination of his imaginative search. The old fisherman is destroyed but not defeated because he learns to accept his loss, to renounce pride without sacrificing honor, to have faith in nature and in the resources of his own mind. In spite of Hemingway's nominal Catholicism, he never achieved for himself the faith, peace, and hope he expressed in the character of Santiago.

Hemingway lived a life of action that finally consumed more energy than it produced. Sometime around 1930, he had begun to identify his own, real life with his public image as an international celebrity, a world traveler, hunter, fisherman, aficionado. In his work this identification led to the Narcissus principle, with fortunate exceptions like *For Whom the Bell Tolls* and *Old Man*. His real face began to acquire the features of the public mask he had adopted; the man became inseparable from his legend. Hemingway resembled an actor whose performance was his own life. The performance ended badly because life is rarely well written, and because the author had always lived and created according to the rules of tragedy. His death was an act in harmony with his myth. To paraphrase Jean Cocteau's words on Victor Hugo, Hemingway was a madman who believed he was Hemingway. Although we recognize the poetic justice of his tragic death, we cannot avoid remembering other great artists who were able to transcend their attachment to youthful vigor and continue creating until an advanced age—Goya and Picasso, to recall only two Spaniards whom Hemingway admired.

Scott Fitzgerald once wrote, "Show me a hero and I will write you a tragedy." Ernest Hemingway may have been one of the last twentieth-century heroes, probably our last heroic writer. He began writing at a moment in Western history after World War I when heroism was moribund. With all the strength and energy of his native land, he declared that the Old World and its high culture were dead. Whether he knew it or not, his life and writing implied a return to the pre-Christian, masculine ideal of the Greeks, with their exaltation of the intelligent mind within a strong body. For one of the few times since the Renaissance, a major author attempted to destroy his own tradition and to create a new basis for experience and art in the body as well as the mind or soul. Like the greatest Spanish novelist, Cervantes, Hemingway's life embodied the ideal of *armas y letras*, soldiering and writing, action and thought, but with greater emphasis on the body and with a modern distrust of reason. His prose had its seat in the muscles and in the rhythms of the blood. On his first trip to Spain after the Great War, Hemingway discovered a way of life even more ancient than the Greeks', one which preserved heroism in the art of bullfighting, the culture of death, the tragic sense of life. As he came to know the country and its people, he also discovered "feminine" elements which deepened his vision; they would be revealed in the magnificent character of Pilar in *For Whom the Bell Tolls*. In the Spaniards' tribal society, in their fiesta spirit, in their sense of the sacred, in their magical use of language, in the "secret things"—earth, sun, wine and food, the bull, blood, cojones, sexuality—he found an antidote to the decay of values in the modern world, to the decline in courage whose consequences we are perhaps only beginning to understand in the final years of the century.

After his fifteen-year exile from Franco's Spain, much of it spent in the Hispanic atmosphere of Cuba, Hemingway returned to the peninsula in 1953. Spain had been forever scarred by civil war and was finally entering the modern world amid forces inimical to its ancient, heroic values. Hemingway's aging and the failure of his inspiration coincided with Franco's dictatorship, the corruption of bullfighting, the tourist boom, and the modernization of Spanish life. The result was an end of the fertile symbiosis between the man and the land that had nourished one of the most original creations in modern literature. Hemingway's Spanish myth had been destroyed.

When he shot himself on that bright, cloudless summer morning, Hemingway had cancelled his reservations for another trip to Spain only a few days earlier. He died four days before the annual explosion of San Fermín and was buried on the very day he had planned to be in Pamplona. The hour of his death was appropriate—dawn, hour of the hunt and the encierro, the running of the bulls through the streets of Pamplona. Because of the time and manner of his suicide, some have attributed it to the Hispanic code of machismo which prefers oblivion to a life without physical strength, sexual potency, arrogance, and pride. When he heard the news of Hemingway's death, intuiting at once that it was self-inflicted, the great bullfighter Juan Belmonte stated laconically, *"Bien hecho"* ("Well done"). The torero knew the writer had killed himself with a gesture of grace and honor, with plenty of cojones. A man like the old jut-jawed matador could appreciate life only as long as he enjoyed health, sex, and sensual pleasures; when he could no longer do so, Belmonte also shot himself, less than a year later.

We might have expected more from a creator like Hemingway. His suicide was a personal as well as a Spanish tragedy. His flawed attempt to relive the old days of ferias and fiestas, in the dangerous summers of 1959–60, no doubt precipitated his decline. His misguided association with the corrupt "death and money business" of bullfighting in the final years of his life was partly responsible for his disenchantment with the country he loved more than any other except his own. Yet even if he had not returned to Spain, his demise was imminent: he had lost the power to create. If Hemingway had been able to maintain the balance between his head and his body, between his conscious and his unconscious mind that had enabled him to invent the most revolutionary prose of his time, he might have continued living and writing. Before we ascribe his fall to some kind of Hispanic code of masculine behavior, we should remember that he chose to die in his own country, not in Spain. In the vast, empty landscape of the American West, he had his final vision of nada. As he had told Spanish journalists in 1960 when a rumor of his death was circulating, "I will not die in Spain. Spain is a country for living, not for dying." The overall movement of Hemingway's Spanish experience was toward an affirmation of life despite, and because of, the culture of death and the tragic sense. If it had not been for his Spanish experience, he might never have been able to grow beyond his early preoccupation with death to affirm the power of life, nature, and love in works like *The Sun Also Rises, Death in the Afternoon, For Whom the Bell Tolls, The Old Man and the Sea*.

It would be difficult to imagine Hemingway in the new Spain of multinational corporations, consumerism, pollution, and tourism beyond his imagination. Video machines now flash and bleep in some of his favorite old bars. Yet he would be happy to find the country ruled by a liberal democracy for the first time since the days of the Republic, and by a good king for the first time in this century. With the instinct of a fighting bull for his *querencia*, Hemingway would find the secret places again. He would discover that the wine and the food are as marvelous as when he was twenty-two. He would be pleased by the new athletic revolution among Spanish youths, by the women whose legs seem to get longer every year. He would see the old faces that were young once, but everyone would remember how they were at the finest time in their lives. As he had his protagonist say in his last posthumous novel, *The Garden of Eden* (1986), "The country is here. . . . It's always here." He would know that Spain is changed, of course, perhaps now as much as we are older. He would know that after a glass of Valdepeñas, it gets very much the same as it was before. We've seen it all go and we'll watch it go again.

To put it in a very Spanish manner, Hemingway was much Hemingway. We could say of him, with words similar to those of Lorca in his elegy for the bullfighter who also died a violent, tragic death:

> It will be a long time, if ever, before there is born
> an American so strong, so rich in adventure.

Notes

Abbreviations used in the notes:

AMF	*A Moveable Feast*
ARIT	*Across the River and Into the Trees*
By-Line	William White (ed.), *By-Line: Ernest Hemingway*
CSS	*The Complete Short Stories of Ernest Hemingway*, The Finca Vigía Edition
DIA	*Death in the Afternoon*
"DS"	"The Dangerous Summer"
FTA	*A Farewell to Arms*
FWBT	*For Whom the Bell Tolls*
GHOA	*Green Hills of Africa*
GOE	*The Garden of Eden*
iot	*in our time*
IOT	*In Our Time*
JFK	Hemingway Collection, John F. Kennedy Library, Boston
Islands	*Islands in the Stream*
Letters	Carlos Baker (ed.), *Ernest Hemingway: Selected Letters 1917–1961*
Life Story	Carlos Baker, *Ernest Hemingway: A Life Story*
MWW	*Men Without Women*
NANA	North American Newspaper Alliance
NAS	*The Nick Adams Stories*
OMATS	*The Old Man and the Sea*
SAR	*The Sun Also Rises*
SS	*The Short Stories of Ernest Hemingway*
TFC	*The Fifth Column and the First Forty-nine Stories*
TFC & 4 Stories	*The Fifth Column and Four Stories of the Spanish Civil War*
THAHN	*To Have and Have Not*
TSTP	*Three Stories and Ten Poems*
TDS	*Toronto Daily Star*
TSW	*Toronto Star Weekly*
WTN	*Winner Take Nothing*

All quotations from Hemingway's letters, manuscripts, and texts are verbatim, with no corrections of grammar, spelling, or punctuation.

Preface
(pp. xi–xvii)

Epigraph: cited in Fraser Drew, "Hemingway's Generosity and Humility," *Mark Twain Journal* (Summer 1962), p. 19.

Paraphrase of EH: EH to Bernard Berenson, 20–22 Mar. 1953 (*Letters*, p. 812).

Pursuit as happiness: title of Part IV, *GHOA* (p. 215).

EH created style for our time: Archibald MacLeish, "His Mirror Was Danger," *Life* (14 July 1961), p. 71; "Years of the Dog," in *The Human Season: Selected Poems 1926–1972* (Boston: Houghton Mifflin, 1972), p. 38.

To live right with our eyes: EH, "On Writing," *NAS*, p. 239. Originally the coda to "Big Two-Hearted River," written in 1924.

The "Spanish thing": EH's expression for the Spanish Civil War, in EH to John Dos Passos, 26 Sept. 1936 (*Letters*, pp. 454–55).

María's razor blade: *FWBT*, pp. 170–71.

Picasso on beginnings: cited in Camilo José Cela, "Literatura y sociedad," lecture delivered at University of Kentucky, 3 Nov. 1981.

Struggle between feminine and masculine in EH's boyhood: Philip Young, *Ernest Hemingway: A Reconsideration* (University Park: Pennsylvania State University Press, 1969), p. 238. Here Young is comparing EH to Mark Twain. For a more complete discussion of the masculine/feminine throughout the writer's career, see Kenneth S. Lynn, *Hemingway: The Life and Work* (New York: Simon and Schuster, 1987).

"Everything went to hell in the

family": EH to Carlos Baker, 30 June 1951 (quoted in *Life Story*, p. 493).

EH to Sherwood Anderson: 7 Sept. 1926 (*Letters*, p. 218).

William Carlos Williams on pure products of America: "To Elsie," in *Selected Poems* (New York: New Directions, 1969), p. 28.

EH's lack of literary education until after he left America for Europe: see Michael S. Reynolds, *The Young Hemingway* (London and New York: Basil Blackwell, 1986), pp. 49–50, 184, 194.

Vargas Llosa on EH's "prehistory": "La prehistoria de Hemingway," *El País*, Madrid (7 Apr. 1986), pp. 11–12.

Artist must destroy or perpetuate: EH, "Gattorno: Program Note," *Esquire* (May 1936), p. 141.

EH's American Guernica: Young, *EH: A Reconsideration*, p. 252.

Hawthorne on America: Preface to *The Marble Faun* or *The Romance of Mount Beni* (Boston and New York: Houghton Mifflin, 1888), p. 15.

EH to Faulkner: 23 July 1947 (*Letters*, p. 624).

Spain as last good country: EH to James Gamble, 12 Dec. 1923; to Howell Jenkins, 9 Nov. 1924; to Gertrude Stein and Alice B. Toklas, 15 July 1925; to Maxwell Perkins, 24 July 1926 (*Letters*, pp. 107, 131, 168, 212). The phrase "the last good country" is from the title of EH's short story in *NAS*, written between 1952 and 1958. See Philip Young and Charles W. Mann, *The Hemingway Manuscripts: An Inventory* (University Park: Pennsylvania State University Press, 1969), p. 47.

EH on "secret things" of Spain: "African Journal," Part 3, *Sports Illustrated* (10 Jan. 1972), p. 24. EH also says that Africa has "the secret things." He wrote this between 1954 and 1958.

Spanish friends call EH "Ernesto": James M. Markham, "Hemingway's Spain," *New York Times* (24 Nov. 1985), Travel Section, p. 15.

EH's love of Spain: EH, "DS," Part I, *Life* (5 Sept. 1960), p. 78; EH to Bronislaw Zielinski, 24 June 1959 (JFK).

EH's "Spanish" appearance: author's interviews with Miguel Fernández, maître d'hotel, Hotel Suecia, Madrid; Pedro Gálvez, Hotel Palace, Madrid; Mariano Martín and Pablo Vela, Cervecería Alemana, Madrid, Feb.–May 1980.

Frederic Henry passes for "Latin": FTA, p. 195.

Dark or night side of EH's personality ("black ass"): "Black Ass at the Cross Roads," CSS, pp. 579–89.

Fiesta concept of life: EH, AMF, p. 210. EH used the phrase negatively here with reference to the idle rich Americans in Europe. From now on I will speak of the more positive "fiesta sense of life" as opposed to the well known "tragic sense of life." See Allen Josephs, *White Wall of Spain: The Mysteries of Andalusian Culture* (Ames: Iowa State University Press, 1983), pp. 128, 151, 153.

EH's cheerless upbringing: see EH to Grace Hall Hemingway, 16 Jan. 1918 (*Letters*, p. 3).

EH on "tribal faith": EH to Thomas Welsh, 19 June 1945 (*Letters*, p. 592).

EH on "fourth or fifth dimension": GHOA, pp. 26–27.

EH's iceberg theory: see DIA, p. 192.

Ancient, secret things in Spain: a recent example is the discovery of El Juyo Cave in northern Spain near Santander. The 14,000-year-old shrine was discovered by a joint

team of Spaniards and Americans and was announced in 1981. See L. G. Freeman and J. González Echegaray, "El Juyo: A 14,000-Year-Old Sanctuary from Northern Spain," *History of Religions* (Aug. 1981), pp. 1–19.

Spanish as "secret language": EH to Edmund Wilson, 8 Nov. 1952 (*Letters*, p. 794).

"The Undiscovered Country": Baker, *Life Story*, p. 348.

"Way past things we know about": EH, *Islands*, p. 196. The passage refers to death.

Spain as continent: MS #49.9 (galleys of Chapter 20, *DIA*), JFK. For this and all items in the Hemingway Collection, the following work is indispensable: Jo August, *Ernest Hemingway: Catalog of the Manuscripts, Correspondence, and Other Material at the John F. Kennedy Library*, 2 vols. (New York: G. K. Hall, 1981).

Spain as rope of sand: "Spain is today, as it always has been, a bundle of small bodies tied together by a rope of sand, and, being without union, is also without strength." Richard Ford, *Gatherings from Spain* (1846; reprint, London: J. M. Dent & Sons, 1970), p. 13.

Robert Browning's heart: "De Gustibus—," in Horace E. Scudder (ed.), *The Complete Poetical Works of Browning* (Boston: Houghton Mifflin, 1895), pp. 178–79.

EH as old Veneto boy: EH to Berenson, 25 Aug. 1949 (*Letters*, p. 666).

EH on heart or soul of a country: MS #49.9.

Figure under the carpet: Leon Edel, "The Figure Under the Carpet," in Marc Pachter (ed.), *Telling Lives: The Biographical Art* (Washington, D.C.:

New Republic Books/National Portrait Gallery, 1979), pp. 27, 32.
EH on serious vs. solemn writer: *DIA*, p. 192.
EH on the part and the whole: *DIA*, p. 278.

Prelude: Madrid, 1984
(pp. 1–7)

Botín's: for a description in the early days of the new democracy, see Allen Josephs, "At the Heart of Madrid," *Atlantic* (July 1979), pp. 74–77.

Chapter 1.
A Strange Country
(pp. 9–18)

Chapter title: "It is a strange country, Spain . . ." MS #49.9 (JFK).
Epigraph: MS #49.9.
EH on SS. *Leopoldina* : Baker, *Life Story*, p. 83.
EH describes Spanish coast: to his family, 20 Dec. 1921; to William B. Smith, Jr., c. 20 Dec. 1921; to Sherwood and Tennessee Anderson, c. 23 Dec. 1921 (*Letters*, pp. 57–59); "At Vigo, in Spain, Is Where You Catch the Silver and Blue Tuna, the King of All Fish," *TSW* (18 Feb. 1922), p. 15, *By-Line*, pp. 16–17.
Vigo as "place for a male": in EH's slang, "male" = "man" or "person."
EH's plans to return to Spain: EH to Smith, c. 20 Dec. 1921 (*Letters*, p. 58).
"Yarrup": EH to Jenkins, 26 Dec. 1921 (*Letters*, p. 60).
EH queries Spaniards about Spain: Luis Quintanilla, "Hemingway en mi recuerdo," *Cuadernos del Congreso por la Libertad de la Cultura*, Paris (Nov. 1961), pp. 45–51.

Stein and Strater talk to EH about bullfighting: *DIA*, pp. 1–2; Emilio Salcedo, "Conversación con Hemingway," *La Gaceta Regional*, Salamanca (15 Sept. 1960), p. 5; Henry Strater to Carlos Baker, 5 May 1953 (quoted courtesy of Professor Baker).
Pound on EH's instincts: quoted in MacLeish, "His Mirror Was Danger," p. 71.
EH on courage of "actual physical conduct . . .": to Edward J. O'Brien, 2 May 1924 (*Letters*, p. 117).
"The first matador got the horn . . .": interchapter 2 of *iot* and IX of *IOT*, first published in *Little Review* (Spring 1923), p. 3, *SS*, p. 159.
Good writing gives kick to the reader: EH to George S. Albee, 1 May 1931 (Univ. of California).
Strater on bullfight crowd: to Baker, 5 May 1953.
EH and Lardner: EH would deny Lardner's influence on *iot* in a letter to Edmund Wilson, 18 Oct. 1924 (*Letters*, p. 129).
EH and Blasco Ibáñez's *Blood and Sand* : EH, "Why Not Trade Other Public Entertainers Among the Nations as the Big Leagues Do Baseball Players?" *TSW* (19 Feb. 1921), p. 13.
American protagonists of *TSTP*: Jim Gilmore ("Up in Michigan") has physical prowess but he is a brute; the aging jockey Butler ("My Old Man") is venal and without honor; the young gentleman ("Out of Season") is fearful and jejune. *SS*, pp. 81–86, 191–205, 173–79.
Wilson on EH and Goya: "Mr. Hemingway's Dry Points," *Dial* (Oct. 1924), p. 341. EH had a two-volume edition of Goya's *La Tauromaquia* in his library at Key West, probably acquired during his trip to Spain in the summer of 1924. See Michael S.

Reynolds, *Hemingway's Reading 1910–1940* (Princeton: Princeton University Press, 1981), p. 131. *La Tauromaquia* is composed of etchings, not lithographs as stated by Wilson.
Story of dishonest mailman: "How'd You Like to Tip Postman Every Time?" *TSW* (11 Mar. 1922), p. 13; in Gene Z. Hanrahan (ed.), *The Wild Years. Ernest Hemingway* (New York: Dell, 1962), pp. 168–69. In a letter to Horace Liveright (15 May 1925), EH would retell the story as if he had witnessed it himself (*Letters*, p. 160).
EH's expectations of Spain: MS #398 ("The first time I went to Spain . . ."), JFK.
"Bull-fights, bandits, and black eyes": Ford, *Gatherings from Spain*, p. 291. Like his protagonist Robert Jordan in *FWBT* (p. 248), EH read Ford; he had the 1849 edition of *Gatherings* in his library at Key West (Reynolds, *Hemingway's Reading*, p. 126). He did not read *Carmen* until after the publication of *SAR*, which some French critics compared to Mérimée's novel. See EH to Perkins, 24 Apr. 1926, and EH to Owen Wister, c. 25 July 1929 (*Letters*, pp. 202, 301).
EH prepares first trip to Spain: MS #546.5 ("Last spring Mac and I decided to go to Spain . . ."), JFK; "Bull Fighting Is Not a Sport—It Is a Tragedy," *TSW* (20 Oct. 1923), p. 23, *By-Line*, p. 90.
EH had only been to Spain on port call: in addition to the four hours he spent in Vigo in December 1921, EH had stopped in the southern Spanish port of Algeciras for "three great days" on the way back from Italy in January 1919. See EH to James Gamble, 3 Mar. 1919; to Grace Quinlan, 8 Aug. 1920 (*Letters*, pp. 21, 36).
Spain in 1920s: see Gerald Brenan,

The Spanish Labyrinth (Cambridge, England: Cambridge University Press, 1969), pp. 57ff.; Salustiano del Campo, *Análisis de la población de España* (Barcelona: Ariel, 1972).
EH's first impressions of Spain: MS #398; "The Soul of Spain with McAlmon and Bird the Publishers," in Nicholas Gerogiannis (ed.), *Ernest Hemingway: 88 Poems* (New York and London: Harcourt Brace Jovanovich/ Bruccoli Clark, 1979), pp. 70–73; EH to Gamble, 12 Dec. 1923; EH to Jenkins, 9 Nov. 1924 (*Letters*, pp. 107, 130).
EH's first bullfight: "Bull Fighting Is Not a Sport," *By-Line*, pp. 91–95; EH to Gregory Clark, c. July 1923 (JFK). On McAlmon's reaction: *DIA*, p. 466.
EH finds admirable physical conduct in bullfight: EH to O'Brien, 2 May 1924.
Hadley on EH being "atavistic . . .": Hadley Richardson to EH, 4 June 1921, quoted in Peter Griffin, *Along with Youth: Hemingway, the Early Years* (New York and Oxford: Oxford University Press, 1985), p. 184.
Botín's and Gin Bottle King: "Bull Fighting Is Not a Sport," pp. 92–93, 95–96.
EH in Madrid: Baker, *Life Story*, p. 110; *DIA*, pp. 51, 48; "Night Life in Europe a Disease Constantinople's Most Hectic," *TSW* (15 Dec. 1923), p. 21, *The Wild Years*, pp. 149–50; "'Old Constan' in True Light; Is Tough Town," *TDS* (28 Oct. 1922), p. 17, *By-Line*, pp. 53–55; "The Soul of Spain," in Gerogiannis (ed.), *EH: 88 Poems*, p. 72.
Postcard to Stein: 9 June 1923 (Beinecke Rare Book and Manuscript Library, Yale Univ.).
Spain in hot weather: EH to Horne, 18 July 1923 (*Letters*, p. 87).
EH on Andalusia: Baker, *Life Story*,

p. 111; *DIA*, p. 51; MS #203.b (Notes on Spain and bullfighting), JFK.
Ronda: *DIA*, pp. 42–43. The photos described are in the Hemingway Collection (JFK Library). In the MS of *DIA* at the Humanities Research Center, Univ. of Texas, EH tells a curious story about getting hit on the head with a large pebble thrown by washerwomen in Ronda (p. 63).
EH on learning Spanish: MS #49.9.
Castile-Aragón like American west: MS #49.9.
Three peninsulas loved by EH: MS #49.9.

Chapter 2. A Wild Place Up in Navarre
(pp. 22–27)

Title: EH to Isabel Simmons, 24 June 1923 (*Letters*, p. 84).
Epigraph: Salvador de Madariaga, "The World Weighs a Writer's Influence: Spain," *Saturday Review* (29 July 1961), p. 18.
EH imagines Pamplona: to Simmons, 24 June 1923.
Hemingways among first English-speaking tourists at San Fermín: "World's Series of Bull Fighting a Mad, Whirling Carnival," *TSW* (27 Oct. 1923), p. 33, *By-Line*, p. 105; Leah Rice Koontz, " 'Montoya' Remembers *The Sun Also Rises*," in Bertram D. Sarason (ed.), *Hemingway and the Sun Set* (Washington, D.C.: NCR/Microcard Editions, 1972), p. 209; EH to Harvey Breit, 3–4 Nov. 1955 (JFK).
EH on San Fermín, 1923: to William D. Horne, 18 July 1923 (*Letters*, pp. 87–88); "Bull Fighting Is Not a Sport," *By-Line*, p. 95; "World's Series of Bull Fighting," *By-Line*; Mary

Hemingway, *How It Was* (New York: Ballantine Books, 1977), p. 416; EH to Smith, 17 Feb. 1925 (JFK).
EH on Italians: Marcelline Hemingway Sanford, *At the Hemingways: A Family Portrait* (Boston: Atlantic–Little, Brown, 1961), p. 184; EH to Ernest Walsh, c. Aug. 1925 (Univ. of Virginia).
EH on Maera: "World's Series of Bull Fighting," *By-Line*, pp. 105–07; *DIA*, p. 82.
EH on bullfighting as "stalwart pre-natal influence": to Simmons, 24 June 1923. The child Mrs. Hemingway was carrying in Pamplona would be baptized John Hadley Nicanor. EH believed children's names "have got to *have Spanish* in them to really come off" (emphasis his): to Stein and Toklas, 9 Nov. 1923 (*Letters*, p. 102).
EH's new images of Pamplona: to Horne, 18 July 1923 (*Letters*, p. 88).
EH on Spain and Spaniards: MS #398 ("The first time I went to Spain . . ."), JFK; to Gamble, 12 Dec. 1923 (*Letters*, p. 107); to Dr. C. E. Hemingway, 7 Nov. 1923 (*Letters*, p. 100); to Jenkins, 9 Nov. 1924 (*Letters*, p. 131); to Smith, 17 Feb. 1925.
Three peninsulas in EH's life: MS #49.9 (JFK); EH to Jenkins, 9 Nov. 1924.
Loyola, and Spain as open wound: *DIA*, pp. 274–75; "Gattorno: Program Note," *Esquire* (May 1936), p. 111.

Chapter 3. The Bullfight and the Prose of Ecstasy
(pp. 29–42)

EH's whole inner life bullfighting: "On Writing," *NAS*, p. 236.
EH's writing, the bullfight, and sex:

"On Writing," NAS, pp. 236–39 (written c. Aug. 1924); EH to Charles Scribner, 2 June 1948 (*Letters*, p. 636); MS of *DIA* (Univ. of Texas), p. 249; EH to Perkins, 15 Jan. 1928 (*Letters*, p. 270); *AMF*, p. 6; MS #354a ("The Dangerous Summer"), p. 772 (JFK).

Five bullfight miniatures of *iot*: "They whack—whacked the white horse . . .," "The crowd shouted all the time . . .," "If it happened right down close . . .," "I heard the drums coming down the street . . .," "Maera lay still . . ." (*iot*), SS, pp. 165, 171, 181, 189, 207.

EH's description of Villalta: "If it happened right down close . . .," original Chap. 14 of *iot* (SS, p. 181). This description was hardly surpassed by the lengthier one in *DIA*, pp. 221–22. For the aficionados old enough to have seen Villalta in person, or for those like myself who have seen him on film, Hemingway's description is eerily exact. Villalta died in 1980, still a hero, especially in his adopted hometown of Madrid.

Blood as symbol of life and death in *iot*: as in "Indian Camp," the first story of *IOT*. There an Indian slits his throat with a razor as his wife is delivered of a baby by Caesarean section.

"Tight and hard" prose of *iot*: EH to John Dos Passos, 22 Apr. 1925 (Dos Passos Collection, Univ. of Virginia). EH is referring here to *IOT* (1925), which incorporated the sketches of the earlier book.

Pound's Imagism as closest source of EH's early style: see Harold Hurwitz, "Hemingway's Tutor, Ezra Pound," in Linda Wagner (ed.), *Hemingway: Five Decades of Criticism* (East Lansing: Michigan State University Press, 1974), pp. 8–20; Wirt Williams,

The Tragic Art of Ernest Hemingway (Baton Rouge and London: Louisiana State University Press, 1981), pp. 17–20.

EH learned "rhythms in prose" from Stein: EH to W. G. Rogers, 29 July 1948 (*Letters*, p. 649).

EH's definition of *templar*: "An Explanatory Glossary," *DIA*, p. 454.

Pound on "absolute rhythm": quoted in William Pratt (ed.), *The Imagist Poem* (New York: E. P. Dutton, 1963), p. 27.

EH's description of Algabeño: "World's Series of Bull Fighting," *By-Line*, p. 108.

P. Young on the "Hemingway style": *EH: A Reconsideration*, pp. 44–46, 207.

Pedro Romero in *SAR*: pp. 219, 218.

A complete faena in *DIA*: pp. 206–7.

Ecstatic prose and integration with the world: at the end of *FWBT*, Robert Jordan feels "completely integrated now" (p. 471).

Carl Jung on the psychological and the visionary artist: "Psychology and Literature," *The Spirit in Man, Art, and Literature*, in *Collected Works*, 18 vols. (New York: Pantheon Books, 1966), 15:90.

Orthodoxy of bullfight: "Bull Fighting Is Not a Sport," *By-Line*, p. 96; Unamuno, "Carta a un torero," in *Obras completas*, 16 vols. (Madrid: Afrodisio Aguado, 1958), 11:913; Ángel Capellán, "Hemingway and the Hispanic World," Ph.D. diss., New York University, 1977, p. 352, revised and published in book form under same title (Ann Arbor, Mich.: UMI Research Press, 1985).

EH and Nietzsche: EH checked out *Thus Spake Zarathustra* during May–September 1926 (Reynolds, *Hemingway's Reading*, p. 163), and

had a copy in his library at the Finca Vigía, Cuba (published by Boni & Liveright, n.d.); see also James D. Brasch and Joseph Sigman, *Hemingway's Library: A Composite Record* (New York and London: Garland, 1981), p. 272. Nietzsche's theory of the Apollonian vs. the Dionysian is contained in *The Birth of Tragedy from the Spirit of Music*, in *The Philosophy of Nietzsche* (New York: Modern Library, 1954), pp. 947–1088.
EH on poetry and prose: to Breit, 3 July 1956 (*Letters*, p. 862); to Arnold Gingrich, 22 Oct. 1938 (*Letters*, p. 472).
"Night Before Battle": published originally in *Esquire* (Feb. 1939), pp. 27–29, 95, 97, reprinted in *TFC & 4 Stories*, pp. 110–39. See EH to Gingrich, 22 Oct. 1938.
Dactylic rhythm and religious expression: see Julian Jaynes, *The Origin of Consciousness in the Breakdown of the Bicameral Mind* (Boston: Houghton Mifflin, 1976), p. 362.
William James, emotion and bodily sensation: Harry Levin, "Observations on the Style of EH," in Carlos Baker (ed.), *Hemingway and His Critics: An International Anthology* (New York: Hill and Wang, 1961), p. 112.
"Old, primitive sensation": Leicester Hemingway, *My Brother, Ernest Hemingway* (Cleveland: World, 1961), p. 127.
"Godlike attribute" of administering death: *DIA*, p. 233.
"Big Two-Hearted River" *(IOT)*: SS, p. 228. See Young, *EH: A Reconsideration*, p. 46. There is a tentative use of ecstatic prose in EH's newspaper article, "There Are Great Fish in the Rhone Canal," *TDS* (10 June 1922), p. 5, *By-Line*, p. 34.

"Cross Country Snow" *(IOT)*: SS, p. 183.
"The Short Happy Life of Francis Macomber": SS, p. 21.
"Fathers and Sons" *(WTN)*: SS, p. 497.
M. Cowley on "primitive" Hemingway: Introduction, Viking Portable *Hemingway* (New York: Viking, 1944), pp. vii–xxiv.
EH on his God: to Arthur Mizener, 12 May 1950 (*Letters*, p. 694).

Chapter 4. The Messiah of Bullfighting
(pp. 47–53)

Epigraph: Madariaga, "The World Weighs a Writer's Influence: Spain," *Saturday Review* (29 July 1961), p. 18.
Ronda style of bullfighting: *DIA*, p. 446.
Cayetano Ordóñez as new messiah of bullfighting: *DIA*, p. 88.
EH watches dressing of C. Ordóñez in Hotel Quintana: although there is no evidence that Hemingway actually witnessed the ceremony, it is very likely that he did: he was a friend of the hotel's owner, Juanito Quintana, and C. Ordóñez fought no fewer than four corridas during the feria of 1925 (7, 9, 11, and 12 July).
Original beginning of *SAR*: one surviving manuscript and three typescripts describe the dressing of the bullfighter in the hotel (MS #193, 195, 197, 197a, JFK). A similar scene appears in the published version of *SAR*, Chap. XV (p. 163). It is likely but not certain that these drafts preceded the published version.
EH changes bullfighter's name from Guerrita to Pedro Romero: see Allen

Josephs, *"Toreo:* The Moral Axis of *The Sun Also Rises," Hemingway Review* (Fall 1986), pp. 91, 95–96.

EH to Sylvia Beach on writing and bullfight: 3 Aug. 1925 (Princeton Univ.).

Composition of SAR: Baker, *Life Story,* p. 154; Frederic Joseph Svoboda, *Hemingway and "The Sun Also Rises": The Crafting of a Style* (Lawrence: University Press of Kansas, 1983).

SAR notebooks: MSS #193–194 (JFK).

Niño de la Palma's first serious goring: *DIA,* pp. 89–90.

Niño's decline: Sam Adams, "The Sun Also Sets," *Sports Illustrated* (29 June 1970), pp. 57–60, 62–64, reprint in Sarason (ed.), *Hemingway and the Sun Set,* pp. 212–21; EH to Breit, 3–4 Nov. 1955 (JFK).

Paris as EH's wasteland in *SAR*: see John McCormick, *The Middle Distance: A Comparative History of American Imaginative Literature: 1919–1932* (New York: Free Press, 1971), p. 53.

EH's withering view of Paris in early journalism and *SAR*: "American Bohemians in Paris a Weird Lot," *TSW* (25 Mar. 1922), p. 15, *By-Line,* pp. 23–25; "The Mecca of Fakers is French Capital," *TDS* (25 Mar. 1922), p. 4; Aaron Lantham, "A Farewell to Machismo," *New York Times Magazine* (16 Oct. 1977), p. 81.

"Who has vitality in Paris?": EH to Fitzgerald, c. 24 or 31 Oct. 1929 (*Letters,* p. 310).

Jake Barnes's summer trip from France to Spain as pilgrimage: see H. R. Stoneback, "From the rue Saint-Jacques to the Pass of Roland to the 'Unfinished Church on the Edge of the Cliff,'" *Hemingway Review* (Fall 1986), pp. 2–29.

Pedro Romero *(SAR)* named after historical bullfighter: for information on the real Romero, see José María de Cossío, *Los toros: Tratado técnico e histórico,* 7 vols. (Madrid: Espasa-Calpe, 1945), 3:825–34.

American ambassador in *SAR*: Ferdinand J. Watson, the American ambassador to Spain, was guest of honor at San Fermín in 1925. See Baker, *Life Story,* p. 152, and José María Iribarren, *Hemingway y los Sanfermines* (Pamplona: Editorial Gómez, 1970), p. 57.

Pedro Romero as ithyphallic authority: Lawrence's theory is cited in Young, *EH: A Reconsideration,* p. 70.

Hemingway's (and Jake Barnes's) senses came alive in Spain: Mary Hemingway, "Hemingway's Spain," *Saturday Review* (11 Mar. 1967), pp. 48–49.

Chapter 5. This Is Country (pp. 61–65)

Mood of *SAR* brightens for trip to Burguete: Carlos Baker, *Hemingway: The Writer as Artist* (Princeton: Princeton University Press, 1973), p. 83.

Real objects in Spain vs. artificial in France: in addition to the novel itself, see EH, MS #714 ("Spain 2"), JFK.

Passage from epilogue of *DIA*: pp. 274–75.

Avaricious Parisians in first part of *SAR*: Jake's concierge and the patronne of the dancing club, for example.

Mountains vs. plains in *SAR*: Baker, *The Writer as Artist,* pp. 82–86.

Problems of chronology in Burguete section: see Michael S. Reynolds, "Words Killed, Wounded, Missing in Action," *Hemingway notes* (Spring 1981), p. 6.
Hemlock forests of northern Michigan: "The Last Good Country," NAS, pp. 89–91.
"Big Two-Hearted River": SS, pp. 209–32.
Relationship between Jake and nature: Professor William Robinson's untitled and unpublished essay on *FTA* was very helpful to me here. The next quotation ("pulling the blanket. . .") is from his essay.
EH on making country in words: "On Writing," NAS, p. 239.
Burguete in 1924 like being in heaven: EH to Hadley Mowrer, 26 July 1939 (*Letters*, p. 493).
EH aware of historical past, Roncesvalles: EH to Smith, 6 Dec. 1924 (*Letters*, p. 136).
EH to Perkins on the monumental and epic: 5–6 Jan. 1932 (*Letters*, p. 352).

Chapter 6.
The Fiesta Sense of Life
(pp. 70–73)

"Unearthly and unbelievable" quality of fighting bull: *DIA*, p. 113.
Jung on universal hero: Carl G. Jung (ed.), "Approaching the Unconscious," in *Man and His Symbols* (New York: Doubleday, 1964), p. 79.
Bullfight "only place where you could see life and death": *DIA*, p. 2.

Chapter 7. The Tragic Sense
of Life
(pp. 79–82)

Jake Barnes does not participate in encierro: neither is there any evidence that EH himself ran the bulls. He did go into the "amateurs" in the bullring of Pamplona (after the running of the fighting bulls), in which brave cows with padded horns are used. After EH's death, his friend, the matador Antonio Ordóñez (son of Cayetano Ordóñez, Niño de la Palma), noted: "It is very strange that, in spite of his close contact with the bullfight, he, himself, never tried to fight, not even with a calf." "Hemingway and I," *Diario de Málaga* (n.d.). This article is contained in a folder labeled "Bullfight Materials" (JFK).
Anti-taurine waiter in *SAR*: as well as recalling similar characters from Blasco Ibáñez's novels (like *Blood and Sand*), this character foreshadows the anarcho-syndicalist waiter in EH's story "The Capital of the World," first published as "The Horns of the Bull," *Esquire* (June 1936), pp. 31, 190–93, later under the new title in SS, pp. 38–51.
Fatal goring witnessed by EH at San Fermín, 1924: Iribarren, *Hemingway y los Sanfermines*, p. 47. For the autobiographical element behind the story of the bull's ear in SAR (p. 199), see EH to Stein and Toklas, 15 July 1925 (*Letters*, p. 167), and Baker, *Life Story*, p. 152.
Vicente Girones episode in *SAR*: see Cathy M. Davidson, "Death in the Morning: The Role of Vicente Girones in *The Sun Also Rises*," *Hemingway notes* (Fall 1979), pp. 11–13.
Federico García Lorca's lament

for bullfighter: "Llanto por Ignacio Sánchez Mejías," in *Obras completas*, 2 vols. (Madrid: Aguilar, 1975), 2:558.
Wilson on Vicente Girones/Robert Cohn: *The Wound and the Bow: Seven Studies in Literature* (New York: Oxford University Press, 1947), p. 218. The following quotation by Wilson refers to *IOT* but could be extended to nearly all of EH's fiction (p. 216).
SAR **as "jazz superficial story":** EH to Perkins, 16 Nov. 1926 (*Letters*, p. 226).
SAR **as tragedy:** EH to Perkins, 19 Nov. 1926 (*Letters*, p. 229).
Baker on *SAR* **as tragicomedy:** *The Writer as Artist*, p. 96.
Wirt Williams on *SAR* **as "first major revelation of H.'s tragic vision":** *The Tragic Art of EH*, p. 40.

Chapter 8. Over the Wind-Blown Fields of Grain (pp. 84–89)

Epigraph: Blaise Pascal, *Pensées*, Louis Lafuma (ed.) (Paris: Editions du Luxembourg, 1952), fragment 60.
MS of *SAR* **on France, Spain, and San Sebastián:** MS #194.6 ("Fiesta, A Novel"), JFK, p. 30. The quotation about getting "all straightened inside" is from the same manuscript, p. 35.
Nick Adams on diving and being underwater: "Summer People," NAS, p. 222.
EH and El Escorial: for the novelist's negative opinion of the monastery, see EH to Dos Passos, 22 Sept. 1936 (Dos Passos Collection, Univ. of Virginia).
Spanish contemporary of EH on El Escorial: Juan Gil-Albert, fragment of *España: empeño de una ficción*, in *Revista de Occidente*, Madrid

(Oct.–Dec. 1980), pp. 128–29.
Jake eats large meal at Botín's: I am indebted to Richard Sugg's fine interpretation of this scene in "Hemingway, Money and *The Sun Also Rises*," *Fitzgerald/Hemingway Annual* (1972), pp. 260, 267.
EH on death as two bicycle policemen: "The Snows of Kilimanjaro," *Esquire* (Aug. 1936), p. 200, SS, p. 74.

Chapter 9. Of Bulls and Men (pp. 91–125)

Epigraph: *Letters*, pp. 236–37.
EH probably began notes for bullfight book before *SAR*: MS #295 ("Bullfighting Manuscript Notes"), JFK. See also Robert W. Lewis, "The Making of *Death in the Afternoon*," in James Nagel (ed.), *Ernest Hemingway: The Writer in Context* (Madison: University of Wisconsin Press, 1984), pp. 36–37; Susan Beegel, "The Death of El Espartero: An Historic Matador Links 'The Undefeated' and *Death in the Afternoon*," *Hemingway Review* (Spring 1986), pp. 12–23.
EH's project for bullfight book (1925): EH to Dos Passos, 22 Apr. 1925 (Dos Passos Collection, Univ. of Virginia). EH denied the rumor about this book in a letter to Carlos Baker, 1 Apr. 1951 (*The Writer as Artist*, p. 145n).
EH and Doughty's *Travels in Arabia Deserta*: EH to Perkins, 15 Apr. 1925 (*Letters*, p. 156).
R. Ford on bullfight: *Gatherings from Spain*, p. 339.
Robert Jordan on Spain: *FWBT*, p. 248.
Antonio Gala on bullfight: *Charlas con Troylo* (Madrid: Espasa-Calpe, 1981), p. 164.

EH said bullfight always a tragedy
and tragedy requires dignity: "Bull-
fighting, Sport and Industry," *Fortune*
(Mar. 1930), p. 83; *DIA*, p. 159.
References to suicide in *DIA*: pp. 3,
20, 122.
Dr. Hemingway and killing cleanly:
M. Hemingway Sanford, *At the
Hemingways*, p. 81.
EH "cared about" his father: EH
to Perkins, 16 Dec. 1928 (*Letters*,
p. 291).
Mencken on *DIA*: "The Spanish
Idea of a Good Time," *The American
Mercury* (Dec. 1932), pp. 506–7;
reprint in Robert O. Stephens (ed.),
*Ernest Hemingway: The Critical
Reception* (New York: Burt Franklin,
1977), p. 123.
EH and "Narcissus principle": Baker,
The Writer as Artist, pp. 385–86, 388.
Baker sees *TFC* (1938) as the first
indisputable example of the principle
in EH's work, but I believe it is already
evident in *DIA*.
**Américo Castro and "Spanish in-
tegralism":** see *Sobre el nombre y
el quién de los españoles* (Madrid:
Taurus, 1973), p. 321.
Salinas on culture of death: "Lorca
and the Poetry of Death," in Manuel
Durán (ed.), *Lorca: A Collection of
Critical Essays* (Englewood Cliffs,
N.J.: Prentice-Hall, 1962), pp. 102–4,
106.
Hemingway, death, and immortality:
see Sean O'Faolain, *The Vanishing
Hero: Studies in Novelists of the
Twenties* (Boston: Little, Brown,
1957), p. 127; John McCormick
and Mario Sevilla Mascareñas, *The
Complete Aficionado* (Cleveland:
World, 1967), pp. 236–37.
Unamuno on immortality: *Del sen-
timiento trágico de la vida en los
hombres y en los pueblos* (1913), tr.

Anthony Kerrigan, *The Tragic Sense of
Life in Man and Nations* (Princeton:
Princeton University Press, 1972).
Deleted sentence from *DIA* **on im-
mortality:** MS, p. 272 (Humanities
Research Center, Univ. of Texas).
**Montherlant compared to Heming-
way re bullfight:** McCormick, *The
Middle Distance*, pp. 71–72; Mario
Praz, "Hemingway in Italy," in Baker
(ed.), *Hemingway and His Critics*, pp.
117–18.
**EH on death during the composition
of** *DIA*: EH to Fitzgerald, 13 Sept., c.
24 or 31 Oct. 1929; EH to Archibald
MacLeish, 30 June 1930, 14 Mar.
1931; EH to Waldo Peirce, 15 Apr.
1932 (*Letters*, pp. 306, 310, 326, 338,
359).
EH and typesetter for *DIA*: EH to
Perkins, 28 June 1932 (*Letters*, pp.
361–62); Baker, *Life Story*, p. 229.
EH's improvised composition of *DIA*:
see MS (Univ. of Texas), where it is
obvious that EH divided his material
into chapters afterwards.
Lorca on bullfight as religious drama:
"Teoría y juego del duende," *Obras
completas*, 1 : 1077.
Origin of bullfight in nature rituals:
see Ángel Álvarez de Miranda, *Ritos y
juegos del toro* (Madrid: Taurus, 1962);
McCormick and Mascareñas, *The
Complete Aficionado*, p. 27.
Survival of totem banquet in Spain:
Pedro Caba, "A Half-Philosophical
Theory," in *Los toros/Bullfighting*
(Madrid: Indice, 1974), pp. 38–39.
Burgess and eating meat of bull:
Ernest Hemingway y su mundo
(Madrid: Ultramar, 1980), p. 71
(trans. of *Ernest Hemingway and His
World* [London: Thames & Hudson,
1978]).
"Sangre de Toro" wine: produced by
Torres vinters, Catalonia.

Passage on Cagancho's faena added to original draft: MS, pp. 9ff. (Univ. of Texas).
Lorca on duende: "Teoría y juego del duende," *Obras completas*, 1:1067–79.
Robert Jordan on "La Gloria": *FWBT*, p. 380.
Montherlant on sun and shade: *Chaos and Night* (New York: Macmillan, 1964), p. 44.
Montherlant's *The Bullfighters (Les Bestiares)* checked out by EH: Richard Layman, "Hemingway's Library Cards at Shakespeare & Co.," *Fitzgerald/Hemingway Annual* (1975), p. 192.
Blood, wine, sun in the eucharist: I am indebted to Fernando Claramunt for the association between the host and the solar circle. See his "Los toros desde la psicología," in Cossío, *Los toros*, 7:20.
EH on cojones and sense of death: "Chroniques: And to the United States," *The Transatlantic Review* (May–June 1924), p. 355.
EH on critics as eunuchs: Rodrigo Royo, "Las pequeñas confesiones de Hemingway," *Arriba*, Madrid (5 Oct. 1956), n.p. In a poem beginning "Little Mr. Wilson . . . ," published posthumously, EH spoke of "All the ball-less critics / All their cuntless wives." Gerogiannis (ed.), *EH: 88 Poems*, p. 97.
Christianity replaced cults of bull-gods with worship of lamb: Claramunt, "Los toros desde la psicología," p. 20.
EH accused of sounding like Baedeker *cum* Duncan Hines: Young, *EH: A Reconsideration*, p. 96.
Aranjuez as Spanish Versailles: see for example Gerald Brenan, *The Face of Spain* (New York: Pellegrini & Cudahy, 1951), pp. 285–88.

Deleted passage on beautiful Spanish women, *DIA*: MS, p. 54 (Univ. of Texas).
Spain lost its virginity before any other country: EH to Isidore Schneider, 23 Mar. 1926 (JFK).
EH divides aficionados in two groups: DIA, MS, p. 8 (Univ. of Texas).
EH on Maera's death: *DIA*, MS, p. 109 (Univ. of Texas).
"Personal element" in bullfight: *DIA* MS, p. 121 (Univ. of Texas).
Honor vs. *pundonor* in Spanish: see *Diccionario de la lengua española* (Madrid: Real Academia Española, 1970), p. 1082; Capellán, "Hemingway and the Hispanic World," pp. 293–94.
Frederic Henry on "abstract words": *FTA*, pp. 184–85. See also Keneth Kinnamon, "Hemingway, the *Corrida*, and Spain," *Texas Studies in Literature and Language* (Spring 1959), p. 55.
EH used "A Natural History of the Dead" indirectly in *DIA*: EH to Everett R. Perry, c. 7 Feb. 1933 (*Letters*, p. 380).
EH admits complicity in paying off bullfight critics: "DS," MS #354a, p. 10 of insert to p. 14 (JFK).
EH on "Story of 2 fairies" for *DIA*: MS, p. 218 (Univ. of Texas).
Huxley, "Foreheads Villainous Low": in *Music at Night and Other Essays* (New York: Fountain Press, 1931), pp. 111–15.
EH and Goya: see EH to Breit, 21 June 1952 (*Letters*, pp. 767–68); José Luis Castillo-Puche, "Hemingway, peregrino en España," *ABC* (25 June 1984), p. 3; "Hemingway y los toros a través de Goya," *Diario de Navarra* (7 July 1984), pp. 16–17; "La influencia de Goya en la obra de Hemingway," lecture delivered by Sr. Castillo-Puche at the International Hemingway

Conference, Madrid, 26 June 1984. Goya's nickname, "D. Francisco de los Toros": Mario Lepore, *The Life and Times of Goya* (New York: Curtis Books, 1966), p. 42.

Dr. Hemingway taught son about killing: M. Hemingway Sanford, *At the Hemingways*, p. 81.

EH not great admirer of gypsies: evident from several passages in *DIA*, and from the portrayal of the cowardly, irresponsible Rafael in *FWBT*.

"To get Spain into a book is hard": *DIA*, MS, p. 73 (Univ. of Texas).

EH to Gingrich on last chapter, *DIA*: 4 Dec. 1932 (*Letters*, p. 378).

Lewis on *DIA* as a book about EH and his love affair with Spain: "The Making of *DIA*," in Nagel (ed.), *EH: The Writer in Context*, p. 39.

Death of novillero, Pedro Carreño: see Cossío, *Los toros*, 3:174–75.

Epilogue to *DIA* included in anthology of verse: Selden Rodman (ed.), *100 Modern Poems* (New York: Pellegrini & Cudahy, 1949), pp. 66–67.

Prose of *DIA* as poetry: Donald Junkins, "Hemingway's Contribution to American Poetry," *Hemingway Review* (Spring 1985), p. 22; "Hemingway's Bullfight Poems," *Hemingway Review* (Spring 1987), pp. 38–45.

Madrid, 1983
(pp. 127–31)

EH had hunting boots for first African safari made at García Tenorio's, Madrid: Quintanilla, "Hemingway en mi recuerdo," *Cuadernos . . .* (Nov. 1961), p. 49; EH to Pauline Hemingway, c. Oct. 1933 (JFK).

Chapter 10. A Clean, Well-Lighted Place
(pp. 132–39)

"A Clean, Well-Lighted Place": first published in *Scribner's Magazine* (Mar. 1933), pp. 149–50, *SS*, pp. 379–83.

"To a Tragic Poetess": (1926); in Gerogiannis (ed.), *EH: 88 Poems*, pp. 88, 150.

EH's later essay (for "A Clean, Well-Lighted Place"): MS #251 ("The Art of the Short Story"), JFK; published in *The Paris Review*, No. 79 (1981), pp. 85–102.

Michener on ambiente: *Iberia: Spanish Travels and Reflections* (New York: Random House, 1961), pp. 53–54.

Goya's "Nada" or "Ello dirá": etching #69, *The Disasters of War*. See Emily Stipes Watts, *Ernest Hemingway and the Arts* (Urbana: University of Illinois Press, 1971), p. 74; Pierre Gassirer and Juliet Wilson, *The Life and Complete Works of Goya* (New York: Reynal & Company, 1971), p. 220.

Brenan on *no* and *nada* in Spanish: *The Face of Spain*, p. 289.

Abstract, philosophical definition of "nada": *Diccionario de la lengua española*, p. 909.

Heidegger on being vs. nothingness: see Marjorie Grene, "Martin Heidegger," in *The Encyclopedia of Philosophy*, 8 vols. (New York: Macmillan Publishing Co. and The Free Press, 1967), 3:461–63.

Spanish mystics and nada: see Francisco Ynduráin, "España en la obra de Hemingway," *De lector a lector* (Madrid: Escelicer, 1973), p. 210.

Baker on nada: *The Writer as Artist*, p. 124.

EH on decorum and dignity in Spain: "The Capital of the World," first

published as "The Horns of the Bull," *Esquire* (June 1936), pp. 31, 190–93, *SS*, pp. 38–51.
EH's triangulation process: Baker, *The Writer as Artist*, p. 123.
EH on living "right" with one's eyes: "On Writing," *NAS*, p. 239.
One could live in Spain for eight pesetas a day: see EH to Dos Passos, 26 June 1931 (*Letters*, p. 342). It is interesting that a 1960 Spanish translation of "A Clean, Well-Lighted Place" increased the old man's tip to a full peseta to compensate for inflation. A less intelligent change in this version is the cutting of the last several hundred words of the story; it ends with the two waiters in the clean, well-lit café saying good night to each other, thus omitting the entire passage on nada—unacceptable to the censors in Franco's Spain. "Un lugar limpio y bien iluminado," in *Relatos* (Barcelona: Luis de Caralt, 1960), pp. 97–101. I am indebted to Professor Bernard Oldsey for making me aware of this translation, and for his excellent treatment of "Clean" in his *Hemingway's Hidden Craft: The Writing of "A Farewell to Arms"* (University Park: Pennsylvania State University Press, 1979).
EH on pride and honor in *DIA*: pp. 91–92.
EH on "grace under pressure": EH to Fitzgerald, c. 20 Apr. 1926 (*Letters*, p. 200), his first mention of the famous phrase.
EH to Dos Passos on "gigantic bloody emptiness and nothingness": 11 Feb. 1936 (Dos Passos Collection, Univ. of Virginia).
EH on thinking "of other people" and getting "into somebody else's head": "Monologue to the Maestro: A High Seas Letter," *Esquire* (Oct.

1935), pp. 21, 174a, 174b, *By-Line*, pp. 220, 219.
EH to Fitzgerald on aging: 13 Sept. 1929 (*Letters*, p. 306).
EH on a fine performance enroute to the grave: EH to Perkins, 7 Dec. 1926 (*Letters*, p. 238).

Chapter 11.
The Undiscovered Country
(pp. 150–87)

Epigraphs: Camus, Preface to "L'Espagne libre," *Essais* (Paris: Gallimard, 1965), p. 1604; Ford, *Gatherings from Spain*, p. 350.
EH says no right or left in literature: to Paul Romaine, 6 July 1932 (*Letters*, p. 363). The following quotation on government is from EH to Dos Passos, 30 May 1932 (*Letters*, p. 360).
EH's sole political belief in liberty, etc.: to Ivan Kashkin, 19 Aug. 1935 (*Letters*, p. 419).
Brenan on Spanish tribal system: *The Face of Spain*, p. 262.
The "Spanish thing": EH to Perkins, 26 Sept. 1936 (*Letters*, pp. 454–55).
Religious conversions among writers in Spanish war: see Hugh Thomas, *The Spanish Civil War* (New York: Harper and Brothers, 1961), p. 392n.
EH's change in religious beliefs in Spanish Civil War: EH to Mrs. P. Pfeiffer, 2 Aug. 1937 (*Letters*, p. 461), 18 Aug. 1939 (Princeton Univ.); to Thomas Welsh, 19 June 1945 (*Letters*, p. 592).
EH on "ideology boys": to Perkins, 8 Dec. 1939 (*Letters*, p. 498).
EH's attempt to save his youthful experience in Spain: Eric Nepomuceno, *Hemingway: Madrid no era una fiesta* (Madrid: Altalena, 1978), p. 66.
"The Spain years": EH to General

Charles T. Lanham, 2 Nov. 1946 (*Letters*, p. 614).

EH would have hated to miss Spanish war: to Perkins, 26 Sept. 1936.

Experience in war invaluable to a writer: EH to Charles A. Fenton, 18 June 1952 (*Letters*, p. 765).

Connolly on EH and Spanish war: review of *THAHN, New Statesman & Nation* (16 Oct. 1937), p. 606.

Malraux and "gigantic masterpisses": EH to Perkins, 5 May 1938 (*Letters*, p. 467). The quotation on the "old stuff" below is from the same letter.

FWBT most important thing EH had ever done: EH to Thomas Shevlin, 4 Apr. 1939 (*Letters*, p. 484). The quotation below on a "real one" is from the same letter.

EH accused of not knowing terrain or facts of war: for example see Ricardo de la Cierva, *Cien libros básicos sobre la guerra de España* (Madrid: Publicaciones Españolas, 1966), pp. 302–3.

EH based FWBT on actual Loyalist offensive: see Thomas, *The Spanish Civil War*, pp. 443–44.

EH on writing to "make it round and whole and solid": "Monologue to the Maestro," *By-Line*, p. 216 (complete reference in Notes to Ch. 10).

Buckley on "third Spain" in FWBT: "La Guerra Civil española y el papel de Hemingway," lecture delivered at First International Hemingway Conference, Madrid, 29 June 1984.

Mountain setting of FWBT looks back to SAR and FTA: Baker, *Writer as Artist*, p. 257.

EH's Indians and Spaniards in FWBT as noble savages: see John J. Allen, "The English of Hemingway's Spaniards," in Sheldon Norman Grebstein (ed.), *Studies in "For Whom the Bell*

Tolls" (Columbus, Ohio: Merrill, 1971), p. 92.

Unamuno on intrahistoria: *En torno al casticismo,* in *Obras selectas* (Madrid: Editorial Plenitud, 1960), pp. 47–144. EH knew Unamuno's work and claimed to have seen him in person, probably in Paris. See EH to Berenson, 20–22 Mar. 1953 (*Letters*, pp. 814–15).

EH on Barco de Ávila, summer 1931: to Dos Passos, 26 June 1931 (*Letters*, p. 342).

Anselmo, Santiago, FWBT and OMATS: these two characters seemed to be linked in EH's imagination. An early draft of *OMATS* begins, "The lines around the eyes of Anselmo . . ." (MS #551, JFK).

EH's "Under the Ridge": *Cosmopolitan* (Oct. 1939), pp. 34–35, 102–6, *TFC & 4 Stories*, pp. 140–51.

EH on horse contractors in bullfight: *DIA*, p. 187.

EH's ability to speak to Spaniards in appropriate tone: attested to by the bullfighter Antonio Ordóñez in his statement at the opening of the International Hemingway Conference, Madrid, 25 June 1984.

EH boasts about his Spanish to Faulkner: 23 July 1947 (*Letters*, p. 624). EH does not state specifically that the foreign language he learned so well was Spanish, but this is the only plausible interpretation.

EH's secret wish to have been born in Spain and write in Spanish: EH to Berenson, 2 Feb. 1954 (*Letters*, p. 828); Baker, *Life Story*, p. 197. The quotation below on English as a "bastard tongue" is from the same letter to B.B.

Spanish a more "poetic" language than English, French: Jorge Guillén,

quoting Wladimir Weidle in *Language and Poetry: Some Poets of Spain* (Cambridge: Harvard University Press, 1961), p. 214. Weidle refers only to English and French; I have extended his idea to German and Italian.
EH on "secret meanings" in Spanish from talk of thieves, etc.: to Wilson, 8 Nov. 1952 (*Letters*, p. 794).
EH on Spanish, Wakamba: to Berenson, 2 Feb. 1954.
Drunken scene after kudu hunt in *GHOA*: pp. 239–44.
EH on Spanish as "roughest language": to Charles Scribner, 9–10 July 1950 (*Letters*, p. 704). See also *ARIT*, p. 93.
Ford on Spaniards' cursing and blasphemy: *Gatherings from Spain*, pp. 77–79.
EH's "Defense of Dirty Words": subtitled "A Cuban Letter," *Esquire* (Sept. 1934), pp. 19, 158b, 158d.
EH's early experiments in transposed dialogue: see "Wild Night Music of Paris Makes Visitor Feel a Man of the World," *TSW* (25 Mar. 1922), p. 22, *The Wild Years*, pp. 79–81. This is the earliest example I have found in EH's work.
C. Scribner, Jr., on use of Spanish in *FWBT*: Introduction to *The Enduring Hemingway: An Anthology of a Lifetime in Literature* (New York: Scribner's, 1974), p. xxvi.
Fenimore on language of *FWBT*: "English and Spanish in *For Whom the Bell Tolls*," in John K. M. McCaffery (ed.), *Ernest Hemingway: The Man and His Work* (Cleveland and New York: World, 1950), pp. 205–20.
María's nickname ("Rabbit"): two unpublished items in the Hemingway Collection suggest quite strongly that "Rabbit" was a nickname used by EH

for Martha Gellhorn; see MSS #522a ("It snowed all afternoon . . .") and #824 ("We used to quarrel before attacks . . ."), JFK. See also Allen Josephs, "Hacia un estudio de la España de Hemingway," *Insula*, Madrid (Feb. 1977), pp. 14–15.
Lisca on "little rabbit": conversation with author in Madrid during International Hemingway Conference, June 1984.
Spanish translator of *FWBT* **obliged to "correct" original**: the two examples described here are from Lola de Aguado's translation, *Por quién doblan las campanas* (Barcelona: Círculo de Lectores, 1972), pp. 187, 12 (*FWBT*, pp. 156, 3).
EH's faulty use of Spanish pronouns in correspondence: see for example EH to Antonio Gattorno, 3 June 1935 (JFK).
EH to Perkins on "thees" and "thous" in *FWBT*: 26 Aug. 1940 (*Letters*, p. 513).
Other techniques to create heroic tone in *FWBT*: see Betty Moore, "Ernest Hemingway and Spain: Growth of a 'Spanish' Prose Style," *es* (Publicaciones del Departamento de Inglés, Universidad de Valladolid) (Sept. 1979), pp. 227–53.
EH's "The Denunciation," etc.: *Esquire* (Nov. 1938), pp. 39, 111–14, *TFC & 4 Stories*, pp. 89–100; *TFC* (1938), *TFC & 4 Stories*, pp. 3–85; "The Butterfly and the Tank," *Esquire* (Dec. 1938), pp. 51, 186, 188, 190, *TFC & 4 Stories*, pp. 101–9; "Night Before Battle," *TFC & 4 Stories*, pp. 110–39 (complete reference in Notes to Chap. 3); "Under the Ridge," *Cosmopolitan* (Oct. 1939), pp. 34–35, 102–6, *TFC & 4 Stories*, pp. 140–51.
Connection between cursing and

destiny of characters in *FWBT*:
see Robert O. Stephens, "Language
Magic and Reality in *For Whom the
Bell Tolls*," *Criticism* (Spring 1972),
pp. 159–60.
Jung on synchronicity: Fore-
word to the *I Ching or Book of
Changes*, Bollingen Series XIX
(Princeton: Princeton University
Press, 1967), p. xxiv; "Synchronicity:
An Acausal Connecting Principle,"
*The Structure and Dynamics of the
Psyche*, in *Collected Works*, 18 vols.
(New York: Pantheon Books, 1960),
8:471–531.
**EH on thinking of other people
and getting in characters' heads**:
"Monologue to the Maestro," *By-Line*,
pp. 219–20 (complete reference in
Notes to Chap. 10).
Deleted passage from *DIA* ("comport-
ing oneself like a man"): MS #24.00,
Chap. 20 (JFK). For a different ver-
sion of the same story about Rafael el
Gallo, see EH to Scribner, c. 15 Aug.
1940 (*Letters*, p. 508).
Flanner on *OMATS*: Baker, *Life
Story*, p. 656 (quoted from Flanner to
Solita Solano, c. Sept. 1952).
EH on secret of *OMATS*: Baker,
Life Story, p. 656 (quoted from Mary
Hemingway's diary entry of 25 Aug.
1952).
**EH says knowledge of Spanish neces-
sary to "know how things really were
in Spain"**: to Lambert Davis, 7 May
1940 (Boston Univ.).
EH and the Virgen del Pilar: so fond
was he of Spain's national patroness
that EH planned to name a daughter
Pilar, but of course his wives bore him
only sons. He had to be content with
baptizing his 38-foot cabin cruiser
after the Virgen del Pilar. When EH
equipped this vessel as a Q-boat to
pursue German submarines off Cuba

in 1941, there was a poetic justice:
another "Pilar" was fighting against
the fascists thousands of miles from
Guadarrama.
**EH on "Emerson, Hawthorne, Whit-
tier, and Company"**: GHOA, p. 21.
Campbell and shaman's function: *The
Masks of God: Primitive Mythology*
(New York: Viking, 1959), p. 252.
EH answers survey by Jolas: c. late
Mar. [?] 1938 (*Letters*, p. 465).
Barea on Pilar and Pablo: "Not Spain
but Hemingway," in Grebstein (ed.),
Studies in FWBT, pp. 82–83.
EH answers Spanish reader of *FWBT*:
to José Alemany, 8 Nov. 1940 (JFK).
**EH on Pastora Imperio in unpub-
lished passage of *DIA***: MS, p. 54
(Univ. of Texas).
Cante hondo and bullfighting: see my
*The Tragic Myth: Lorca and "Cante
Jondo"* (Lexington: University Press of
Kentucky, 1978), p. 47.
Starkie on flamenco and toreo: "Cante
Jondo, Flamenco and the Guitar,"
Guitar Review (1956), p. 6.
**Lorca on duende and "culture of the
blood"**: "Teoría y juego del duende,"
Obras completas, 1:1068. The follow-
ing quotation on duende as "the spirit
of the earth" is from the same page.
Pilar on the "darkness in us" (deleted
passage): MS #85 (*FWBT*), p. 301
(JFK). No chapter is indicated by the
author.
**Gypsy Rafael's song on sun and
moon**: see EH, NANA dispatch,
Teruel front, 19 Dec. 1937, repro-
duced in Margaret Calien Lewis,
"Ernest Hemingway's *The Spanish
War*: Dispatches from Spain, 1937–
38," M.A. thesis, University of Louisville, 1969, p. 108.
**Jordan, María, and "most absurd
love scene . . ."**: Leslie Fiedler, "Men
Without Women," in Robert P. Weeks

(ed.), *Hemingway: A Collection of Critical Essays* (Englewood Cliffs, N.J.: Prentice-Hall, 1962), p. 86.
Baker on origins of María's character: CB to author, 4 Mar. 1980.
Jordan, María, and reconciliation of Protestants, Catholics: see F. I. Carpenter, "Hemingway Achieves the Fifth Dimension," in Baker (ed.), *Hemingway and the Critics*, p. 198. The passage from the typescript of *FWBT* is found in Chap. 42, p. 27 (JFK).
Spanish people "will rise again": EH, "On the American Dead in Spain," *New Masses* (14 Feb. 1939), p. 3.
Like Hemingway, R. Jordan learns everybody cries in war: in the posthumous "Landscape with Figures," a short story dealing with the Spanish Civil War, the narrator says, "In a war everybody of all ranks including generals cries at some time or another." *CSS*, p. 593.
Wilson on "amoeba-like" María: "Hemingway: Gauge of Morale," in *The Wound and the Bow*, p. 239.
María belongs to EH's line of European heroines: Edwin Sheffield Gleaves, Jr., "The Spanish Influence on EH's Concepts of Death, *Nada*, and Immortality," Ph.D. diss., Emory University, 1964, p. 128.
EH on capea or bull-baiting in *DIA*: p. 22.
Difference between mass murder and bullfight: see Baker, *Writer as Artist*, p. 261.
Massacre in Ronda, 1936: see Thomas, *The Spanish Civil War*, p. 176. Thomas fails to advise his readers that his source was the highly partisan biography of a Nationalist leader by José María Pemán, *Un soldado en la historia: Vida del*

Capitán-General Varela (Cadiz: n.p., 1954).
Multiple Spanish influences on EH's massacre scene: Capellán, "Hemingway and the Hispanic World," p. 662.
EH and Baroja, Valle-Inclán: for evidence of EH's familiarity with these authors, see Reynolds, *Hemingway's Reading*, entry nos. 366–69, 2138–39, pp. 96, 195; Brasch and Sigman, *Hemingway's Library*, nos. 387, 389–90, 393, 6767–68, pp. 23, 380.
Autumn reminded EH of death: see EH to Fitzgerald, 13 Sept. 1929: "Summer's a discouraging time to work—You dont feel death coming on the way it does in the fall when the boys really put pen to paper." (*Letters*, p. 306).
EH defends "smell of death" passage: EH to Scribner, c. 15 Aug. 1940 (*Letters*, pp. 508–9).
EH on transformation of Pamplona youths into requetés: see Royo, "Las pequeñas confesiones de Hemingway," *Arriba* (5 Oct. 1956), n.p.
EH and first wife get drunk on train: EH to Stein and Toklas, 15 July 1925 (*Letters*, pp. 167–68); *DIA*, p. 270.
Koestler on abominable acts in Spanish war: *Spanish Testament* (London: V. Gollancz Ltd., 1937), p. 130.
Deleted passage on Jordan's emotions after last love scene: MS #83 (*FWBT*), Chap. 36, p. 5 (JFK).
Jordan on "Mother earth" in deleted passage: MS #83, Chap. 42, p. 9 (JFK).
EH on "feeling of life and death" in bullfight: *DIA*, p. 4.
Jordan on "no victory" (deleted passage): MS #83 (*FWBT*), Chap. 43, p. 83 (JFK).

Author's note ("People are not as they end up . . ."), typescript: written on a small piece of paper inserted after Chap. 24 (JFK).

EH's "On the American Dead in Spain": *New Masses* (14 Feb. 1939).

Jordan's inclination toward death: see Young, *EH: A Reconsideration*, pp. 107–8.

Ronda, 1980
(pp. 189–90)

EH on the modern face of bull-fighters: "DS," MS #354a, p. 795 (JFK).

Antonio Ordóñez's son-in-law Paquirri: Francisco Rivera ("Paquirri") was killed by a bull in Pozoblanco (Cordova), 3 Oct. 1984.

Chapter 12. Dangerous Summers
(pp. 191–206)

Epigraphs: MS #49.9 (galleys of *DIA*), JFK; Matthew J. Bruccoli (ed.), *The Notebooks of F. Scott Fitzgerald* (New York: Harcourt Brace Jovanovich/Bruccoli Clark, 1978), p. 58.

EH's first meeting with A. Ordóñez: "DS," Part I, *Life*, p. 86.

EH's plans for appendix to *DIA*: "DS," Part I, *Life*, p. 91.

Mary calls Ordóñez EH's "pet": *How It Was*, p. 583.

L. Hemingway on EH and "kid brothers": *My Brother*, p. 130.

EH compares A. Ordóñez to his sons: to P. Hemingway, 5 Aug. 1959 (*Letters*, p. 895).

Description of P. Romero, *SAR*: pp. 163, 175, 185.

EH on friendship with "mystery": to

Adriana Ivancich, 28 Oct. 1952 (Univ. of Texas).

EH to female admirer on Ordóñez: to Monique de Beaumont, 31 Aug. 1959 (quoted in Bruccoli and C. E. Frazer Clark, *Hemingway at Auction: 1930–1973* [Detroit: Gale Research Co., 1973], p. 227).

EH on "mystery" in Ordóñez's toreo: "DS," MS #354a, pp. 201–2 (JFK).

EH compares Ordóñez to northern Cheyenne: to Juanito Quintana, c. May 1959 (quoted in José Luis Castillo-Puche, *Hemingway, entre la vida y la muerte* [Barcelona: Destino, 1968], p. 219).

EH to C. Baker on Ordóñez: 8 Dec. 1959 (quoted courtesy of Prof. Baker).

Ordóñez possibly never read any books except EH's novels: EH to Breit, 3–4 Nov. 1955 (JFK).

EH would make Ordóñez's toreo "permanent": "DS," MS #354a, p. 747.

EH did not discuss politics with Ordóñez: affirmed by the bullfighter in his statement at the opening of the International Hemingway Conference, Madrid, 25 June 1984.

EH on Ordóñez's mixing him up as father: EH to Breit, 3–4 Nov. 1955.

EH on C. Ordóñez, 1959: "DS," MS #354a, p. 257. Cayetano died on 30 Sept. 1961.

"Strange summer of 1959": M. Hemingway, *How It Was*, pp. 591, 594, 596, 598–99, 620.

EH says following bullfighter like "being married to an alcoholic": EH to Charles Scribner, Jr., 27 Aug. 1959 (Princeton Univ.).

Photographs of EH during bullfight season, 1959: see Peter Buckley, *Ernest* (New York: Dial Press, 1978). Buckley's observation on EH is on p. 157.

EH's bibulous letters: see for example, EH to De Beaumont, 20 Sept. 1959 (JFK).

Life contracts EH to write "DS": M. Hemingway, *How It Was*, pp. 599–600.

EH regrets accepting *Life* contract: to Lanham, 16 Jan. 1961 (Princeton Univ.).

Ordóñez punished for infractions: mid-September 1959. See EH to Lanham, 16 Sept. 1959 (Princeton Univ.); "DS," Part III, *Life* (19 Sept. 1960), p. 95; M. Hemingway, *How It Was*, p. 602.

EH wants to begin "DS" in Spain: Baker, *Life Story*, p. 549.

EH "working like a steam engine" in Cuba: EH to Nathan (Bill or Negro) Davis, 1 Apr. 1960 (Princeton Univ.).

EH's letters to Davis (25 Feb., 12 Mar., 1 Apr. 1960): Bruccoli and Clark, *Hemingway at Auction*, pp. 125–26.

EH claims fewer than half of Ordóñez's bulls tampered with: "DS," Part III, *Life*, p. 76.

EH on standing for the "complete bullfight": *DIA*, p. 162.

EH admits he lost detachment from bullfighters' point of view: "DS," MS #354a, second page insert to p. 680.

EH's "partner" A. Ordóñez: "DS," Part I, *Life*, p. 86.

"Shaved" horns become "altered" in *Life*: MS #354a, p. 390; "DS," Part II, *Life* (12 Sept. 1960), p. 75.

EH doesn't want Ordóñez's "place in history" to be denied him: "DS," MS #354a, pp. 71–72.

EH calls Manolete "great bullfighter with cheap tricks": "DS," Part I, *Life*, p. 86.

EH had only seen Manolete perform once: to Lanham, 19 Feb. 1947 (Princeton Univ.). I am grateful to Professor Jeffrey Meyers for pointing out this letter to me. See his *Hemingway: A Biography* (New York: Harper & Row, 1985), p. 520. EH admitted Manolete had drawn the two worst bulls that afternoon in Mexico in "DS," Part I, *Life*, p. 85.

EH to Patrick Hemingway on Ordóñez's defective killing: 5 Aug. 1959 (*Letters*, p. 895).

Cau on Ordóñez's killing: *Las orejas y el rabo* (Barcelona: Plaza y Janés, 1962), p. 32. For other treatments of Ordóñez as bullfighter, especially as swordsman, see L. Jiménez Martos, *Tientos de los toros y su gente* (Madrid: Rialp, 1981), p. 181; Néstor Luján, *Historia del toreo* (Barcelona: Destino, 1967), p. 401; Michener, *Iberia*, pp. 492, 513–15; Shay Oag, *In the Presence of Death: Antonio Ordóñez* (New York: Coward-McCann, 1969); Kenneth Tynan, *Bull Fever* (New York: Harper and Brothers, 1955), p. 191.

EH on "deadly rivalry" between Ordóñez and Dominguín: "DS," Part I, *Life*, p. 91. EH also calls the bullfight a "game of death" (MS #354a, p. 221).

Ordóñez quoted on rivalry: Cau, *Las orejas y el rabo*, p. 79.

Dominguín on rivalry: Franco Pierini, "Luis Miguel replica a Hemingway," *Gaceta Ilustrada*, Madrid (5 Nov. 1960), p. 53. To my knowledge, the statements by both bullfighters are translated into English for the first time here.

EH on "death and money business": MS #354a, p. 416.

Castillo-Puche on EH's self-deception: " 'El verano peligroso' de Hemingway," lecture delivered at Univ. of Arkansas, 8 Apr. 1985. I am grateful to Sr. Castillo-Puche for allowing me to see the typescript of his lecture.

EH's reaction to Mary's criticism of "DS": *How It Was*, pp. 610–11.

EH's esthetic of profusion: I have borrowed this term from Douglas Day's excellent *Malcolm Lowry: A Biography* (New York: Laurel, 1975), p. 204.

EH hired to write "DS" when death of Ordóñez or Dominguín seemed possible: EH to William Lang, 3 Jan. 1960 (JFK).

EH to Thompson (*Life*): rough draft of letter inserted in MS of "DS"; typed letter dated 31 Mar. 1960 (JFK).

Ordóñez's "dark side": "DS," Part II, *Life*, p. 78. EH refers to the torero's "pride of the devil" in Part II, p. 68.

EH's description of virgin forest of Irati: "DS," Part II, *Life*, p. 75. Following quotation about the fiesta of San Fermín is on the same page.

EH on gun licenses at Spanish customs, Algeciras: "DS," Part I, *Life*, p. 88.

EH and Jesuit Seminary Fund Association: "DS," MS #354a, pp. 396, 416.

EH's money clip stolen, Murcia: "DS," MS #354a, p. 765.

EH's idea on fireworks and violence: "DS," MS #354a, p. 441.

EH on wrongness of looking without seeing: see "African Journal," Part 2, *Sports Illustrated* (3 Jan. 1972), p. 46. The following quotation is from "DS," MS #354a, pp. 815–16.

EH calls summer of 1959 one of his last: "DS," MS #354a, p. 773.

EH on moral of "DS": MS #354a, pp. 927–28.

Summer of 1959 dangerous for EH alone: Castillo-Puche, "Por fin se publicará 'El verano peligroso,' polémica obra de Hemingway," *Ya*, Madrid (12 Jan. 1985), p. 1.

EH to Quintana on writing "DS": 1 June 1960 (JFK).

Castillo-Puche on tragedy produced over pages of MS, "DS": "'El verano peligroso' de Hemingway" (lecture).

Ordóñez-Dominguín create "exploitable rivalry": EH to M. Hemingway, 25 Sept. 1960 (*Letters*, p. 907).

Horn-shaving, summer 1960: EH to Aaron (A. E.) Hotchner, 7 Aug. 1960 (JFK).

Filth in and out of the bullring: "DS," MS #354a, p. 732. The following quotation by EH on right and wrong merging into greyness is on the same page.

EH to Buckley on Girón brothers and bullfighting: 4 June 1957 (JFK).

EH fears he might not be allowed to return to Spain: to Lanham, 16 Sept. 1959 (Princeton Univ.).

EH loathes "whole damned bull business": this paragraph is based on excerpts from EH to M. Hemingway, 15 Aug., 3 Sept., 7 Sept., 23 Sept. 1960, in M. Hemingway, *How It Was*, pp. 619–21; and on EH to Mary, 25 Sept. 1960 (*Letters*, p. 908).

EH's reaction to publication of "*DS*": Baker, *Life Story*, p. 554.

Dominguín on EH as better journalist than novelist: reported by the press at the time of "DS"'s publication in Spanish by *Life* (31 Oct., 14 Nov., 28 Nov. 1960). See also Ordóñez to EH, 8 Dec. 1960 (JFK). Dominguín had called Hemingway "the Nobel of the Marshall Plan" even earlier; the matador repeated the expression more recently in Luis Reyes, "Dominguín destruye la leyenda de su amigo Hemingway," *Tiempo*, Madrid (25 June 1984), p. 109.

EH accused of writing pornography in *FTA*: Lucio del Amo, "Hemingway tiene su saldo en contra," *Informaciones*, Madrid (22 Nov. 1960), p. 8. The same journalist accused EH of sinning from lack of faith. EH attended Pío Baroja's funeral in Madrid, Oct. 1956; see my *Hemingway en España* (Madrid: Castalia, 1989).

Kennedy on book publication of "The Dangerous Summer": "The Last Olé," *New York Times Review of Books* (9 June 1985), p. 32. Because of the unauthoritative nature of the book, I have used not it but the original manuscript in my treatment of the work.

EH on divisiveness of Spaniards: to Sidney James, c. Feb. 1953 (JFK).

Epilogue: All Stories End in Death
(pp. 207–12)

Title: *DIA*, p. 122. The narrator says to the Old Lady: "Madame, all stories, if continued far enough, end in death. . . ."

Epigraphs: the first is written on a small piece of paper inserted after Chap. 24 of the typescript, *FWBT* (JFK; see end of Chap. 11, above); the second is from L. Hemingway, *My Brother*, p. 18.

EH on literary life and death: F. Vizcaíno Casas, "Me gustaría tener una muerte literaria," *ABC*, Madrid (30 Jan. 1954), p. 27.

Rilke on "one's own death" (*der eigene Tod*): see *The Book of Hours* (1905; partially translated in *Poet Lore*, 26, no. 1 [1915]: 121), and *The Notebooks of Malte Laurids Brigge* (1910; New York: W. W. Norton, 1949).

Spanish writer on intensity of Hem- ingway's life and death: Fernando Claramunt, "El paraíso español de Hemingway," *Cruz Ansata*, Puerto Rico (1983), 131.

EH desisted from suicide because he knew "how swell life gets again": EH to Isidor Schneider, c. early Oct. 1926 (JFK). EH referred to "juice(s)" several times: see his letters to Dos Passos, 11 Feb. 1936 (Dos Passos Collection, Univ. of Virginia), and to Charles Scribner, Jr., 6 July 1960 (*Letters*, p. 906). He referred to fucking, fighting, and writing in the same letter to Dos Passos.

EH to MacLeish on thinking with head vs. bones: c. May 1943 (*Letters*, p. 545).

Whitman and problem of aging body: see Arthur Wrobel, "Whitman and the Phrenologists: The Divine Body and the Sensuous Soul," *PMLA* (Publications of the Modern Language Association of America) (Jan. 1974), pp. 17–22.

EH on "death loneliness . . . every day that is wasted": AMF, pp. 165–66.

EH had misfortune of outliving his talent: these words were applied by Hemingway to Kipling in "Defense of Dirty Words," *Esquire* (Sept. 1934), p. 158b.

EH's life finally consumed more energy than it produced: see Alberto Moravia, "Nothing Amen," in *Man as an End: A Defense of Humanism* (New York: Farrar, Straus and Giroux, 1966), pp. 231–36.

Cocteau on Hugo: cited in Andrés Amorós, *Introducción a la literatura* (Madrid: Castalia, 1979), pp. 98–99.

Fitzgerald on hero and tragedy: Bruccoli (ed.), *The Notebooks of F. Scott Fitzgerald*, p. 51.

Decline in courage in final quarter of twentieth century: "A decline in courage may be the most striking feature that an outside observor notices in the West today. . . ." Aleksandr I. Solzhenitsyn, A *World Split Apart* (Commencement Address, Harvard University, 8 June 1978) (New York: Harper and Row, 1978), p. 9.

EH's plans for trip to Pamplona, July 1961: see Capellán, "Hemingway and the Hispanic World," p. 48.

Belmonte's reaction to EH's suicide: told by the American bullfighter John Fulton, in Michener, *Iberia*, p. 498. Belmonte shot himself on 8 Apr. 1962.

"Death and money business" of bullfighting: "DS," MS #354a, p. 416.

EH on Spain as "country for living not dying": cited in P. Félix García,

"País para vivir," *ABC* (5 July 1961), p. 1; and in Castillo-Puche, *Hemingway, entre la vida y la muerte*, p. 31.

"The country is here . . ." (quotation from EH's last posthumous novel): *GOE*, p. 53. The editing of this book was as severe and questionable as that of *The Dangerous Summer*.

Hemingway was much Hemingway: I have translated the words of Fernando Claramunt in his article, "España en las cartas de Hemingway," *Historia y Vida*, Barcelona-Madrid (Sept. 1982), p. 122.

Lorca on death of Sánchez Mejías: "Llanto por Ignacio Sánchez Mejías," *Obras completas*, 1:558. Of course I have altered the original to fit Hemingway.

Select Bibliography

This is not a complete record of works relating to Hemingway and Spain, nor of those I have consulted. It includes all published references listed in the notes, in addition to other sources, but neither unpublished sources nor correspondence. The major repositories of Hemingway's unpublished works and correspondence can be found in Audre Hanneman, *Ernest Hemingway: A Comprehensive Bibliography* (Princeton: Princeton University Press, 1967), and *Supplement to Ernest Hemingway: A Comprehensive Bibliography* (Princeton: Princeton University Press, 1975). For the extensive holdings in the Hemingway Collection, see Jo August, *Ernest Hemingway: Catalog of the Manuscripts, Correspondence, and Other Material at the John F. Kennedy Library*, 2 vols. (New York: G. K. Hall, 1981).

Writings by Hemingway

"Judgment of Manitou." *Tabula* (Feb. 1916), pp. 9–10. Reprinted in *Ernest Hemingway's Apprenticeship, Oak Park, 1916–1917*, edited by Matthew J. Bruccoli, pp. 96–97. Washington, D.C.: Bruccoli Clark/NCR Microcard Editions, 1971.

"Sepi Jingan." *Tabula* (Nov. 1916), pp. [8]–9. Reprinted in Bruccoli, ed. *Ernest Hemingway's Apprenticeship*, pp. 101–3.

"Why Not Trade Other Public Entertainers Among the Nations as the Big Leagues Do Baseball Players?" *Toronto Star Weekly* (19 Feb. 1921), p. 13.

"At Vigo, in Spain, Is Where You Catch the Silver and Blue Tuna, the King of all Fish." *Toronto Star Weekly* (18 Feb. 1922), p. 15. Reprinted in *By-Line: Ernest Hemingway*, edited by William White, pp. 16–17. New York: Scribner's, 1967.

"Queer Mixture of Aristocrats, Profiteers, Sheep and Wolves at the Hotels in Switzerland." *Toronto Star Weekly* (4 Mar. 1922), p. 25. Reprinted in *By-Line*, pp. 18–19.

"How'd You Like to Tip Postman Every Time?" *Toronto Star Weekly* (11 Mar. 1922), p. 12. Reprinted in *The Wild Years: Ernest Hemingway*, edited by Gene Z. Hanrahan, pp. 168–69. New York: Dell, 1962.

"American Bohemians in Paris a Weird Lot." *Toronto Star Weekly* (25 Mar. 1922), p. 15. Reprinted in *By-Line*, pp. 23–25.

"The Mecca of Fakers Is French Capital." *Toronto Daily Star* (25 Mar. 1922), p. 4. Reprinted in *By-Line*, pp. 23–25.

"There Are Great Fish in the Rhone Canal." *Toronto Daily Star* (10 June 1922), p. 5. Reprinted in *By-Line*, pp. 33–35.

"Germans Are Doggedly Sullen or Desperate over the Mark." *Toronto Daily Star* (1 Sept. 1922), p. 23. Reprinted in *The Wild Years*, pp. 113–15.

"Once over Permit Obstacle, Fishing in Baden Perfect." *Toronto Daily Star* (2 Sept. 1922), p. 28. Reprinted in *The Wild Years*, pp. 119–23.

"Crossing to Germany Is Way to Make Money." *Toronto Daily Star* (19 Sept. 1922), p. 4. Reprinted in *By-Line*, pp. 45–48.

"'Old Constan' in True Light; Is Tough Town." *Toronto Daily Star* (28 Oct. 1922), p. 17. Reprinted in *By-Line*, pp. 53–55.

"Betrayal Preceded Defeat, Then Came Greek Revolt." *Toronto Daily Star* (3 Nov. 1922), p. 10. Reprinted in *The Wild Years*, pp. 200–2.

"Mussolini, Europe's Prize Bluffer More like Bottomley than Napoleon." *Toronto Daily Star* (27 Jan. 1923), p. 11. Reprinted in *By-Line*, pp. 61–65.

"The first matador got the horn . . ." *Little Review* (Spring 1923), p. 3. Reprinted in *The Short Stories of Ernest Hemingway*, p. 159. New York: Scribner's, 1967.

"Up in Michigan," "Out of Season," "My Old Man." *Three Stories and Ten Poems* (1923). Reprinted in *The Short Stories*, pp. 81–86, 173–79, 191–205.

"Bull Fighting Is Not a Sport—It Is a Tragedy." *Toronto Star Weekly* (20 Oct. 1923), p. 23. Reprinted in *By-Line*, pp. 90–98.

"World's Series of Bull Fighting a Mad, Whirling Carnival." *Toronto Star Weekly* (27 Oct. 1923), p. 33. Reprinted in *By-Line*, pp. 99–108.

"Night Life in Europe a Disease; Constantinople's Most Hectic." *Toronto Star Weekly* (15 Dec. 1923), p. 21. Reprinted in *The Wild Years*, pp. 149–56.

"The Revolutionist," "They whack—whacked the white horse . . . ," "The crowd shouted all the time . . . ," "If it happened right down close . . . ," "I heard the drums coming down the street . . . ," "Maera lay still . . ." *in our time* (1924). Reprinted in *The Short Stories*, pp. 157–58, 165, 171, 181, 189, 207.

"Chroniques: And to the United States." *The Transatlantic Review* (May-June 1924), pp. 355–57.

"Tackling a Spanish Bull Is 'Just Like Rugby'; Hemingway Tells How He Surprised the Natives." *Toronto Star Weekly* (2 Aug. 1924), p. 34.

"The Soul of Spain with McAlmon and Bird the Publishers." *Querschnitt*, Part I (Autumn 1924), pp. 229–30. *Querschnitt*, Part II (Nov. 1924), p. 278. Reprinted in *Ernest Hemingway: 88 Poems*, edited by Nicholas Gerogiannis, pp. 70–73. New York and London: Harcourt Brace Jovanovich/Bruccoli Clark, 1979.

"Pamplona Letter." *Transatlantic Review* (Oct. 1924), pp. 300–2.

"Indian Camp," "The Doctor and the Doctor's Wife," "Soldier's Home," "Cross Country Snow," "Big Two-Hearted River." *In Our Time* (1925). Reprinted in *The Short Stories*, pp. 91–95, 99–103, 145–53, 183–88, 209–18.

The Sun Also Rises. New York: Scribner's, 1926; rpt. 1970.

"The Real Spaniard." *Boulevardier* (Oct. 1927), p. 6.

"The Undefeated," "Hills Like White Elephants," "The Killers," "Che Ti Dice La Patria," "Banal Story." *Men Without Women* (1927). Reprinted in *The Short Stories*, pp. 235–66, 273–78, 279–89, 290–99, 360–62.

A *Farewell to Arms*. New York: Scribner's, 1929; rpt. 1969.

"Bullfighting, Sport and Industry." *Fortune* (Mar. 1930), pp. 83–88, 139–40, 142, 144, 146, 150.

Death in the Afternoon. New York: Scribner's, 1932; rpt. 1969.

"A Clean, Well-Lighted Place." *Scribner's Magazine* (Mar. 1933), pp. 149–50. Reprinted in *The Short Stories*, pp. 379–83.

"Marlin off the Morro: A Cuban Letter." *Esquire* (Autumn 1933), pp. 8, 39, 97. Reprinted in *By-Line*, pp. 137–43.

"Fathers and Sons." *Winner Take Nothing* (1933). Reprinted in *The Short Stories*, pp. 488–99.

"The Farm." *Cahiers d'Art* (1934), pp. 28–29.

"The Friend of Spain: A Spanish Letter." *Esquire* (Jan. 1934), pp. 26, 136. Reprinted in *By-Line*, pp. 144–52.

"A Paris Letter." *Esquire* (Feb. 1934), pp. 22, 156. Reprinted in *By-Line*, pp. 153–58.

"Notes on Dangerous Game: The Third Tanganyika Letter." *Esquire* (July 1934), pp. 19, 94. Reprinted in *By-Line*, pp. 167–71.

"Defense of Dirty Words: A Cuban Letter." *Esquire* (Sept. 1934), pp. 19, 158b, 158d.

Luis Quintanilla Catalogue (20 Nov.–4 Dec. 1934). Pierre Matisse Gallery, New York, pp. [2]–[3]. Article [Program Notes]. *Esquire* (Feb. 1935), pp. 26–27.

"Monologue to the Maestro: A High Seas Letter." *Esquire* (Oct. 1935), pp. 21, 174a, 174b. Reprinted in *By-Line*, pp. 213–20.

Green Hills of Africa. New York: Scribner's, 1935; rpt. 1963.

"Gattorno: Program Note." *Esquire* (May 1936), pp. 111, 141.

"The Horns of the Bull." *Esquire* (June 1936), pp. 31, 190–93. Reprinted as "The Capital of the World" in *The Short Stories*, pp. 38–51.

"The Snows of Kilimanjaro." *Esquire* (Aug. 1936), pp. 27, 194–201. Reprinted in *The Short Stories*, pp. 52–77.

"The Short Happy Life of Francis Macomber." *Cosmopolitan* (Sept. 1936), pp. 30–33, 166–72. Reprinted in *The Short Stories*, pp. 3–37.

North American Newspaper Alliance (NANA) dispatches: Valencia, 18 Mar. 1937; Guadalajara front, 23 Mar. 1937; Madrid, 27 Mar., 14 Apr., 21 Apr., 30 Apr. 1937; New York, 23 May 1937; Teruel front, 23 Sept. 1937; Madrid, 30 Sept., 6 Oct. 1937; Teruel front, 19 Dec. 1937; Teruel, 24 Dec. 1937; Barcelona, 4 Apr. 1938; Tortosa, 10 Apr. 1938; Ebro Delta, 18 Apr. 1938; Madrid, 10 May 1938. Reprinted in Margaret Calien Lewis, "Ernest Hemingway's *The Spanish War*: Dispatches from Spain, 1937–38." M.A. thesis, University of Louisville, 1969.

"The Chauffeurs of Madrid." NANA dispatch, 23 May 1937. Reprinted in *By-Line*, pp. 268–74.

"Fascism Is a Lie." *New Masses* (22 June 1937), p. 4.

To Have and Have Not. New York: Scribner's, 1937; rpt. 1965.

"The Time Now, the Place Spain." *Ken* (7 Apr. 1938), pp. 36–37.

"Dying, Well or Badly." *Ken* (21 Apr. 1938), p. 68.

"The Cardinal Picks a Winner." *Ken* (5 May 1938), p. 38.

"Old Man at the Bridge." *Ken* (19 May 1938), p. 36. Reprinted in *The Short Stories*, pp. 78–80.

The Spanish Earth. Cleveland: J. B. Savage, 1938.

"Treachery in Aragon." *Ken* (30 June 1938), p. 26.

"Call for Greatness." *Ken* (14 July 1938), p. 23.

"The Denunciation." *Esquire* (Nov. 1938), pp. 39, 111–14. Reprinted in *The Fifth Column and Four Stories of the Spanish Civil War*, pp. 89–100. New York: Scribner's, 1969.

"The Butterfly and the Tank." *Esquire* (Dec. 1938), pp. 51, 186, 188, 190. Reprinted in *The Fifth Column and Four Stories,* pp. 101–9.

"Night Before Battle." *Esquire* (Feb. 1939), pp. 27–29, 91–92, 95, 97. Reprinted in *The Fifth Column and Four Stories*, pp. 110–39.

"On the American Dead in Spain." *New Masses* (14 Feb. 1939), p. 3.

"Under the Ridge." *Cosmopolitan* (Oct. 1939), pp. 34–35, 102–6. Reprinted in *The Fifth Column and Four Stories*, pp. 140–51.

For Whom the Bell Tolls. New York: Scribner's, 1940; rpt. 1968.

The Old Man and the Sea. New York: Scribner's, 1952; rpt. n.d.

"A Visit with Hemingway: A Situation Report." *Look* (4 Sept. 1956), pp. 22–31. Reprinted in *By-Line*, pp. 470–78.

"Un lugar limpio y bien iluminado." Spanish translation of "A Clean, Well-Lighted Place." In Ernest Hemingway, *Relatos*, pp. 97–101. Barcelona: Luis de Caralt, 1960.

"The Dangerous Summer." *Life*, Part I (5 Sept. 1960), pp. 78–109; Part II, "The Pride of the Devil" (12 Sept. 1960), pp. 60–82; Part III, "An Appointment with Disaster" (19 Sept. 1960), pp. 74–96.

Islands in the Stream. New York: Scribner's, 1970.

A Moveable Feast. New York: Scribner's, 1971.

"African Journal." *Sports Illustrated*, Part 1 (20 Dec. 1971), pp. 5, 40–52, 57–66; Part 2 (3 Jan. 1972), pp. 26–46; Part 3 (10 Jan. 1972), pp. 22–30, 43–50.

"The Indians Moved Away," "The Last Good Country," "Summer People," "On Writing." *The Nick Adams Stories*, pp. 34–36, 70–132, 217–28, 233–41. New York: Scribner's, 1972.

Por quién doblan las campanas. Translation of *For Whom the Bell Tolls.* Translator, Lola de Aguado. Barcelona: Círculo de Lectores, 1972.

"To a Tragic Poetess" ["Little Mr. Wilson"]. In Gerogiannis, ed. . . . *88 Poems*, pp. 87–88, 97.

The Dangerous Summer. New York: Scribner's, 1985.

The Garden of Eden. New York: Scribner's, 1986.

"Black Ass at the Cross Roads," "Landscape with Figures." *The Complete Short Stories of Ernest Hemingway*, The Finca Vigía Edition, pp. 579–89, 590–96. New York: Scribner's, 1987.

Secondary Sources

Adams, Sam. "The Sun Also Sets." *Sports Illustrated* (29 June 1970), pp. 57–60, 62–64. Reprinted in Sarason, ed., *Hemingway and the Sun Set*, pp. 212–21.

Allen, John J. "The English of Hemingway's Spaniards." In Grebstein, ed., *Studies in "For Whom the Bell Tolls,"* pp. 91–93.

Álvarez de Miranda, Ángel. *Ritos y juegos del toro.* Madrid: Taurus, 1962.

Amorós, Andrés. *Introducción a la literatura.* Madrid: Castalia, 1979.

Baker, Carlos. *Ernest Hemingway: A Life Story.* New York: Scribner's, 1969.

———. *Hemingway: The Writer as Artist.* 4th ed. Princeton: Princeton University Press, 1973.

———, ed. *Ernest Hemingway: Selected Letters 1917–1961.* New York: Scribner's, 1981.

———, ed. *Hemingway and His Critics: An International Anthology.* New York: Hill and Wang, 1961.

Barea, Arturo. "Not Spain but Hemingway." In Grebstein, ed., *Studies in "For Whom the Bell Tolls,"* pp. 80–90.

Baroja, Julio Caro. *Los Baroja.* Madrid: Taurus, 1972.

Beegel, Susan. "The Death of El Espartero: An Historic Matador Links 'The Undefeated' and *Death in the Afternoon.*" *Hemingway Review* (Spring 1986), pp. 12–23.

Benson, Jackson J. *Hemingway: The Writer's Art of Self-Defense.* Minneapolis: University of Minnesota Press, 1969.

Brasch, James D., and Joseph Sigman. *Hemingway's Library: A Composite Record.* New York and London: Garland, 1981.

Brenan, Gerald. *The Face of Spain.* New York: Pellegrini & Cudahy, 1951.

———. *The Spanish Labyrinth.* Cambridge, England: Cambridge University Press, 1969.

Browning, Robert. "De Gustibus—." *The Complete Poetical Works of Browning,* edited by Horace Scudder, pp. 178–79. Boston: Houghton Mifflin, 1895.

Bruccoli, Matthew J., ed. *The Notebooks of F. Scott Fitzgerald.* New York: Harcourt Brace Jovanovich/Bruccoli Clark, 1978.

———, and C. E. Frazer Clark, Jr., eds. *Hemingway at Auction: 1930–1973.* Detroit: Gale Research Co., 1973.

Buckley, Peter. *Ernest.* New York: Dial Press, 1978.

Burgess, Anthony. *Ernest Hemingway y su mundo.* Madrid: Ultramar, 1980. Translation of *Ernest Hemingway and His World.* London: Thames & Hudson, 1978.

Caba, Pedro. "A Half-Philosophical Theory." In *Los toros/Bullfighting,* pp. 38–39. Madrid: Indice, 1974.

Campbell, Joseph. *The Masks of God: Primitive Mythology.* New York: Viking, 1959.

Camus, Albert. Preface to "L'Espagne libre." *Essais,* pp. 1604–8. Paris: Gallimard, 1965.

Capellán, Angel. "Hemingway and the Hispanic World." Ph.D. diss. New York University, 1977.
———. *Hemingway and the Hispanic World.* Ann Arbor, Mich.: UMI Research Press, 1985.
Carpenter, F. I. "Hemingway Achieves the Fifth Dimension." In Baker, ed., *Hemingway and His Critics*, pp. 192–201.
Castillo-Puche, José Luis. *Hemingway, entre la vida y la muerte.* Barcelona: Destino, 1968. Translation of *Hemingway in Spain.* New York: Doubleday, 1974.
———. "Hemingway, peregrino en España." *ABC*, Madrid (25 June 1984), p. 3.
———. "Hemingway y los toros a través de Goya." *Diario de Navarra* (7 July 1984), pp. 16–17.
———. "Por fin se publicará 'El verano peligroso,' polémica obra de Hemingway." *Ya*, Madrid (12 Jan. 1985), Cultural Supplement, pp. 1–2.
Castro, Américo. *Sobre el nombre y el quién de los españoles.* Madrid: Taurus, 1973.
Cau, Jean. *Las orejas y el rabo.* Barcelona: Plaza y Janés, 1962.
Claramunt, Fernando. "El paraíso español de Hemingway." *Cruz Ansata*, Puerto Rico (1983), pp. 127–36.
———. "España en las cartas de Hemingway." *Historia y Vida*, Barcelona-Madrid (Sept. 1982), pp. 114–22.
———. "Los toros desde la psicologia." In Cossío, *Los toros*, 7:1–181.
Coates, Robert M. "Bullfighters." *New Yorker* (1 Oct. 1932), pp. 61–63. Review of *Death in the Afternoon.* Reprinted in Stephens, ed., *Ernest Hemingway: The Critical Reception*, pp. 115–16.
Connolly, Cyril. Review of *To Have and Have Not.* *New Statesman & Nation* (16 Oct. 1937), p. 606.
Cossío, José Maria de. *Los toros. Tratado técnico e histórico.* 7 vols. Madrid: Espasa-Calpe, 1984.
Cowley, Malcolm. Introduction, Viking Portable *Hemingway.* New York: Viking, 1944, pp. vii–xxiv.
———. "A Portrait of Mr. Papa." In McCaffery, ed., *Ernest Hemingway: The Man and His Work*, pp. 34–56.
Davidson, Cathy M. "Death in the Morning: The Role of Vicente Girones in *The Sun Also Rises.*" *Hemingway notes* (Fall 1979), pp. 11–13.
Day, Douglas. *Malcolm Lowry: A Biography.* New York: Laurel, 1975.
De la Cierva, Ricardo. *Cien libros básicos sobre la guerra de España.* Madrid: Publicaciones Españolas, 1966.
Del Amo, Lucio. "Hemingway tiene su saldo en contra." *Informaciones*, Madrid (22 Nov. 1960), p. 8.
De la Mora, Constancia. *In Place of Splendor: The Autobiography of a Spanish Woman.* New York: Harcourt, Brace, 1939.
Del Campo, Salustiano. *Análisis de la población de España.* Barcelona: Ariel, 1972.

Desnoes, Edmundo. *Inconsolable Memories*. New York: New American Library, 1967.

Diccionario de la lengua española. Real Academia Española. Madrid: Espasa-Calpe, 1970.

Dos Passos, John. *The Best Times: An Informal Memoir*. New York: New American Library, 1966.

————. *Rosinante to the Road Again*. New York: Doran, 1922.

Drew, Fraser. "Hemingway's Generosity and Humility." *Mark Twain Journal* (Summer 1962), p. 19.

Eby, Cecil D. *Between the Bullet and the Lie: American Volunteers in the Spanish Civil War*. New York: Holt, Rinehart and Winston, 1969.

Edel, Leon. "The Figure Under the Carpet." In *Telling Lives: The Biographical Art*, edited by Marc Pachter, pp. 16–34. Washington, D.C.: New Republic Books/National Portrait Gallery, 1979.

Ehrenburg, Ilya. *Memoirs: 1921–1941*. Cleveland and New York: World, 1964.

Erikson, Erik H. *Childhood and Society*. New York: W. W. Norton, 1963.

Fenimore, Edward. "English and Spanish in *For Whom the Bell Tolls*." In McCaffery, ed., *Ernest Hemingway: The Man and His Work*, pp. 205–20.

Fenton, Charles A. *The Apprenticeship of Ernest Hemingway: The Early Years*. New York: Farrar, Straus & Young, 1954.

Ferreras, Juan Ignacio. "Entre la nada y el estilo." *El País*, Madrid (1 July 1984), p. 39.

Fiedler, Leslie. "Men Without Women." In Weeks, ed., *Hemingway: A Collection of Critical Essays*, pp. 86–92.

Ford, Richard. *Gatherings from Spain*. 1846; reprint London: J. M. Dent & Sons, 1970.

Freeman, L. G., and J. González Echegaray. "El Juyo: A 14,000-Year-Old Sanctuary from Northern Spain." *History of Religions* (Aug. 1981), pp. 1–19.

Fuentes, Norberto. *Hemingway en Cuba*. Havana: Editorial Letras Cubanas, 1984. Translation, *Hemingway in Cuba*. Secaucus, N.J.: Lyle Stuart, 1984.

Gala, Antonio. *Charlas con Troylo*. Madrid: Espasa-Calpe, 1981.

García, P. Félix. "País para vivir." *ABC* (5 July 1961), p. 1.

García Lorca, Federico. "Teoría y juego del duende." In vol. 1, pp. 1067–79, *Obras completas*. 2 vols. Madrid: Aguilar, 1975.

————. "Llanto por Ignacio Sánchez Mejías." In vol. 2, pp. 549–58, *Obras completas*.

Gassirer, Pierre, and Juliet Wilson. *The Life and Complete Works of Goya*. New York: Reynal & Company, 1971.

Gil-Albert, Juan. Fragment of *España: empeño de una ficción*. *Revista de Occidente*, Madrid (Oct.–Dec. 1980), pp. 128–29.

Gleaves, Edwin Sheffield, Jr. "The Spanish Influence on Ernest Hemingway's Concepts of Death, *Nada*, and Immortality." Ph.D. diss., Emory University, 1964.

Goñi, Fermín. " 'Sanfermines,' un acontecimiento popular con seis siglos de historia." *El País* (5 July 1981), pp. 20–21.

Grebstein, Sheldon Norman, ed. *Studies in "For Whom the Bell Tolls."*
Columbus, Ohio: Merrill, 1971.

Grene, Marjorie. "Martin Heidegger." In vol. 3, pp. 461–63, *The Encyclopedia of Philosophy.* 8 vols. New York: Macmillan and The Free Press, 1967.

Griffin, Peter. *Along with Youth: Hemingway, the Early Years.* New York and Oxford: Oxford University Press, 1985.

Guillén, Jorge. *Language and Poetry: Some Poets of Spain.* Cambridge: Harvard University Press, 1961.

Hawthorne, Nathaniel. *The Marble Faun* or *The Romance of Mount Beni.* Boston and New York: Houghton Mifflin, 1888.

Hemingway, Leicester. *My Brother, Ernest Hemingway.* Cleveland: World, 1961.

Hemingway, Mary. "Hemingway's Spain." *Saturday Review* (11 Mar. 1967), pp. 48–49, 102–4, 107.

———. *How It Was.* New York: Ballantine Books, 1977.

———. "The Lost Resorts: Havana." *Saturday Review* (2 Jan. 1965), pp. 40–41, 70, 72, 74.

Hotchner, A. E. *Papa Hemingway: A Personal Memoir.* New York: Random House, 1966.

Hurwitz, Harold. "Hemingway's Tutor, Ezra Pound." In Wagner, ed., *Hemingway: Five Decades of Literary Criticism,* pp. 17–20.

Huxley, Aldous. "Foreheads Villainous Low." *Music at Night and Other Essays.* New York: Fountain Press, 1931.

Iribarren, José María. *Hemingway y los Sanfermines.* Pamplona: Editorial Gómez, 1970.

Jaynes, Julian. *The Origin of Consciousness in the Breakdown of the Bicameral Mind.* Boston: Houghton Mifflin, 1976.

Jiménez Martos, L. *Tientos de los toros y su gente.* Madrid: Rialp, 1981.

Josephs, Allen. "At the Heart of Madrid." *Atlantic* (July 1979), pp. 74–77.

———. "Hacia un estudio de la España de Hemingway." *Insula,* Madrid (Feb. 1977), pp. 14–15.

———. "Hemingway's Poor Spanish: Chauvinism and Loss of Credibility in *For Whom the Bell Tolls.*" In Noble, ed., *Hemingway: A Revaluation,* pp. 205–23.

———. "*Toreo*: The Moral Axis of *The Sun Also Rises.*" *The Hemingway Review* (Fall 1986), pp. 88–99.

———. *White Wall of Spain: The Mysteries of Andalusian Culture.* Ames: Iowa State University Press, 1983.

Jung, Carl, ed. "Approaching the Unconscious." In *Man and His Symbols,* pp. 18–103. New York: Doubleday, 1964.

———. Foreword to the *I Ching or Book of Changes,* pp. xxi–xxxix. Princeton: Princeton University Press, 1967.

———. "Psychology and Literature." *The Spirit in Man, Art, and Literature.* Vol. 15, pp. 84–105, in *Collected Works.* 18 vols. New York: Pantheon Books, 1966.

———. "Synchronicity: An Acausal Connecting Principle." *The Structure and*

Dynamics of the Psyche. Vol. 8, pp. 471–531, in *Collected Works.* New York: Pantheon Books, 1960.

Junkins, Donald. "Hemingway's Bullfight Poems." *Hemingway Review* (Spring 1987), pp. 38–45.

———. "Hemingway's Contribution to American Poetry." *Hemingway Review* (Spring 1985), pp. 18–23.

Kennedy, William. "The Last Olé." *New York Times Book Review* (9 June 1985), pp. 1, 32–33, 35. Review of *The Dangerous Summer.*

Kert, Bernice. *The Hemingway Women.* New York and London: W. W. Norton, 1983.

Kinnamon, Keneth. "Hemingway, the *Corrida,* and Spain." *Texas Studies in Literature and Language* (Spring 1959), pp. 44–61.

Koestler, Arthur. *Spanish Testament.* London: V. Gollancz Ltd., 1937.

Koontz, Leah Rice. " 'Montoya' Remembers *The Sun Also Rises.*" In Sarason, ed., *Hemingway and the Sun Set,* pp. 207–11.

Lanthan, Aaron. "A Farewell to Machismo." *New York Times Magazine* (16 Oct. 1977), pp. 66–69, 79–82.

Layman, Richard. "Hemingway's Library Cards at Shakespeare & Co." *Fitzgerald/Hemingway Annual* (1975), pp. 191–207.

Lepore, Mario. *The Life and Times of Goya.* New York: Curtis Books, 1966.

Levin, Harry. "Observations on the Style of Ernest Hemingway." In Baker, ed., *Hemingway and His Critics,* pp. 93–115.

Lewis, Robert W. "The Making of *Death in the Afternoon.*" In Nagel, ed., *Ernest Hemingway: The Writer in Context,* pp. 31–52.

Llona, Victor. "The Sun Also Rose for Ernest Hemingway." *Fitzgerald/Hemingway Annual* (1972), pp. 159–71.

Lynn, Kenneth S. *Hemingway: The Life and Work.* New York: Simon and Schuster, 1987.

Luján, Néstor. *Historia del toreo.* Barcelona: Destino, 1967.

McCaffery, John K. M., ed. *Ernest Hemingway: The Man and His Work.* Cleveland and New York: World, 1950.

McCormick, John. *The Middle Distance: A Comparative History of American Imaginative Literature: 1919–1932.* New York: Free Press, 1971.

———, and Mario Sevilla Mascareñas. *The Complete Aficionado.* Cleveland: World, 1967.

MacLeish, Archibald. "His Mirror Was Danger." *Life* (14 July 1961), pp. 71–72.

———. "Years of the Dog." In *The Human Season: Selected Poems 1926–1972,* p. 38. Boston: Houghton Mifflin, 1972.

Madariaga, Salvador de. "The World Weighs a Writer's Influence: Spain." *Saturday Review* (29 July 1961), p. 18.

Markham, James M. "Hemingway's Spain." *New York Times* (24 Nov. 1985), Travel Section, p. 15.

Mencken, H. L. "The Spanish Idea of a Good Time." *The American Mercury* (27 Dec. 1932), pp. 506–7. Review of *Death in the Afternoon.* Reprinted in Stephens, ed., *Ernest Hemingway: The Critical Reception,* pp. 123–24.

Meyers, Jeffrey. *Hemingway: A Biography.* New York: Harper & Row, 1985.

Michener, James. *Iberia: Spanish Travels and Reflections.* New York: Random House, 1961.

Montherlant, Henry de. *Chaos and Night.* New York: Macmillan, 1964.

———. *Les Bestiares.* Paris: B. Grasset, 1926.

Moore, Betty. "Ernest Hemingway and Spain: Growth of a 'Spanish' Prose Style." *es* (Publicaciones del Departamento de Inglés, Universidad de Valladolid) (Sept. 1979), pp. 227–53.

Moradell, Borau. "Hemingway descubre, entusiasta, el paisaje aragonés." *Heraldo de Aragón*, Saragossa (14 Oct. 1956), p. 9.

Moravia, Alberto. "Nothing Amen." In *Man as an End: A Defense of Humanism*, pp. 231–36. New York: Farrar, Straus and Giroux, 1966.

Nagel, James, ed. *Ernest Hemingway: The Writer in Context.* Madison: University of Wisconsin Press, 1984.

Nepomuceno, Eric. *Hemingway: Madrid no era una fiesta.* Madrid: Altalena, 1978.

Nietzsche, Friedrich. *The Philosophy of Nietzsche.* New York: Modern Library, 1954.

Noble, Donald R., ed. *Hemingway: A Revaluation.* Troy, N.Y.: Whitson Publishing Company, 1983.

Oag, Shay. *In the Presence of Death: Antonio Ordóñez.* New York: Coward-McCann, 1969.

O'Faolain, Sean. *The Vanishing Hero: Studies in Novelists of the Twenties.* Boston: Little, Brown, 1957.

Oldsey, Bernard. *Hemingway's Hidden Craft: The Writing of "A Farewell to Arms."* University Park: Pennsylvania State University Press, 1979.

Ordóñez, Antonio. "Hemingway and I." *Diario de Málaga* (n.p., n.d.). Hemingway Collection, JFK.

Pascal, Blaise. *Pensées.* Louis Lafuma, ed. Paris: Editions du Luxembourg, 1952.

Pemán, José María. *Un soldado en la historia: Vida del Capitán-General Varela.* Cadiz: n.p., 1954.

Pérez Gállego, Cándido. "Aportación española al estudio de Hemingway: Notas para una bibliografía." *Filología Moderna*, Madrid (Oct. 1961), pp. 57–71.

Pierini, Franco. "Luis Miguel replica a Hemingway." *Gaceta Ilustrada*, Madrid (5 Nov. 1960), pp. 52–54.

Pratt, William, ed. *The Imagist Poem.* New York: E. P. Dutton, 1963.

Praz, Mario. "Hemingway in Italy." In Baker, ed., *Hemingway and His Critics*, pp. 116–30.

Quintanilla, Luis. "Hemingway en mi recuerdo." *Cuadernos del Congreso por la Libertad de la Cultura*, Paris (Nov. 1961), pp. 45–51.

Rahv, Philip. "Paleface and Redskin." In *Image and Idea: Twenty Essays on Literary Themes*, pp. 1–6. New York: New Directions, 1957.

Redman, Ben Ray. "Spokesman for a Generation." *Spur* (1 Dec. 1929), pp. 77, 186.

Reyes, Luis. "Dominguín destruye la leyenda de su amigo Hemingway." *Tiempo*, Madrid (25 June 1984), pp. 106–10.

Reynolds, Michael. *Hemingway's Reading 1910–1940*. Princeton: Princeton
University Press, 1981.
———. *The Young Hemingway*. London and New York: Basil Blackwell, 1986.
———. "Words Killed, Wounded, Missing in Action." *Hemingway notes*
(Spring 1981), pp. 2–9.
Rilke, Rainer Maria. *The Book of Hours*, 1905. Partially translated in *Poet Lore*,
26, no. 1 (1915): 121.
———. *The Notebooks of Malte Laurids Brigge*. 1910; reprint New York:
W. W. Norton, 1949.
Rodman, Selden, ed. *100 Modern Poems*. New York: Pellegrini & Cudahy,
1949.
Ross, Lillian. *Portrait of Hemingway*. New York: Simon and Schuster, 1961.
Royo, Rodrigo. "Las pequeñas confesiones de Hemingway." *Arriba*, Madrid
(5 Oct. 1956), n.p.
Salcedo, Emilio. "Conversación con Hemingway." *La Gaceta Regional*,
Salamanca (15 Sept. 1960), p. 5.
Salinas, Pedro. "Lorca and the Poetry of Death." In *Lorca: A Collection of
Critical Essays*, edited by Manuel Durán, pp. 100–7. Englewood Cliffs, N.J.:
Prentice-Hall, 1962.
Samuelson, Arnold. *With Hemingway: A Year in Key West and Cuba*. New
York: Random House, 1984.
Sanford, Marcelline Hemingway. *At the Hemingways: A Family Portrait*.
Boston: Atlantic–Little, Brown, 1961.
Sarason, Bertram D., ed. *Hemingway and the Sun Set*. Washington, D.C.:
NCR/Microcard Editions, 1972.
Scribner, Charles, Jr. Introduction to *The Enduring Hemingway: An Anthology
of a Lifetime in Literature*, pp. xiii–xxix. New York: Scribner's, 1974.
Sheean, Vincent. *Not Peace but a Sword*. New York: Doubleday, Doran, 1939.
Smith, Julian. "Christ Times Four: Hemingway's Unknown Spanish Civil War
Stories." *Arizona Quarterly* (Spring 1969), pp. 5–17.
Solzhenitsyn, Aleksandr I. *A World Split Apart*. Commencement Address,
Harvard University, 8 June 1978. New York: Harper and Row, 1978.
Stanton, Edward F. "The Correspondent and the Doctor: A Spanish
Friendship." *Hemingway Review* (Fall 1981), pp. 53–55.
———. *Hemingway en España*. Madrid: Castalia, 1989.
———. *The Tragic Myth: Lorca and "Cante Jondo."* Lexington: University Press
of Kentucky, 1978.
Starkie, Walter. "Cante Jondo, Flamenco and the Guitar." *Guitar Review*
(1956), pp. 3–14.
Stephens, Robert O. "Language Magic and Reality in *For Whom the Bell Tolls*."
Criticism (Spring 1972), pp. 151–64.
———, ed. *Ernest Hemingway: The Critical Reception*. New York: Burt
Franklin, 1977.
Stoneback, H. R. "From the rue Saint-Jacques to the Pass of Roland to the
'Unfinished Church on the Edge of the Cliff.'" *Hemingway Review* (Fall
1986), pp. 2–29.

Sugg, Richard. "Hemingway, Money and *The Sun Also Rises*." *Fitzgerald/ Hemingway Annual* (1972), pp. 257–67.

Svoboda, Frederic Joseph. *Hemingway and "The Sun Also Rises": The Crafting of a Style*. Lawrence: University Press of Kansas, 1983.

Thomas, Hugh. *The Spanish Civil War*. New York: Harper and Brothers, 1961.

Turnbull, Andrew, ed. *The Letters of F. Scott Fitzgerald*. New York: Scribner's, 1963.

Tynan, Kenneth. *Bull Fever*. New York: Harper and Brothers, 1955.

Unamuno, Miguel de. "Carta a un torero." Vol. 11, pp. 909–13, in *Obras completas*. 16 vols. Madrid: Afrodisio Aguado, 1958.

———. *Del sentimiento trágico de la vida en los hombres y en los pueblos* (1913). Translated by Anthony Kerrigan, *The Tragic Sense of Life in Man and Nations*. Princeton: Princeton University Press, 1972.

———. *En torno al casticismo*. In *Obras selectas*, pp. 47–144. Madrid: Editorial Plenitud, 1960.

Vargas Llosa, Mario. "La prehistoria de Hemingway." *El País* (7 Apr. 1986), pp. 11–12.

Vizcaíno Casas, F. "Me gustaría tener una muerte literaria." *ABC* (30 Jan. 1954), p. 27.

Wagner, Linda, ed. *Hemingway: Five Decades of Literary Criticism*. East Lansing: Michigan State University Press, 1974.

Watson, William Braasch. "Hemingway's Civil War Dispatches." *The Hemingway Review* (Spring 1988), pp. 4–92. The entire issue is devoted to the Spanish Civil War.

Watts, Emily Stipes. *Ernest Hemingway and the Arts*. Urbana: University of Illinois Press, 1971.

Weeks, Robert P., ed. *Hemingway: A Collection of Critical Essays*. Englewood Cliffs, N.J.: Prentice-Hall, 1962.

Williams, Wirt. *The Tragic Art of Ernest Hemingway*. Baton Rouge and London: Louisiana State University Press, 1981.

Wilson, Edmund. "Hemingway: Gauge of Morale." In *The Wound and the Bow: Seven Studies in Literature*, pp. 214–42. New York: Oxford University Press, 1947.

———. "Mr. Hemingway's Dry Points." *Dial* (Oct. 1924), pp. 340–41. Review of *Three Stories and Ten Poems* and *in our time*. Reprinted in Stephens, ed., *Ernest Hemingway: The Critical Reception*, pp. 1–3.

Wrobel, Arthur. "Whitman and the Phrenologists: The Divine Body and the Sensuous Soul." *PMLA* (Publications of the Modern Language Association of America) (Jan. 1974), pp. 17–22.

Wylder, Delbert E. *Hemingway's Heroes*. Albuquerque: University of New Mexico Press, 1969.

Ynduráin, Francisco. "España en la obra de Hemingway." *De lector a lector*. Madrid: Escelicer, 1973.

Young, Philip. *Ernest Hemingway: A Reconsideration*. University Park: Pennsylvania State University Press, 1969).

———, and Charles W. Mann. *The Hemingway Manuscripts*. University Park: Pennsylvania State University Press, 1969.

Acknowledgments

These I wish to thank:

The Ernest Hemingway Foundation for permission to quote from unpublished material and to reproduce photographs from the Hemingway Collection, John F. Kennedy Library.

Naomi B. Pascal, Editor-in-Chief, University of Washington Press, for her imagination, foresight, and faith in this book.

The late Carlos Baker.

The students of my graduate courses on Hemingway and Spain at the University of Kentucky, who have given me many insights on the writer and his works.

Richard and Valerie Herr, whose invitation to give a lecture at the Instituto Internacional, Madrid, stimulated my early research.

José Luis Romero, whose friendship of twenty-five years has allowed me to understand many things, of Spain and Spaniards, expressed here.

Dr. Fernando Claramunt, aficionado *nonpareil*, and Pura Albert de Claramunt, whose hospitality and conversations on men and bulls, amid libations of Rioja and Valdepeñas, have graced various stages of the book.

Joaquín González Muela, friend and translator of another version of this work into Spanish, who has proven that *traduttore* is not always the same as *traditore*.

Max Pavón, who taught me enough about running the bulls on the Cuesta de Santo Domingo to prevent the book from being a posthumous one.

José María Torrabadella, Fernando Lizaúr, and the members of the Peña Anaitasuna, Pamplona, whose vitality, joy, and generosity during San Fermín have taught me that Hemingway was right about the Basque and Navarrese peoples.

Antonio González, gracious host and friend, whose restaurant Botín still embodies the best of Hemingway's favorite city in Spain, Madrid.

Félix and the late Carlos García Tenorio of Madrid, whose conviviality and craft led Hemingway to call them the best bootmakers in the world.

Ángel Pérez Escudero and his wife, Ciriaca, who saved me from pneumonia in San Ildefonso de la Granja.

Frank Burke, Luis Costa, Walter Foreman, Eric Furr, Michael Impey, John Muniak, Armando Prats, Alison Rieke, Alan Ross, Michael Shotwell, David Spaeth, and Arthur Wrobel, who have read portions or all of the manuscript and given me what every author needs: intelligent advice and suggestions.

I also wish to thank:

María Elena Arizmendi; Julio Caro Baroja; José Luis Castillo-Puche; Camilo José Cela; Alberto Flores of the Bar El Patio, Madrid; Pedro Gálvez of the Hotel Palace, Madrid; Miguel Fernández, maître d'hotel, and Jesús Fernández Jiménez, manager of the Hotel Suecia, Madrid; Antonio González, Jr.; Edward

Hagemann; Jo August Hills; Elizabeth Holdridge Dos Passos; Manolo Jiménez
and the other owners of the restaurant El Callejón, Madrid; Paqui Lahortiga;
Peter Lisca; Asenchi Madinaveitia Sánchez-Arcas; Mariano Martín and Pablo
Vela of the Cervecería Alemana, Madrid; James E. Nagel; Joan L. O'Connor;
Bernard Oldsey; Alfonso Ordóñez; Lillian Palmer; Juan Posada, matador de
toros and bullfight critic; Marilyn Raugust; Joseph Ricapito; William Robinson;
Alfonso Carlos Saiz Valdivielso, bullfight critic and editor of *Clarín Taurino*;
David Schoonover; Paul Smith (University of California, Los Angeles); Paul
Smith (Trinity College, Connecticut); William Watson.

I wish to express my gratitude to the University of Kentucky Research
Foundation and to the National Endowment for the Humanities for assistance
which covered my travel and research expenses.

I would like to thank my friends at the Interlibrary Loan Office of the
University of Kentucky Library, for searching and finding dozens of books and
journals wherever they were to be found. I also wish to thank the following
institutions: John F. Kennedy Library, Princeton's Firestone Library, Yale's
Beinecke Rare Book and Manuscript Library, the University of Texas'
Humanities Research Center, the Library of Congress, Boston University's
Mugar Memorial Library, the University of California's Bancroft Library,
Dartmouth College's Baker Memorial Library, the Diputación Foral
(Pamplona), the University of Florida Library, the Hemeroteca Municipal
(Madrid), the Hemeroteca Nacional (Madrid), the University of Indiana's Lilly
Library, the Instituto Internacional (Madrid), Knox College's Seymour Library,
the University of Maryland's McKeldin Library, Southern Illinois University's
Morris Library, the University of Virginia's Alderman and Clifton Waller Barrett
Libraries.

Index

Page numbers of photographs are printed in boldface type.